# THE BOOK
# THAT JESUS WROTE

## *JOHN'S GOSPEL*

## Barbara Thiering

## CORGI BOOKS

**THE BOOK THAT JESUS WROTE**
**A CORGI BOOK : 0 552 14665 X**

First publication in Great Britain

Published by arrangement with
Transworld Publishers (Australia) Pty Ltd.

PRINTING HISTORY
Corgi edition published 1998

Set in 11/12pt Plantin by
Phoenix Typesetting, Ilkley, West Yorkshire.

Corgi Books are published by Transworld Publishers Ltd,
61–63 Uxbridge Road, London W5 5SA,
in Australia by Transworld Publishers (Australia) Pty Ltd,
15–25 Helles Avenue, Moorebank, NSW 2170
and in New Zealand by Transworld Publishers (NZ) Ltd,
3 William Pickering Drive, Albany, Auckland.

Reproduced, printed and bound in Great Britain by
Cox & Wyman Ltd, Reading, Berks.

Dr Barbara Thiering was a member of the University of Sydney's School of Divinity for twenty-two years and is now a full-time writer and researcher. Her scholarly articles and books on the Dead Sea Scrolls have earned her a world reputation, and she is the author of the best-selling *Jesus the Man: A New Interpretation from the Dead Sea Scrolls* and *Jesus of the Apocalypse: The Life of Jesus after the Crucifixion*. She lives in Sydney and has a grown family.

Acclaim for *Jesus the Man*:

'[The] sensational nature [of the book's findings] may disguise the strength of the research and scholarship, which Thiering has deployed in the course of her narrative'
Peter Ackroyd, *The Times*

'The impact of *Jesus the Man* by Barbara Thiering may turn out to be as profound as that of Darwin's Origin of the Species on theories of human evolution'
*Focus* Magazine

'Some will see her as an anti-Christ, a mischievous scholar determined to destroy Christianity. To others she will be a source of comfort and peace enabling them to live Christian lives without having to accept as fact Jesus's divinity, his miracles, the virgin birth and resurrection'
The *Australian* Magazine

'This massive work of courage and conviction throws much of what the Church teaches out the stained-glass window'
*Sunday Age*, Melbourne

'This work of courage by Barbara Thiering has left critics applauding her ability to bring to light such a contro-versial topic' *Gisborne Herald*

*Also by Barbara Thiering*

JESUS THE MAN
JESUS OF THE APOCALYPSE

*and published by Corgi Books*

# Contents

# Preface

The Dead Sea Scrolls, found fifty years ago, were at first hailed as the greatest discovery ever made about Christian origins. Then, by a decade later, they had all but disappeared from public view, and had been endorsed by many scholars as having little to do with the history of Christianity. Now, we have come full circle again, with a guarded agreement that they are very close indeed to the background of the earliest Church.[1]

This book continues the project of applying to the New Testament the insights and information that the Scrolls have given us. It has been argued, in earlier books and in *Jesus the Man* and *Jesus of the Apocalypse*, that we now have the key to discovering a wealth of new facts about the real Jesus. Despite all appearances, his history is set out in the gospels and Acts of the New Testament, in a way that was accessible to Christian leaders, but in the disguise of miracles and supernatural acts for the 'babes in Christ'. Parts of that history are also found in related books that have been thought by biblical scholars to be irrelevant.

Jesus was not a supernatural figure, but he was a very great figure. The further stages of the research, applied now to the gospel of John, give an understanding of the mind of a man who was born into a turning point of history, and who had the wit, the determination, and the heroism, to turn it in a productive direction, a direction that laid the foundations of western culture. Through his own book, as the gospel of John may be seen to be, he transformed a noble former religion into a universal one. He becomes vividly present to us as the processes of his thought appear.

Christianity, in the sense that Jesus understood it, but not in the sense of a demand to believe the unbelievable, shines out from the book that he wrote and the subsequent books that he inspired. It is not in the surface stories, which are mostly incredible, but in something in those stories, when they were read by people in his day who had access to certain special knowledge.

The present work, like its predecessors, depends on applying to the text of some books of the New Testament a technique that is defined in the Dead Sea Scrolls, called the pesher technique. The method is such that the results, which give an actual history, are proveable, and are not a matter of subjective interpretation. In *Jesus the Man*, the parts of the results giving a chronology were set out, and in *Jesus of the Apocalypse* a full demonstration on the text of the Book of Revelation was given.

This work brings out the results of the application of the method to the gospels, so as to show the basic stages of their construction. It adds further detail about the pesher method, which should be of general interest to readers of the English text, and would enable scholars to test the method on the Greek text,

8

for it is the Greek text that supplies the pesher.

An outline of the basic history, summarized from the previous two books, is supplied in More about the Pesher (p. 245)

The author wishes to thank once more the team that has helped in the publication of this research: Judith Curr, Shona Martyn, Jo Jarrah, Maggie Hamilton and Rowan Ayers.

If it were possible, the writers of supportive letters from all over the world would be thanked by name, but since that is not possible, let me say that they have given me a sense of community that was at times deeply needed. We are in the process of one of the great changes in the language of religion, not in religion itself, which is a fundamental human drive, but simply in its cultural form. Such a change does not happen lightly, but when it is based on new knowledge, as all the great changes have been, it will inevitably make its way. It is good indeed to be part of it, and of a world community that is allowing it to happen.

# CHAPTER 1

# The Conception

It was early April, AD 33. In a room with walls made of rough stones, its roof thatched with reeds, sat a man with bandaged hands. Inside the bandages, his hands were crushed and broken, great wounds in the palms, where nails had been driven through. He would never use his hands again.

The man was Jesus. About a fortnight before, he had been crucified, beginning the process of capital punishment which the Romans employed to destroy enemies of the empire. But the process had been halted, for him and for the two other men who had been put on crosses with him. The sentence of the other two had been changed to burial while still alive, their legs broken so they could not escape from the cave in which they would be placed. Jesus had been given a different option: suicide by drinking poison.

But now he was here, in the stone buildings not far from the place where the executions had begun. One of the others who had suffered with him had gone into hiding, but Jesus was permitted to stay here, under official protection, in the secluded state of a man living in a monastery. The monastery was beside the Dead Sea.

It was already known in Jerusalem that this man Jesus, who was widely known as the 'the Christ' (the descendant of David), had been put on a cross, had apparently died after only a few hours, had been put in a burial cave, and a day or so later had been seen with his friends. The report found its way into the notes of the Jewish historian Josephus.

There had been no miracle. The poison Jesus had drunk needed time to work, and before it could take full effect he was given a massive dose of a purgative. He had made an undignified, but real, recovery. His stomach tissues and digestive tract had been damaged, and as he sat in his room he was still convalescent, nursing his helpless hands. But he had been through the profoundest spiritual experience a human can have. In utter desolation at the betrayal that had put him on the cross, at his own failure, he had surrendered to despair, had asked for the poison with the pre-arranged words 'I thirst', had become unconscious from the drug mixed with the poison, and had begun to sink down into death. His last sensations must have been the puncturing of his side, the spurt of blood from the wound, and the rough handling as he was lifted down from the cross.

Then, in the darkness of the cave, came the renewal of sensation, a stinging in his loins, and the glimmering of consciousness. Is this life, still? His friend Simon Magus, sitting beside him with his own ankles broken, continued to revive him, and his energy returned, warmth, and then hope. He had been given back the gift of life, he was cared for, there was no more betrayal, no despair. It was a resurrection in everything but the physical sense.

And now, as he recovered in the weeks that followed, in the quietness of the monastery, came a surge of mental energy such as he had never known. He must, he would, let out the words and thoughts that had been thronging in his head. He had something urgent to say, and he had devised the method by which it must be said. His hands could not write, but his attendant, a Gentile called Philip, would write it down for him. It would be in Greek, a language he spoke well enough, and with which Philip could help. Its nuances would serve his purpose; Hebrew and Aramaic were not flexible enough.

After what he had been through, there were things that had to be said, some of them to everyone, some of them to certain people only. To everyone, he must say: despair is not the end, failure is not the end. Life is more powerful than death, life will come back again. And the effective way to say it was as a drama, in which he himself was the central player. Every human being came to moments such as he had been through – humiliated, defeated, blackly despairing. But the dark winter is followed by spring, never forget that. Since the beginning of human history the resurrection of life had been celebrated in a spring festival, the enactment of renewed hope in nature teaching the renewal of hope for humanity.

But there was more. Survival and truthfulness went together. There was something about lying that destroyed individuals and societies. You could get away with a lie for the moment, it might even lead to great success, and there were necessary political lies. But when the falsehood is found out and trust is broken, it can never be repaired.

Simon Magus, Simon the Magician, was the very embodiment of the problem, and in fact of every problem a religious institution could have. Simon the gnostic, Simon the Great Power of God, called by many the Holy God. The powerful intellect – he would eventually give rise to the legend of Faust – through whom came great good and greater evil. It was Simon, Simon the Zealot, who had been crucified on the central cross, the ringleader of the triumvirate of zealots whom Pilate had rounded up. Placed in the cave beside Jesus, Simon had used his medical knowledge to save his life. It was Simon who was the 'young man' in the cave, not actually young in years, but reduced to the status of novice through the failure of the zealot uprising that had brought them all there.

It was he, still sitting in the cave after Jesus had been taken away, who said to the returning women: 'He is risen!' His words, like so many of the words that he and Jesus used when they joked together in their community, had a double meaning. They loved verbal puzzles, double meanings, plays on words. To anyone who knew the special sense of certain terms, 'he is risen' simply meant 'he is promoted, by being restored to the status of a celibate in a monastery'. But to those who had no knowledge of their institution and its special language, the words could be taken to mean that Jesus had risen from the dead, for it had been believed by some that he was dead when he was placed in the cave. Simon fully intended that they should be taken in this sense. The news of a resurrection should be spread to the outside world, and Simon himself given the credit of being the incarnation of a heavenly visitant, one through whom a resurrection had been brought about. It would give him enormous power. He foresaw his return to the headship of the mission in which they were all engaged, with greatly enhanced political strength, and with him would be Jesus, now receiving the devotion of ordinary members, the man who, through his agency, had come back from the dead.

Simon had long practised the art of manipulating the truth in order to win the reverence of uncritical minds. According to one of the many reports of his activities, he made claims to magical arts that were a guarantee of success in the pagan world. He contrived to make statues walk, roll on fire without being burnt, fly through the air, make loaves out of stones, turn into a serpent or a goat, open lockfast gates, and melt iron. At banquets in his house he made dishes appear in the air with no carriers.[1] Such tricks were part of Simon's opening ploy. He then went on to teach his initiates a sophisticated gnostic system of thought that drew its ingredients from Greek philosophy and oriental wisdom. He was at the forefront of the mission to the Diaspora, of which Jesus was a part. Hellenized Jews and Gentiles found Simon's philosophy more stimulating than traditional religion, and some were prepared to treat him as an incarnation of the divine. They extended this reverence also to his mistress Helena, who was said to be the divine Thought of God, the incarnation of Wisdom, the female aspect of God.

To Jesus, at the headquarters of the mission near the Dead Sea, Simon and Helena had been good companions, helping him in his protest against the restrictions placed on Gentiles. He differed sharply from Simon politically, maintaining that the Roman

15

world was to be gained for God by evangelism and teaching, not by force of arms. But although at the political level Jesus opposed Simon, at the personal level he felt the pull of Simon's immense knowledge and the freedom from tradition that it promised. Now, Simon had saved his life. And had told a tremendous lie, which was at the same time poetically true.

There was a way of rising above this dilemma to a new creative act. A project had been forming in his mind during the previous years, that of writing a new scripture. A new scripture, replacing the Old Testament around which everything in Judaism centred. A New Testament. He had already seen that there was no hope of retaining a Jewish identity among the hundreds of thousands of Gentile members to whom he was promising equality, a freedom from the inferior position to which the Jewish leaders of the mission were relegating them. A new religion was already forming, one that accepted the intellectual, spiritual and ethical concepts of Judaism, but rejected the requirement of circumcision, dietary laws, observance of the sabbath, and attendance at the synagogue. A new religion had to have a new scripture. It would be to throw away thousands of years of tradition, it would be close to blasphemy for those to whom the Jewish Law was the very voice of God. But the Law no longer spoke vital truth, not even to many Jews.

Moreover, there was ready to hand the very instrument Jesus needed to deal with Simon's fabrications. It was common for thinking people everywhere, in both pagan and Jewish circles, to assume that their sacred scriptures had a second level of meaning, discernible by those with higher knowledge. Philo the Jew of Alexandria had devoted his life to 'discovering' the level in the Old Testament that set out the truths of Platonic, Stoic and Pythagorean philosophy. He was so convinced of its existence that he condemned people who saw only the ordinary meaning of the Old Testament as 'self-satisfied pedantic professors of literalism'.[2] But Philo and those like him saw only allegorical truths. In the circles in which Jesus moved, a different sort of hidden meaning had been found in Old Testament scripture. It was believed to contain statements in historical form. For those who had the key, it contained descriptions of events experienced by present day leaders. Written long ago, they functioned as prophecies. But the essential point was their definition as history. Scripture looked like one thing to ordinary outsiders, who would see in it only the familiar moral and ethical truths, but it also contained factual descriptions of events, able to be perceived by those with an insider's knowledge.[3]

Jesus was a teacher, as all members of the mission were. Their work was to teach those who came to the monasteries for learning. There, not only the Law of Moses was taught, but also knowledge which was said to be higher: astronomy, medicine, mathematics, natural science, philosophy. As teachers, they had found that knowledge must be graded. It took years to master the more difficult parts, and such mastery was built on more elementary knowledge. Their novices were first taught elementary matters including Moses' laws, then went on to further years of study of the higher subjects until they reached graduation.

Some men who visited the monastery for short periods, but normally lived in the world, were given some learning, but only of the elementary kind, and were forbidden to go further. A sharp division had grown up between these and the more advanced scholars. The visitors were likened to young children, to 'babes', and were said to be 'fed with milk, not with meat'.[4]

It would be ideal for Jesus' purpose to construct his new scripture in the same way. It would contain religious truths for the 'babes', including the great truth of spiritual resurrection. And, because there was something urgently to be said to the scholars and leaders, to counter Simon's corrupted gnosticism, it would also contain historical statements. It would give a real history, of what had happened to Jesus, and a true account of the formation of his emerging party. But this time the history would really be there, and not have to be read into it, because it had been very carefully placed there.

The concept grew in Jesus' mind, and he began to sketch his ideas. How should he deal with this false claim to a miracle? By having any number of miracles, so cheapening the very notion.

Jesus walked up and down his room (for his feet had not been nailed), looking out of its window space at the blue surface of the Dead Sea. He began to act a part. He would be a clown. A magician. Jesus the Magus. Like Simon Magus, except that Simon expected people to really believe his tricks, consciously practising sleight of hand. Jesus' claims to magic tricks would be so absurd that no-one would believe them. Then, the people who thought twice, who knew that he had something valuable to say, would look again, look behind the appearances, to discover something else.

What should he say he had done, the magician? Amazing things. He had turned water into wine, no less. Jars of water were standing there, and when they were poured out, the water had turned into wine. And, still making up for food shortages, on another occasion he had fed 5000 people with five loaves and two fish. Moreover, there had been large quantities of fragments left over. Then he went on to walk on water. People living near the Dead Sea could float on its surface without sinking, but he had gone one better and walked on the sea. Then, he had healed people just by saying words. One sick man had been miles away, and his word alone had healed him. Another sick man had been waiting thirty-eight years beside a pool, and in all that time no-one had come to let him down into its healing waters, but Jesus simply spoke to him, and he lifted up his stretcher and walked. With a blind man, he spat on his eyes, and the spittle healed him. And, just to round it all off, in the seventh marvel he raised a man from the dead. The man was in a cave, had been there four days, and Jesus simply said 'Come forth!' and out came the man, dressed in his graveclothes but alive.

Who would believe it? Many people would, or at least have a feeling of awe, when the stories were read in the dim and mysterious atmosphere of a place of sacred worship. He had often listened to equally absurd stories from the Old Testament that were received with devout attention by the congregation. Elisha had made an axe float on water. The Israelites in the wilderness had been fed with manna come down from heaven. The waters of the Red Sea had parted, letting 600,000 Israelites through, then had closed over Pharaoh's army. The sun had stood still when Joshua held his hands up.[5] During worship, disbelief was suspended, and these stories were accepted as a sign of God's power. But Jesus, and other men like him who spent their days in a learned community, had often expressed their disbelief to each other, perhaps made jokes about it, while at the same time not disturbing the naive whom they were concerned to educate. Pagan writers of their time were equally disbelieving of their own sacred stories, advising each other not to take them seriously.[6]

It had long been the custom to justify such stories by finding hidden meanings in them. But now, Jesus the clown, the Magus, was inventing his own stories, drawing on his considerable sense of humour. And putting his own meanings into them. For those who were accustomed to using reason, and had access to the written text so that they could study it, a rewarding exercise was being prepared. When the point had been seen, the magician would dissolve, and behind him another man would appear: a thinker, a reformer, a liberator, and, if it was believed that membership of his community gave salvation, a redeemer.

The clues were placed everywhere, directed at the thinking, critical mind. For a start, there were seven miracles, a sure sign of a literary unit, something constructed. The reader was directed to count them. After the first one, 'this was the first sign Jesus did . . .' After the second, 'this was the second sign . . .', to make sure the total was not missed. In biblical conventions, seven meant a unity. A unity was being presented for consideration.

Then, the stories were full of extraneous detail or strange reactions that the critical mind could hardly pass over without questioning. In the miracle of turning water into wine, it was very precisely stated that there were six waterpots there, holding two or three measures each. Why such detail? Then, when the wine was poured out, the ruler of the feast did not even comment on the miracle, but complained that Jesus had kept the good wine till last. Did nobody notice there had been a miracle? Or was there, perhaps, something better to comment on?

When the man was healed at a distance, an exact time was given, 'yesterday at the seventh hour' (1pm). Why? And why was it said that the man in the next story had lain beside the pool for thirty-eight years? Not even a round number was used, the usual way of expressing a long time.

The figures really ran riot in the feeding of the multitude: five loaves, two fish, 5000 men, twelve baskets of fragments left over. Moreover, in a parallel account that was not found in John but was added when the story was given in Mark, it was said that on another occasion there were 4000 men, seven loaves, a few fish, and seven baskets of fragments were left over. This story was immediately followed by a riddle, listing all the numbers, with Jesus directly saying that it was a riddle to be solved by those who were astute enough to work it out.[7]

When Lazarus was raised from the dead, a puzzling reaction by the Jews was included in the story. Together with the high priest Caiaphas, they said that this was a matter for great concern, for 'the

Romans will come and take away our place and our nation'. Why should the Romans do this because a man was raised from the dead? Moreover, the Jews then proceeded to plot the destruction of both Jesus and Lazarus. Why such inappropriate reactions to a man who had been brought back from death? There is more than a hint of a political setting for the story, but such a setting seems hardly relevant to its theme.

It can be imagined that as Jesus paced the room and the stories shaped themselves in his head, he saw himself laughing with Philip about the absurdities, working with him in companionship while between them they got the detail down. In the detail they would be setting out the real history, every fact of time, place and organization, to be understood by the members of the monastic schools. It was, in fact, necessary to know that the waterpots held two or three measures each, and that the good wine had been left till last. An understanding of the numbers of the loaves was basic to the monastic system and a key to the whole hierarchy.

But then he saw the obvious objection: he would be deceiving. Ordinary people who revered him believed that they could trust his words, simply as they stood. When they found that the sense was double, they might lose respect for the outer form, which for them was intended to be valid. They might lose respect for him too. He would be looked on by his enemies as the Deceiver, and there would be another reason for calling him the Man of a Lie, apart from the meaning 'bastard' which his enemies used against him because of his alleged illegitimacy.[8]

But, he might reason, he was simply employing an educational process. The stories were a necessary first step, leading on to higher knowledge. Children began with myths and stories, awakening in them a sense of awe. Then they went on to understand and prefer abstractions. Pre-literate adults were like children, and the greatest gift one could give them was the educational process. Was it a deception to begin as one would with children?

The stories could be said to deceive. But Nature itself deceives. The world looks flat, and many an ordinary person in the Hellenistic world would defend the belief that it was flat; nothing could be more obvious. Only after close observation, thought and reasoning – such as the fact that the shadow of the earth on the moon at a time of solar eclipse is curved – would it be known to a select few that it was spherical. Pythagoras and his school had known it.[9] They knew that learning often took people beyond what was obvious. And when a man followed where knowledge led, he became a new person, a freer and more powerful person. In a way, knowledge gave salvation, salvation from a more primitive self.

Then Jesus foresaw another criticism: he would be accused of contempt for the ignorant, for the 'babes'. He had certainly often supressed feelings of contempt, when he found that others could not see what he could see, and that their blindness was crippling, even endangering them. At council meetings, he was given to outbursts of scorn at the self-serving policies of some of the speakers, at their confusions, at their inability to make distinctions. They called him arrogant, resenting his witticisms at their expense.[10]

Yet, he would reason further, it was this very exercise of using your mind, of thinking hard and long, of pursuing knowledge, that people most desired. They would do anything to better themselves with knowledge. The Greco-Roman world was living at a time of the first great flowering of science, resulting in enthusiasm for the power of the human intellect. It was recognized that science depended on close observation, on asking questions, on reasoning through consistently to the end, to achieve evidenced knowledge, gained by scientific method. He would be giving them a carefully constructed set of exercises to teach such methods, and, moreover, in a school that gave them not only learning but also religious insight. In the Greek world philosophers were the saints, and he would be adding ethics and spirituality. Any initial reservations would surely be overcome when such riches were being offered.

Somewhere in his book he would admit that he had written it. It must be done very carefully, indirectly, for the ordinary reader believed that he was dead, and moreover that a work of scripture came by divine revelation, not contrivance. A means was available to him, through a man who was the chief of his Gentile followers, a man named John Mark. The gospel was to be attributed to him, called by his name. Because of John Mark's special relation to Jesus, being his 'eunuch', the term for a celibate 'male-female' who acted as go-between in his dynastic marriage, he was obliged to speak as if he were two people, and one who did not speak for himself but in the persona of another. When he

24

spoke as if he were the husband, he said 'we'. So characteristic was this usage that 'we' came to be a kind of name for him.

Later, when the book of Acts was written, Jesus allowed this meaning of 'we' to become close to obvious, for anyone who assumed the unity and proper grammatical form of the book. Acts, normally giving a history in the third person, suddenly began to use 'we' as the subject of events. 'We' first appeared when the party of missionaries was invited by the 'man of Macedonia' to come over to Philippi. 'When he (Paul) had seen the vision, immediately we sought to go on into Macedonia . . .' Then the 'we' form continues for a time but is dropped, to reappear in the account of the voyage to Rome. 'We' by now referred to Luke, himself the 'man of Macedonia'. The continuing use of 'we' from the time the voyage to Rome began meant that Jesus was on board the ship, accompanying Paul and his party to Rome.[11]

In the opening chapter of John, 'we' appears in what has previously been a third person account: 'The Word became flesh and dwelt among us, and we beheld his glory'. John Mark is introducing himself as the close associate of Jesus, the Word. Then, in the last verses of the book, in the place of a signature and postscript, appear the words: 'One having written these things, and we know that his witness is true'. John Mark is the subject of the first phrase, the ostensible author, and in the second phrase he speaks for Jesus, not himself, confirming the accuracy of the record.

Jesus would not remain content with just giving a

record of what had happened, or with such broadly philosophical theories as are found in the Sayings in John's gospel. When, in the following decade, he met up with Paul, formerly the zealot nationalist Saul, his thoughts would be directed to the great themes that were to become central to Christianity. Foremost among these was the atoning power of suffering, which his personal history had illustrated. When it was seen as the final chapter of Old Testament religion, which taught that the repeated sacrifice of an animal was a way of removing sin, his hours of unmerited suffering on the cross would be interpreted as the final, once-for-all sacrifice, removing the need for repeated sacrifices, enabling Judaism to break out of its ritual mould to become a universal religion.

If Paul, with his acute awareness of the politics of the change, found the words in his Epistles, it was Jesus behind him who helped him shape them. Paul all but admits the presence of Jesus, with whom he had frequent discussions, when he is giving advice about marriage. 'To the married I give charge, not I but the Lord . . .'; and 'To the rest I say, not the Lord . . .' At the end of one of his epistles, written in Ephesus, he sent a code message to Jesus in Corinth, 'Maranatha', Aramaic for 'Our Lord, come!', intending that Jesus should come to Ephesus the following year.[12]

In a sense, then, Jesus' authorship lies behind the whole of the New Testament, either in the books that he composed or guided, or in the books that relied on his method but set out a different viewpoint. His Church became more than his book, and sometimes left his book behind. But it remained an invitation to the questing intelligence, an education out of religious childhood into the maturity of knowing that God cannot be encapsulated in human history.

# CHAPTER 2

# How He Invented the Language

In the course of those months in AD 33 when Jesus was composing his gospel, he invented a whole new language of double meanings. Others who followed him with subsequent gospels, and he himself in later years, would add to it, but its ground rules were laid down in what came to be called John's gospel.

The basic principle was that a term could have both a general, moral meaning and a special, technical meaning, and both meanings were valid. An example is the word 'enemy' (*echthros*). Its general meaning was as it appears, and 'love your enemies' was a Christian moral precept. But when the special meaning of 'love' (*agapaō*) was known, meaning 'admit to the Agape meal', the communal meal of ascetic initiates, and when it was taken with the special sense of 'enemies', meaning 'Romans', the political enemies of the Jews, then 'love your enemies' also meant 'admit Romans to the Agape meal'. This was a political statement, highly provocative to the zealot ascetics among whom Jesus preached this doctrine, and it gave important historical information – that Jesus was a political rebel who taught friendship with the Romans occupying his country.

The first step in recording any history is to give the time when it happened, the next step to give the place, the next to give the persons to whom it happened. For each of these steps a language was crafted.

One of the central concerns of the monastic schools to which Jesus belonged was the measurement of time. It was these schools whose main centre was at Qumran near the Dead Sea where they produced the Dead Sea Scrolls, from which a mass of new information has become available. One of the main reasons why they had separated from other Jews was that they observed a different calendar. Following the sun rather than the moon, as they believed that heaven required, they relied on a solar calendar which had long been in use. Its chief characteristic was its perfect regularity and symmetry, and it led to an orderly mode of life which was part of the monastic discipline. Prayers must be said at every hour of the day, and especially at the high points of day – sunrise, noon and sunset. Devices had been developed which acted as a clock, and the prayers of the ascetics, rising at the fixed times of day and night, were the human voice of the clock.[1]

The high points of the year were the equinoxes and solstices, and at these seasons special days were inserted into the calendar. In every quarter year, leading up to the equinox or solstice, there were three months of thirty days each, giving a year of 360 days, and to bring the year to a more accurate 364 days four days were inserted at the high points. These were considered the great days, when, if heaven were to act to fulfil prophecy, its interventions would come. Such a day, if a fulfilment occurred, was the great 'Today' to which prophecy looked forward.

Seasonal councils were held around this day, lasting three days. Following the theme of 'Today', the day preceding was called 'Yesterday', and the day after called 'Tomorrow'. In Jesus' new language, these words were used with an absolute, not a relative sense, and so were a means of naming an absolute date. The word for 'today' (*sēmeron* in Greek) names the great day, called the 31st, as it was added to the previous month of thirty days. The word for 'yesterday' (*echthes*) names the 30th of the month. The word for 'tomorrow' (*aurion*) names the 1st of the next month.

This means that the text of the gospel contains, in disguised form, actual dates of days, contrary to all appearances. When the man in the story of the distant healing was said to have been healed 'yesterday', it indicated to those who understood the calendar that the event in question occurred on the day that was the solar 30th at one of the seasons, and it is possible from further information to work out that it was Thursday, 20 September, AD 31. Because of such information, many dates can be worked out, including that of the crucifixion – Friday, 20 March, AD 33.

The solar calendrists did not have names for the days of the week, rather they simply numbered them. Another device was developed for naming these days, using terms which again seem to be relative, not absolute. When the text reads 'three days', it is to be read as 'Day 3', Tuesday. All nouns with numbers are to be treated in such a way. The calendar was so regular that dates always fell on the same day of the week, and since all events in the story happened at the seasonal councils, these names of days give dates also. For example, in the Lazarus story, when Jesus stayed in a place 'for two days', the meaning is that he stayed on Day 2, Monday, and knowledge of the calendar, season and year shows that particular Monday in question (Monday, 1 December, AD 32).

Further, hours for prayer were assigned to monastic members according to their position in the hierarchy, the highest members saying prayers at the key points, especially noon. Those lower down the scale prayed at lesser hours, such as the ninth hour, 3 pm, or the tenth hour, 4 pm, for those lower still. Thus, when it is carefully noted in John that certain disciples left the Baptist and joined Jesus at the tenth hour,[2] this information, far from being unrelated and therefore useless, says something important, that they acted at a time for lesser members, in fact that they were Gentiles. When the man in the distant healing story was said to be healed 'yesterday at the seventh hour', his precise status is being given: he was assigned to a somewhat lesser day, but at the hour of 1 pm which positioned him a grade below a person who prayed at noon.

When it came to place, a theory of the unity of all places, which were interrelated with time, made it possible to work them out from a single basis, as will be shown more fully below. Terms for place, apparently vague, had an absolute sense: for example, prepositions with a general meaning, such as 'before' and 'behind', meant the compass points, for in

Hebrew thought the east was 'before' and the west was 'behind', since the ideal position was facing east. Another pair of prepositions meant 'north' and 'south'.

As for persons, many different devices were adopted, one of them to use a variety of different names as pseudonyms for the same person, in the way that the Scrolls do. Detail in the stories about these persons link them together. For example, when the story of the woman with ointment was placed by one gospel in the house of Lazarus of Bethany, and by another gospel in the house of Simon the leper of Bethany, and Lazarus was seen to be a leper in a parable, then it was known that these were names for the same man, for the student of special meanings assumed that the history was entirely consistent with itself and there were no varying accounts, as the modern scholar assumes.

Identities were covered by using terms appearing to be too broad to give information. For example, many plurals were used: 'the scribes', 'the Pharisees', 'the chief priests'. But the plural form was used in a different way, to mean a single person who represented another holding the office. 'The Scribe' was a person who could be identified, and 'the Scribes' was another person reproducing him in his office.

Some persons in the history were so important that they were made almost invisible to the outsider. Chief among these were the Herods – Agrippa Herod, who was present in Judea in the gospel period, attempting to gain support for a restoration of the Herodian monarchy, and his half-uncle, the tetrarch Antipas. They were actually at the centre of

the mission of which Jesus was a part. It had been
founded by Herod the Great, one of its aims being
to bring in revenue from the Diaspora, so that the
property of the mission was owned by the Herod
family and was the subject of dispute between these
two men, who consequently were at the centre of
mission politics. The events actually centred around
these two figures, and all that happened concerning
Jesus was an offshoot of their political struggles.

No word could be more indefinite than 'all' (in
Greek, *pas*). It was an ideal method, then, of designating the Herods, likely to be overlooked by the
casual reader. It suited them, for Herod the Great,
in whose time the mission had been founded,
claimed all positions in the hierarchy, the active
leaders being merely his delegates. When the word
appears, in its different forms, it refers to one of the
Herod family.

The word 'many' is equally imprecise. But, as the
Scrolls have shown us, one of the structures of
the Qumran community, their body of laymen, were
called 'the Many' (*rabbim*). When the Greek equivalent *polloi* appears, it refers to the person who was
the head of the Many, who at this time was Agrippa.
Thus, when John 2:23 reads, 'Many believed in his
(Jesus') name . . . but Jesus did not trust himself to
them', the meaning concerns the attitude of Agrippa
to Jesus, and Jesus' reaction to it. When such words
as 'many' and 'all' appear, they should be seen with a
capital letter – 'Many', 'All' – for they functioned as
names.

# The Gnostic Heavenly Man:
## The Key to All Systems

The ancients had found that even the mysteries of heaven could be mapped. It can be discovered that the student of the gospels was working with a map or diagram, created from the practices of the celibate community. Every day he sat in a room equivalent to one of the rooms in the Qumran buildings, watching the liturgy being conducted, taught to interpret its every detail as part of the order of creation. On the principles of Pythagoreans, who, according to contemporary sources, were the main influence on the Qumran community,[3] all reality was systematized, and could be expressed through a single plan, determined by numbers. The microcosm of the plan was spread out in the room. The student had only to refer to a diagram recording that plan to give him the solution to every problem in the puzzle that he was solving in the gospel text. The plan and its applications gave such unity to the gospels that they acted as a memorable textbook for every aspect of knowledge, liturgy and ministry.

What the student actually saw, when he sat in the original setting at Qumran, was a rectangular room, running north-south, its side walls made of large rough stones plastered together. The remains of the room, which is to be interpreted as a vestry, are still to be seen there, with half the walls standing.[4] If he measured the room, using the cubit measure (18 inches, the standard derived from a man's forearm, or 46 cm), he would find that when the side walls were included it was a square of 12 × 12 cubits, 144 square cubits, as the New Jerusalem was in the plan of the Book of Revelation. It ended with a dais and a projecting step, and further down from the dais ran another room of similar size.

But what he saw in his mind's eye was something far grander than this, nothing less than the plan of the universe. On the model of ancient temples, whose ceilings were patterned with stars to show that the worshipper was in heaven rather than on earth, the room in front of him was interpreted as a heavenly place containing the diagram representing all things (see Figure 1).

Its central depiction was the figure of a man, the Heavenly Man with which the gnostic literature is preoccupied. Philosophers who were at the beginning of the movement of thought that became gnosticism believed that the elect who were given learning in the celibate schools were far more than ordinary men. Through their knowledge they came close to being divine, their heads in heaven. Their ideal could be represented by the figure of a super-human man, 12 cubits high, three times the size of an ordinary man.

But this man was not entirely divine. Seven of his 12 cubits lay in the northern room, bounded by the dais, which represented a line just above his genitals. From his genitals downwards he was human, and in the class of ordinary men treated by the celibates as unclean, his lower 5 cubits being on the projecting step and in the southern room.

Each 1 cubit row in the room was called by a number, for in the interrelationship of time and space they were the cubits on which a man stood to pray at the hours of the day, and they ran downwards from the north. The noon prayer, at the sixth hour

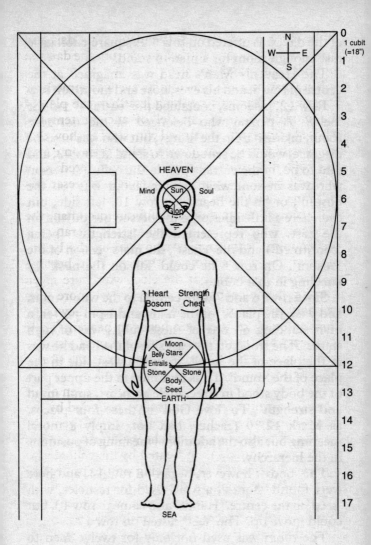

Labels in figure:

0
1 cubit
(=18")
1
2
3
4
5
6
7
8
9
10
11
12
13
14
15
16
17

N
W · E
S

HEAVEN

Mind    Sun    Soul

Glory

Heart    Strength
Bosom    Chest

Moon
Belly    Stars
Entrails
Stone    Stone
Body
Seed
EARTH

SEA

**FIGURE 1  The Heavenly Man**

37

of the day, was offered on row 6. A square cubit gave just enough room for a man to stand.

The Heavenly Man's head was imagined at the centre of row 6, and his eyes, nose and mouth on row 7. Row 12, his loins, contained the 'entrails' and the 'belly'. A person who belonged in the northern room, taking part in the liturgy, but who was in some disgrace, would be sent down to stand at row 12, and said to be 'in the entrails', or 'in the belly'. A person who was in somewhat greater favour was 'on the bosom', or 'in the heart', on row 10, left side, but even here a little inferior to the person beside him on the east, who represented the 'strength', (being 'confirmed') and the 'chest', the male version of the 'bosom'. On row 8 he could 'fall on the neck' by kneeling in that cubit.

Since rows 6 and 7 were central to the whole room and were the places for the noon and 1 pm prayer, a man standing on one of these cubits was of high status. If he stood on the east side of the head he was in the place of the 'soul', if on the west side in the place of the 'mind'. Thus four men in the upper part of the body stood in a rectangle at 'heart, soul, mind and strength'. To 'love God' in these four places, as Mark 12:30 teaches, had not simply a moral meaning but also the additional meaning of positions in the hierarchy.

The 'body', however, began on row 13, and here were found 'stones', a word used for testicles, with 'seed' in the centre. 'Hands' also came to row 13, but could move up. The 'feet' rested on row 17.

The room was used not only for twelve men to offer prayers at the twelve successive hours of the day, but also for the meals of these twelve. It was in this room that the twelve loaves of the Presence were eaten, loaves representing the twelve tribes, which had been offered to God in the sanctuary from earliest Old Testament times. This ceremony became the starting point of the Christian Eucharist.

At meal times a table was placed in the room, across 6 cubits of its 10 cubit width. Six men sat on either side of the table, on seats or parts of a bench, each place a cubit square, with room under the 2 cubit wide table for their feet. They sat very close to each other, expressing the fellowship of a monastic community.

Only these twelve men were privileged to use the north part of the vestry, from row 12 upwards. Row 13 consisted of a 1 cubit wide step, its remains still to be seen, raised a cubit above the floor of the south vestry. If a man was excluded from the meal he was sent as far down as row 13. The excluded man was defined as 'unclean', at the level of the genitals.

Ordinary men who did not have prayer duties and did not take part in the eating of the sacred loaves sat in the south room. The twelve in the northern, upper room formed a ministry, while these were the laity, sharing in the 'uncleanness' of the man in row 13.

These were the congregation of what eventually became a Christian church. The history is of the way these 'unclean', who had come to include Gentiles, broke into the hierarchy and took over all its positions, up to the very highest.

Students of the Kabbalah, the Jewish mystical tradition, will have observed that the Heavenly Man discerned behind the gospels looks like an early form of the human body which kabbalists believed to be the key to all reality. Ten Sephiroth, or Emanations, were attached to the different parts of the body, and in their meaning and combinations metaphysical insights were found. The detail is not the same, but there is sufficient similarity to raise the question of a historical connection. The Kabbalah, written down in the book called Zohar, was believed to have been revealed to Simon ben Jochai, who lived in a cave about AD 70, having escaped a death sentence from Titus, the conqueror of Jerusalem. The possibility would be worth considering that he continued the contemplative tradition of the Therapeuts, a branch of the ascetic movement connected with Qumran whose history was part of theirs. Because of their involvement in zealotry they were pursued by Titus, while the Christians continued the teaching tradition of the same movement.[5]

## The Scheme of the Universe

While the human body was seen as giving the plan of hierarchy, the vestry represented far more. Astronomy was one of the major interests of these celibate schools, and they believed they could depict the universe on the vestry floor. It was represented by a circle, filling the whole of the 12 × 12 cubits, including the side walls, and its centre was in the centre of the Heavenly Man's forehead, with the radii running outwards in the shape of an X, the form of their initiation symbol. An X was put on a man's forehead at the time he reached the highest grade (it was the shape of the archaic letter Taw, the last letter in the Hebrew alphabet, indicating that a man could go no higher in the system of grades called by letters).

At the very centre of the circle, where the noon prayer was said, was the Sun, for their science was based on their solar calendar. Earth was a long way below it, on row 13, the place for the unclean and excluded, for these thinkers held the gnostic view of the baseness of human life. A man who was sent down to row 13 was said to be 'thrown to Earth'. Just above Earth, in row 12, was the place of the Moon and the Stars, well below the Sun, for there was knowledge of the immensity of the solar system.

In the second phase of occupation of Qumran, as the archaeologists have shown, a platform was built in this room, acting as a part roof for the room which had formerly been open, with steps leading up to it outside on the north.[6] The platform became the substitute for the sanctuary, which had formerly been placed in a courtyard running north-south, to which the vestry room was attached. The whole building having become defiled because of the earthquake of 31 BC, all prayers were now said in the vestry, and the platform, which ran down to row 7, was for the use of the very highest priests who had formerly used the sanctuary. This platform came to be called 'Heaven'. When Jesus was 'taken up to Heaven' in the week after the crucifixion, he was simply brought to this platform, where he resumed his position as a person of high rank saying prayers there.

Since the Man was imagined to be standing on the bed of the Sea, the three main positions in the vestry were 'Heaven, Earth and Sea'. When it was said that

41

'God made Heaven, Earth and Sea' (Acts 4:24), the special meaning was that the vestry at Qumran contained the plan of all creation.

At the centre of the larger circle, at the Man's forehead, a 1 cubit circle was conceived, and here stood the priests who were the nucleus of the community, and of the universe, for they were believed to be incarnations of divine beings. Repeated when the platform was built above, the circle lay half on row 6 and half in upper row 7. Its lower half was called the 'Glory' as the place where the light of the Sun was reflected.

'Heaven' was conceived as containing the throne of God, and on occasions a chair for the supreme priest, who claimed to be an incarnation of God, was placed on the platform. Its actual dimension – as always at Qumran – was much smaller than its significance, and the seat filled a square cubit at row 6, while a half cubit for the priest's feet, a footstool, was necessarily in the semicircle below the line. The seat was seen as a reproduction of the throne of God in the true heaven. When God performed the act of creation, it was believed, he stood up at the footstool, which then became the Beginning, the *archē*, the spot where creation began. In the anatomical imagery it was the place of the nose, from which came the breath of God. It was also the place of the Spirit, likened to breath, for the Spirit of God 'moved over the face of the waters' in the Genesis account of creation.

Here, at the 'Beginning', the book of Genesis, meaning 'the beginning', had its place. From this spot the scriptures were read and teaching given from them, and the word 'podium' in the usage of

Christian monasteries retained the association of such a spot with the feet of God. A person who was 'in the Beginning', *en archē*, or who was at 'the Glory', was standing at this podium. The word 'Glory' conveyed the additional sense of the place of enlightenment received through teaching.

## 'All the Kingdoms of the World'

When, at the outset of his ministry, Jesus had been tempted by Satan and taken up to a high mountain where he was shown 'all the kingdoms of the world in a moment of time', he had been, in fact, undergoing a this-worldly experience. 'Satan' was one of the many pseudonyms for Judas Iscariot, and Jesus was discussing with him the politics of the mission to the Diaspora in which they were all involved. Founded some seventy years before, in the time of Herod the Great, to bring Jews into a renewed form of Judaism, the mission had reached the point where some, such as Judas, hoped that it would lead to an actual material empire, a Jewish empire taking over from Rome.

In drawing up the plan of conquest, a map of the world was used, circular as ancient maps usually were. Two cubits in diameter, it corresponded to the circle around the lower body of the Heavenly Man, thus expressing an attitude to the fallen world.

The north, south, east and west points of the world circle were said to represent cities at these compass points, the great capitals of the world where the mission had centres. At the north was Antioch, at the south Alexandria in Egypt, at the east and west Babylon and Rome respectively (see Figure 2).

Within the circle a lesser X reproduced the greater one, its points indicating the NE, NW, SE and SW points of the geographical world. For the mission, these were Damascus to Armenia in the north-east; Ephesus to Illyricum in the north-west; Arabia in the south-east; and Cyrene in the south-west.

This geographical scheme covered the Jewish Diaspora. A word was used for the wider world than that of Judea – the Cosmos, Greek *kosmos*, translated 'the world'. For the monastics living at Qumran, the Diaspora was not a holy place, and those living an ordinary married life were equal to those in the Diaspora, not pure enough to be admitted to the sacred fellowship meal at the table higher in the

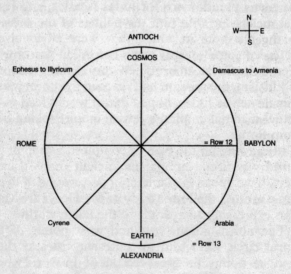

**FIGURE 2  World Map**

44

room, called the Agape meal, from the verb 'to love'. These monastics, including those who became Christian like John Mark, were told, 'Do not love the world', an admonition found in the Epistle of John.

When a man who normally dined at the holy table 'came into the world', he was doing so for the reason that he was temporarily leaving monastic life for marriage. Men like Jesus, who had to continue their great dynasties – Jesus was physically descended from the line of David – lived normally in the monastic community, but had to leave from time to time to cohabit with their wives, simply for the sake of begetting children. The arrangements of his rule, called the second order of Essenes, are given by Josephus. (The Essenes, described by ancient writers and known to have lived at Qumran, formed the nucleus of the ascetic movement to which Jesus belonged.)

The man who was coming 'into the world' expressed it, in the first instance, by coming down to row 12 in the vestry, its lowest point, then stepping outside to row 13, the level of the 'flesh'. From there he went outside the vestry and away from the Qumran buildings, to a building where such men prepared for married life.

## The Outside World: The Pillar Bases Outside

Outside the southern room of the vestry, on its eastern side, are still to be seen two circular pillar bases carved in the Greek style, contrasting sharply with the rough stones of the rest of the building. The top of each pillar base measures just 1 cubit, suggesting that they were used as the cubit measure. One of them has been left upturned by the archaeologists, and it is clear that they are not exactly in their original positions (see Figure 3).[7]

From early Old Testament times there were monthly visitors to the temple, ordinary villagers coming at new moons to see their king, who would permit them to look inside the splendid sanctuary but not go into it, receiving them outside its open door.[8] When the temple priests were exiled and the sanctuary was reduced to the small scale of Qumran,

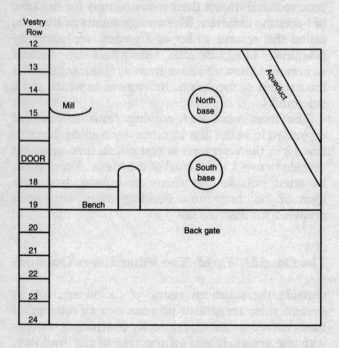

**FIGURE 3  The Pillar Bases**

the practice was continued, now serving a more urgent purpose. Ordinary villagers came from Galilee in the north, bringing the food tithes that they preferred to pay to these, their rightful priests, rather than to the false priesthood using a lunar calendar that had taken over the Jerusalem temple. The grapes and the wheat they brought were used to make the holy loaves and holy wine for use in the monastery. A mill for grinding wheat into flour was found by the archaeologists near the pillar bases.

The pilgrims, as they had now become, were still received outside the door, by the lowest member of the priestly hierarchy, the heir of David, their king in traditional practice. The vestry, which took over the role of the sanctuary after the earthquake, was still not open to them. The king stood on the north pillar base to meet them, and the chief pilgrim stood on the south base, the two being placed in line with the sides of the door of the south vestry. As the monastic system developed, the pilgrims were given instruction, in gratitude for the food tithes. Coming at the new moons, which now became the 1st of the month in the solar calendar, they stayed for the thirty days of the solar month, being given elementary knowledge. The north base was a reproduction 'Moon', the 1 cubit circle that was also depicted in the vestry.

Another feature of this area, still to be seen, is a large stone bench outside the south door of the vestry. Its position suggests a place for outsiders to the congregation. Only initiates were permitted into the south vestry, and outside it sat those who had not yet qualified, or never would. These were classed as 'boys and women'. The 'boys', originally, were literally boys, youths of high or royal birth who had been sent to the monastic school; they were given their elementary instruction in this area. This purpose gave a further set of associations to the area which were retained. The south pillar base was also used as a place for corporal punishment. From hitting with the teacher's measuring rod to flogging, such punishments were built into the monastic system.

The other kind of occupant of the bench was a woman, of the status of a princess or queen, who was also given some instruction. The highest grade for a woman was that of Virgin.

The woman's position was the starting point in the education of Gentiles. As these Jewish monastic schools became increasingly attractive to Gentiles, some came to village synagogues, then accompanied pilgrims to the main centre, staying for further education. Some became proselytes and were treated like Jews, others chose to remain uncircumcised and so were legally the equals of women. The whole of this triangular area, bounded on the east by the aqueduct, developed as a school, for Jewish pilgrims and for Gentiles. It, and places like it, were very probably the schools, described by Josephus, in which a class of men called 'exegetes' taught Jewish traditions.[9]

When uncircumcised Gentiles sought to go on to actual initiation, it was argued by some that at the beginning of creation, in the time of Adam, there had been no covenant of circumcision, and that Gentiles should be allowed into this first covenant. Their school would be like an 'Eden' – a term for Qumran found in the Scrolls[10] – and they would be taught by an 'Adam', a name used for the heir of David in a new role on the north base. They themselves would be likened to an 'Eve', equal to the Virgin, as the female image was retained. The area of the pillar bases then became a 'garden', where the chief Gentile was taught, and the outer hall on the east side of the building, where pilgrims were accustomed to have their meals, was called a larger 'garden', where they were taught in numbers.

On the north base was imagined the 'tree of knowledge'. The south base, where preparation for initiation or 'life' was given to Gentiles, could be called the 'tree of life'. The Book of Revelation retains the Eden imagery up to the very end, giving a description that fits very well the pillar bases – one of them the 'tree of life' – and the aqueduct nearby, which was called 'the river of life'.[11]

But the south base, to which married men had come and which therefore had associations of uncleanness, was also the place where punishment was given, and it was treated by Jewish members as a negative spot. When the country came under Roman occupation and tribute had to be paid to Rome, pilgrims coming to Qumran placed their tribute money here. It was their silent way of saying that it was defiled money. The south base then stood for Caesar, and the representative of Caesar, the Roman governor, could be invited to stand on it. On the principle, frequently used, that a man visiting Qumran brought his home base with him, the south base became the 'praetorium' when the governor used it. Pontius Pilate, brought down to Qumran for the trial of zealots (see Chapter 5), was kept outside the sacred vestry, and stood on this base, going between it and the north base to conduct the hearings. When men were convicted of setting up as rivals to Caesar, they were made to stand on the south base and mocked.

The pesher of the crucifixion story relies on intimate knowledge of this area and of the vestry, where the Last Supper and the hearings before the priests took place. Each gospel tells exactly the same story, using different terms, and the challenge was to identify the times, places and personalities, which are exactly the same in all four accounts.

The pesharist when he had finished had the script of a Passion play, plotting every detail of what had happened on that Thursday evening and Friday morning, enabling it to be re-enacted exactly where it had taken place, or in reproductions of Qumran elsewhere. As the Book of Revelation shows, by AD 44 an actual re-enactment of the crucifixion was held at Qumran, 'that great city . . . called Sodom'. Jesus himself took part.[12] The Christians, having come from the communities of the Therapeuts, who held a re-enactment of the Exodus to symbolize religious salvation, quickly saw the value of having a new drama, to teach the point that salvation now came about through identification with the suffering of Jesus.

# CHAPTER 3

# 'In the Beginning Was the Word'

'In the beginning was the Word, and the Word was with God, and the Word was God.'

The best known part of John's gospel is its opening. Simply as they stand, the words are powerfully evocative of religious feeling. The spiritual person responds to their meaning, that the human is part of the divine. 'Word' – that is what makes us human, that we have speech, and speech expresses reason. There is an immanent Reason in everything, there is meaning, it is not hopeless. This is the insight of faith, carrying the religious person through the darkest of times.

It is the language of Stoic philosophy, and the words 'in the beginning' connect it with the book of Genesis, giving in one phrase the history that married Greek thought to Hebrew scripture at the birth of western culture. But the language is universal, speaking directly to the need of the human to open to the divine. 'The Word was God'. There is that of God in all of us, God is that towards which we are evolving. To listen to the Word, and to glimpse God through the mystery of our inadequacy, is to be moving towards wholeness.

The opening of John's gospel is the best example of the perfect balance that Jesus achieved in his new scripture, between an immediately available meaning that was understood by everyone without particular knowledge, and a historical meaning that lay within the words to a person who had specialized knowledge. For the other meaning of these words is: 'At midnight on 1 March, AD 29, Jesus left the enclosed monastic life and became a village teacher, one who acted also as a priest'.

Words come from mouths, and on the place of the mouth in the diagram of the Heavenly Man stood the heir of David, who, when he brought the message of learning from the monastery into the outside world, was called 'The Word'. 'The Word' remained a code name for Jesus, right up to the year AD 63 when Paul sent a coded message, 'the Word of God is not fettered', meaning that Jesus was not in prison.[1]

In the same cubit, in its upper part, was the *archē*, the Beginning, the footstool where God as Spirit stood to create the world, the podium where a reader of scripture and teacher stood. Jesus as the David was still in a celibate state, entitled to stand at the teaching podium on the platform at Qumran, so 'in the Beginning was the Word'. He would eventually return there after four years outside, being 'brought up to Heaven'. But he was now leaving, for in the following year, when he turned thirty-six, he would have to marry according to the dynastic rule. This day, 1 March, AD 29, was his thirty-fifth birthday.[2]

The chief priest who stood at the centre of row 6 was at the same time 'God'. A Sadducee priest accepted the view, widely held by Diaspora Jews and expressed in the writings of Philo, that a high priest

52

was more than human, could act as an incarnation of God himself, accepting prayers on behalf of God, and was addressed as 'God'. The current Sadducee priest was Jonathan Annas, one of the Annas family who supplied a series of high priests in Jerusalem in the first century AD. At the time Jonathan was aspiring to become high priest – an ambition he achieved some years later – with the support of the ascetic community at Qumran; he was already acting in the role of 'God'. His more liberal view of morality enabled him to accept Jesus as legitimate (Jesus had been conceived before his parents' wedding and was regarded by Pharisees as illegitimate), and Jesus was therefore his lay subordinate in the pair, Priest and King, who were leaders of village communities. As the Scrolls show, the king, who was only a layman, had to accept his subordination to a priest in these priestly communities.[3]

Jesus therefore stood 'towards the God', *pros ton theon*, the phrase usually translated as 'with God'. The preposition *pros* always has the special sense of a position in the cubit south of a northern one. But the wording goes on: 'a God (not 'the God') was the Word'. Another usage is being drawn on here, that a noun without an article means a person in a lower position, or his servant and representative. Jesus himself could act as a representative of 'God', and that meant that he could act as a priest. But he could only do so in the village, when he worked as a teacher, 'God' being far away.

It was this role that was the central concern of Jesus throughout his period outside, and that accounted for much that happened to him. Acting like a priest, teaching Gentiles who became his followers and formed his party, he was treated by them as if he were a real priest, and as if there were no need for any Jewish priest. He accepted the role, for it meant that all men could become priests, not simply those who had been born into the priestly tribe, and it meant also that the Jewish priesthood and the institutional side of the Jewish religion had become obsolete.

So, at the outset of the gospel, he stated his fundamental tenet: 'the Word was a God'.

A few hours later Jesus 'came into the world'. He moved down to the dais edge, as his first step outside the enclosed life. Then later that same day, 'the Word became flesh and dwelt among us'. By noon, Jesus had gone outside the Qumran buildings, to a building further down the coast where a man prepared for marriage.

He then needed a 'eunuch' to act as go-between in his forthcoming marriage, and John Mark, a celibate Gentile, was chosen. When in buildings outside Jesus could still teach at the podium, the 'Glory', so John Mark introduces himself, the 'we' who spoke in the persona of another, by saying 'we beheld his Glory'.

The historical and political dimension was signalled when the prologue, apparently about pure metaphysics, came quickly to the statement: 'There was a man sent from God, whose name was John'. The sudden introduction of John the Baptist seems out of place in the theological context, especially if the Baptist was thought to be of no great significance. From this point on the alert reader was aware that there were two streams of thought, one spiritual, one historical, and in addition he was being told that the Baptist was of importance in the history.

From the following statements about the Light the student knew that although the Baptist had been the supreme priest of the community, known as 'the Light', based on the seven-branched candelabra of the temple, he had now been temporarily displaced by Jonathan Annas, who took over the title. The historical reason was that the Baptist himself had left monastic life for marriage, being thirty-six years old in this year, six months older than Jesus. The political point was that the Baptist agreed with Pharisee views on the illegitimacy of Jesus, whereas Jonathan Annas accepted him as legitimate, so from this moment Jesus could act as the David.

In the remainder of the prologue, the words seem to show the Baptist hailing Jesus as his superior – 'he who comes after me has become before me, for he was my first'. But there is a series of plays on words, which actually mean that Jesus, who should have been in the place of the David, belonged, in the Baptist's opinion, with illegitimates. Such men, who were called 'orphans', were admitted into an Essene monastery as permanent celibates, and were never permitted to go outside to marry.

The prologue, then, gives the first piece of narrative, despite appearances. After that, the book launches into the form of narrative, about the Baptist and Jesus. Each episode happened 'the next day', and this, like all time words, gives a precise set of dates, on Monday, Tuesday and Thursday – 7, 8 and 10 March, AD 29. When the Baptist appeared to be upholding Jesus, he was, in the precise meaning, expressing conflict with him. The history begins with a split between the followers of the Baptist and the followers of Jesus, running parallel to the account in the Dead Sea Scrolls of the conflict between the Teacher of Righteousness and his rival, called 'the Man of a Lie' and 'the Wicked Priest'. From a number of pieces of evidence it is possible to say that the Teacher referred to in the Scrolls was John the Baptist, and the rival teacher Jesus. The Scrolls are telling the same story from the point of view of the Baptist's followers.[4]

# CHAPTER 4

# The Seven Signs

## Anatomy of the Gospel

During the years of his ministry Jesus had said to his Gentile students: 'To you is given the mystery of the kingdom of God', and he went on to illustrate his concept with the example of a parable, something that looked like a simple story but had a second, historical meaning. Scripture itself, they all believed, was a 'mystery', in the sense of a puzzle, with a pesher (solution), the Hebrew word found in the Scrolls for the concealed historical level in scripture. When Jesus added 'Everything is given in parables' (Mark 4:11), he was promising a new scripture, in the form of stories that would have a second layer of meaning. A Christian pesharist would be given a new puzzle to solve.

The additional motive was to do something about the growing rumour of a resurrection that had been started by Simon Magus. Jesus' answer was the seven Signs, all unbelievable miracles, but all with a natural meaning, leading up to the eighth, the resurrection – surely it had a natural solution too.

So he composed his gospel, with its most apparent structure the seven Signs. He did not include any other story claiming as much as the resurrection.

There was no virgin birth. That was still to develop, a belief derived from an actual event but written in such a way as to appear to be supernatural.

Nor did he include any parables, although the concept was known and came to be illustrated in Mark's gospel. He was not, at this point, concerned with past history. The need for recording a complete history of the mission in the form of parables would be seen as time went on.

His plan for his gospel was a simple one. It would fall into two main parts. The first would deal with the years of ministry, and the second with the crucifixion, both being of about equal length. An anatomical image was natural: the seven Signs were like a spine, the crucifixion story like a head, and the long discourses that filled out both parts were like the flesh.

Through the 'spine', the seven Signs, he would record the actual steps in the history of what had happened during those years and, through the discourses, the accounts of the debates that his actions had provoked, furious arguments in the seasonal councils. Each miracle story would record one of the successive changes he had made in the constitution. Each would concern a typical person in the hierarchy, beginning with the lowest and ending with the highest. By the time he had finished, Jesus had overturned all of the established practices of the mission, designed to keep celibate Jews and their priests at the top, and the 'unclean' – married men, women, Gentiles – in an inferior position.

Moreover, he had transformed the offices of the levitical priesthood into the offices of the Christian ministry. When he began, the leading ministers used names of archangels – 'Phanuel' and 'Raphael'; or of the levitical families of the Old Testament – Kohath, Gershon, and Merari. Such names are found in the Scrolls and their related literature, and some make a brief appearance in the New Testament. When Jesus had finished, he had a cardinal, an archbishop, a bishop, a presbyter, a deacon and two kinds of laymen. Beginning at the lowest point, with the laymen, the order went upwards, ending with the cardinal at the seventh Sign. The structure was then ready for the 'head', the Pope, whose position would come about through the 'resurrection', when a layman, Jesus, broke through into an office that had belonged to a high ranking Jewish priest.

Each Sign would, moreover, concern an individual who had played a part in the history of those years, not simply the history of the ministry, but also of the politics that occupied the centre of the stage – the question of the restoration of the Herodian monarchy. Herod Agrippa, returned from Rome, bankrupt, despairing, but still hoping to persuade Rome to restore his family to rule, was at times in alliance with and at others in rivalry with Herod Antipas, the tetrarch of Galilee. Agrippa, with the assistance of another relative, Thomas Herod, wanted a return of the royal Herods, while Antipas wanted a more comfortable existence, keeping the Herodian wealth but letting a Sadducee high priest be the real authority in the country and in the worldwide mission. Agrippa had at first allied with the Pharisees and with the fiery preacher John the Baptist. His monarchist party in the mission had long been led by Judas Iscariot. But part way through these years, when the Baptist was discredited and executed, Agrippa changed sides, in a short-lived alliance with Antipas and the Sadducees. During this brief period many of the reforms of Jesus could be implemented, for Agrippa wanted the favour of Rome. To gain Rome's favour the mission, which by now had an enormous following of Gentiles in the Diaspora, had to give Gentiles higher status, for it was their voice that would be heard in the Roman court.

The seven Signs were: first, turning water into wine; second, healing a man at a distance; third, the man who had been thirty-eight years at the pool and was healed without entering it; fourth, feeding 5000 with five loaves and two fish; fifth, walking on water; sixth, healing a blind man; and seventh, the raising of Lazarus.

## 'Turning Water Into Wine' (John 2:1–12)

In the first miracle, Jesus the magician performs one of his best tricks, inviting his audience either to awed respect, or to critical analysis, according to their preference. He was at a wedding, it says, and his mother was present too. The servants (*diakonoi*, a word that elsewhere means 'deacons') found that they had run out of wine. Mary informed Jesus of this, and he answered her discourteously. But she said to the servants, 'Do what he tells you'. Jesus told them to take the six stone waterpots, fill them with water, draw some out, and bring it to the steward of the feast (*architriklinos*, a word meaning the slave who acted as a kind of butler at a banquet). When he tasted it, he found that the water had become wine. Without mentioning the miracle, he simply called the bridegroom and complained that it was usual to serve the good wine first and the worse wine later, 'when they are drunk', but that he, the bridegroom, had kept the good wine until now. There is no detail after this, and the story ends with the solemn statement: 'This is the beginning of Signs that Jesus did . . . and manifested his glory'.

The modern believer usually prefers not to dwell on the story, apart from including a reference to it in the traditional marriage service. Nor, apparently, did contemporaries repeat it, for nothing like it appears in the other gospels. But its essential point was easily accessible to a pesharist with knowledge of the Qumran initiation system. The earlier stage was a baptism with water, followed two years later by full initiation, the main privilege of which was the receiving of the 'Drink of the Community', the wine at the sacred meal. Only male Jewish celibates received the wine, while unclean persons such as Gentiles, the physically and mentally handicapped, women and married men were confined to the stage of baptism, and not permitted to attend the sacred meal. In Qumran language, 'to turn water into wine' was to say to such unclean persons that they could now become full initiates and receive the communion. That would be to bring about a social revolution, removing the barrier against the unclean, a matter of the greatest consequence and worthy of being presented as a 'miracle'.

Uncircumcised Gentiles were confined to the very lowly position of being merely baptised, denied full membership. They were called 'children', and the distinction was retained within the Christian church, but for real children, who are given baptism only, and later confirmation, with participation in the communion meal of bread and wine. An uncircumsised Gentile – a fully adult man – was now treated as if he were the same as a Jewish celibate, overcoming the tremendous gulf that had been set up by the founders of the mission.

As the sign of his initiation, he was given wine, but not new wine, the drink that is prescribed in the Scrolls. In Judea, new wine was used at the time of the grape harvest in September, and would keep for less than a year afterwards. The highest celibates received their initiation in September, the season of the great Jewish feasts, but lesser grades used March and June. The Scrolls reveal that the feast of Pentecost was one of the initiation seasons, but it was for a lower class, the pilgrims who visited and were given instruction, sometimes advancing to a form of initiation, but one that kept them outside the vestry. They could not use the new wine which by now had become unpalatable, but had to use fermented wine, the drink of ordinary men in the world, treating it as sacred. When Peter was accused of being 'drunk with new wine' at Pentecost,[1] it was a way of saying that he used fermented wine as sacred wine.

For these members, fermented wine was 'good wine', and new wine, by Pentecost when this event took place, was 'worse wine'. It had been the custom to drink fermented wine earlier in the evening at a common meal for satisfying hunger, then to drink the new wine in the later sacred part when the communion was held. When excess was permitted, as in some communities, there was drunkenness, and the taste of the new wine, the 'worse wine' was then disguised. But in Jesus' reform fermented wine, the 'good wine', was 'kept until now', used as the sacred wine, but sipped only, the special meaning of the word 'taste'.

From the start there had been two kinds of uncircumsised Gentiles, those who were attracted by the celibate life, and those who preferred the married state. Of the celibates, some, such as John Mark, would enter monastic institutions, while others lived as individuals, with their own property, learning and teaching in the school system that arose from the practice of instructing pilgrims. John's gospel was written for the celibate kind of Gentile, and the first of the individuals, under John Mark, was the man called Philip, whose skills were lent to Jesus for the recording of his gospel, being rewarded with the title Philip the Evangelist. In acknowledgement, he became the subject of this first sign, recording the advancement of men who had hitherto been treated as outsiders.

### 'Healing at a Distance' (John 4:46–54)

The second Sign, its number indicated by a careful note at the end, appears to show Jesus simply saying a few words, and a man some distance away being healed at the same moment. Jesus was in the same place as for the first Sign, in 'Cana', and was told by a 'royal one' (*basilikos*) that his son was sick, or 'weak', in another village, and about to die. Jesus had to be persuaded by the father, whom he accused of wanting miracles too much, but then he yielded and said, 'Your son lives'. Some servants arrived, saying that the son was alive, and that the fever had left him 'Yesterday, at the seventh hour'. The father 'knew that at that hour Jesus spoke'.

A thoughtful reader might find it strange that Jesus rebuked a dependence on miracles, but then performed one implying the magical power of words. In other healings, he was said to have made contact with the person, laying hands on him. The father, in fact, asked Jesus to 'come down and heal him', but Jesus apparently chose not to. The episode does little to enhance the image of Jesus as a real healer, yet it is underlined as a major Sign.

The history that emerges from a close analysis is much more believable, and much more important. The date was Friday, 21 September, AD 31. The previous night the turning point of political events had occurred. John the Baptist, discredited by the failure of his prophecies, had been condemned to execution. An all-night 'banquet' of the type the Therapeuts observed, actually an abstemious sacred meal and council, had been attended by both Herods, Agrippa and Antipas the tetrarch, who had represented Herodian interests in the country since the abolition of the monarchy in AD 6. Both agreed that the Baptist was better put out of the way; their real reason being that he was jeopardizing their standing with Rome.

The previous day, Thursday, was not simply 'yesterday' in the ordinary sense, but Yesterday, one of the fixed days called Yesterday, Today and Tomorrow, the 30th, 31st, and 1st at the quarters of the solar calendar. The seventh hour of the day was 1 pm, when the second stage of the noon communal meal began. At that hour, on the Thursday, the 'fever' had lost its hold. The word for 'fever' was *pyretos*, from *pyr*, 'fire', and it alluded to John the Baptist, the 'Elijah' who wanted to bring down 'fire from heaven' against Antipas and his wife Herodias, who were likened to Ahab and Jezebel of the Old Testament Elijah story. It had been decided at the Herodian council on the Thursday at 1 pm that John must go, and the events of the night continued the process.

An uncircumcised Gentile would never have been permitted by the Baptist to become equal to a Jewish celibate initiate, a man who was not 'weak' but 'strong'. Some Gentile initiates, as Philip had now become in the previous Sign, were tolerated, but were treated as equal to women. They were 'weak', and still could not be 'confirmed', could not become 'strong' like men and begin their progress up the promotion ladder. The second Sign records how this barrier was overcome for Philip, so that Gentiles were no longer treated as women, and there was no longer a difference between initiates who could not advance and those who were 'confirmed'.

Jonathan Annas, the 'royal one' of the story, had now become Chief Priest in the Baptist's place. As a liberal Sadducee who believed in peaceful relations with Rome, Annas and his whole family were in favour of the promotion of Gentiles, and Jesus agreed with him on this point, although not on other matters. As soon as Jonathan was confirmed in his position as successor to the Baptist, he, with Jesus, gave Philip the full form of initiation.

Jonathan, however, was treated as the leading priest but not as a supreme priest by Agrippa, who claimed that role for himself, as his grandfather Herod the Great had done. For him, Jonathan was a subordinate, equal to a king who was deputy to the supreme priest, so called a 'royal one'. This issue would be one of the causes of the political tensions of these years.

The Jewish male form of initiation was understood as the giving of 'life'. But the consequence of this was that a man could also be 'put to death' spiritually – that is, excommunicated. Previously a Gentile, not having been given 'life', even if he had a form of membership, could not be excommunicated. As the gnostic Gospel of Philip itself states, 'A Gentile cannot "die", for he has never been "born" that he might "die"'.[2]

No sooner had he received his new status, which meant membership of councils, than Philip's hostility towards Agrippa became known. Philip, whose ordinary name was Protos, was to figure later in the history as an enemy of Agrippa: Philip lent Agrippa money and took action against him when the debt was not paid.[3] He appears in Acts as an associate of Simon Magus, Agrippa's great enemy, who eventually brought about his death. Although Jonathan Annas had used his new position to promote Philip, Agrippa claimed the power to override him. He rescinded the promotion, thus excommunicating Philip, who began the series of stages leading downwards: he was 'about to die'.

But Jonathan Annas and Jesus decided to act independently of Agrippa, and reinstate Philip. This was the political point of the story: that Jonathan, with Jesus, defied Agrippa. They knew Agrippa's fickleness, which would be expressed in constant changes of policy throughout his career.

Philip, although apparently still at a distance in the surface story, was, in fact, brought to the building where Jesus and Jonathan were. This is shown by the use of the device called 'the rule of the last referent' (explained on pp. 262–3.) All three were at the first building outside the Qumran monastery, one in which women could live. The remains of this building have been found at Ain Feshkha, two miles down the coast of the Dead Sea from Qumran. It was here that many of the most important events took place. It was in this building that Gentiles, the equals of women, began their instruction, and where they were brought up to higher grades.

When Jesus seemed to be rebuking the *basilikos* about wanting 'signs and wonders', he was talking to Philip, and it was not a rebuke but simply a statement about his form of liturgy.

The person who was at a distance from Philip in this episode was not Jesus, but Agrippa. He arrived at Ain Feshkha to find that the ceremony of reinstatement, at which he should have been present, had taken place without him. He was forced to give in, to preserve his new formal alliance with the Sadducees. But he was permitted to give a ruling on Philip's exact status, which was expressed through his day and hour for prayer.

He ruled that Philip was to keep the times that he had been given at his promotion the previous day, when the Baptist had lost power and the 'fire' had left him. He was to attend councils 'Yesterday', meaning the 30th rather than the 31st, a lesser promotion day as he was still only an initiate, and he was to say his prayer at the seventh hour, 1 pm, meaning that he was a grade below an acolyte who said a prayer as the servant of the supreme priest at noon.

## 'The Man Who Was Thirty-Eight Years at the Pool'
### (John 5:1–18)

Immediately after the second Sign a third is recorded. Jesus came to a pool called Bethsaida, which had five porches, in which lay a multitude of sick people. It was said to be in Jerusalem, using the plural form of the word. A certain man had been lying there for thirty-eight years (why such an exact figure when not even the year of Jesus' ministry is given in this gospel?). Jesus saw him and asked him, 'Do you wish to be healed?' The sick man said, 'Sir, I do not have a man so that when the water is stirred up he should throw me into the pool, but when I come, another goes down before me'. Jesus said: 'Pick up your bed and walk', and the man immediately became whole, picked up his bed, and walked. There followed a lively discussion, not about the healing, but about the fact that the man picked up his bed on the sabbath. The sabbath law decreed that from 6 pm on Friday evening no burden should be lifted up.

The man had apparently suffered from a remarkable lack of charity over a very long time, and it was strange that the pool, even if it did have healing powers, should work for only one at a time. But even to the average member listening to this tale, anyone who had a basic knowledge of the Old Testament, there was a signal in the 'thirty-eight years'. According to the book of Deuteronomy, it was in year 38 of the Exodus that the preparations for crossing the Jordan into the Promised Land began.[4] This man was intended to be associated with a 'Joshua', who had gone down into the waters of Jordan when they parted for the crossing. Something more than a medical marvel was being related here.

It was part of the public history of this period that would-be 'Joshuas' kept appearing, attracting a large following, and demanding that the waters of Jordan should part or the walls of the city fall down.[5] It can now be seen that these demonstrations arose from the community of which Jesus – himself called 'Joshua' – was a member, and that the Joshua theme came from the Exodus liturgy that was observed by the Therapeuts at their pentecontad feasts. They enacted a religious drama of the Exodus as symbolizing religious salvation, with leaders acting the parts of Aaron, Moses, Miriam and Joshua.[6]

Such demonstrations were staged on the 31st at the quarters of the solar calendar, the 'Today', for it had long been believed that heaven, observing this calendar, would intervene in history on this day, and bring 'Joshua' to a political victory. The episode of the man at the pool took place on a 31st, Friday, 21 September (the equinox), three hours after the second Sign. 'Jerusalem', when the plural form of the word was used, meant Qumran, the New Jerusalem which had been built by priests exiled from the real Jerusalem. The leaders who had been at Ain Feshkha had walked up to Qumran, for this was the Jewish end of the year and a great event was to be expected then.

For the version of the chronology held by James the brother of Jesus, this was year 38 of a forty year 'Exodus' that had begun in September, 8 BC. Its forty year point, in September AD 33, is the subject of a story in Acts 3, concerning James, the 'Lame Man'. A triumphant vindication of the work of mission that had been conducted during those years was expected by James on this afternoon at 3 pm, the hour when the sabbath began.

The role of 'Joshua' was primarily that of the Chief Therapeut, who appeared in the demonstrations recorded in public histories. He was expected to take would-be members and lead them through the waters of a river, calling it the 'Jordan', the process giving them a form of initiation, but only to the lifestyle of the Therapeuts, not to coenobitic life. They were permitted to marry, but lived single by choice, devoting their time to learning. Proselytes, Gentiles who fully accepted Jewish identity, were given the same kind of baptism.

The heir of David had been appointed from the start of the mission to baptize pre-proselytes, married Gentiles like the man called James Niceta, who adopted some aspects of Jewish practice and thought, but not a full Jewish identity. When he was in this role, the David either taught the doctrine and lifestyle of the Therapeuts, being called 'Joshua' (Jesus in Greek), or taught the lifestyle of Nazirites, men who took periods of retreat away from marriage. In this role the David was called 'the Nazorean' or the 'Nazirite', so in the combined role he was called 'Jesus the Nazirite'.

When he was fulfilling other roles that his family line determined, his crown prince could act for him, but only as a Nazirite, not as a 'Joshua'. The 'crown prince' of Jesus, his successor, was at present his younger brother James, until Jesus' own son was born. But this title was, for James, only a few hours old. The country was under the rule of a Pharisee high priest, Caiaphas, who from the time of his inauguration in AD 18 had had sufficient influence in the mission, which now exercised considerable political power, to declare Jesus incapable of succeeding his father Joseph, and James to be the true heir. Caiaphas was still high priest, but within the mission Agrippa had just allied with the Sadducee contender for the high priesthood, and a future could be foreseen in which Jesus was the true David.

James had not yet heard the news, which was brought to him when the leaders came up to Qumran. He was acting in the part of a 'Joshua' himself, at a small pool just inside the walls fed by the aqueduct. It was designated a 'Jordan', and he was expecting that a sign from heaven would come to confirm that this was indeed year 38, when the end of the 'Exodus wanderings' had come, and he as Joshua would plunge into the 'Jordan', whose waters would part to let him through to a 'Promised Land'.

The original Joshua had been accompanied by an Aaronite priest, who with other priests stepped down into the waters of Jordan first, bearing the ark of the Covenant.[7] For James, this part should have been played by Caiaphas, but now Jonathan Annas was the favoured priest, and he showed his new authority by going down into the water first. James knew what this meant, that he was no longer the 'Joshua'. In that capacity he had acted as a presbyter, but now he was reduced to deacon. He could teach James Niceta only in his earlier stages, leaving his instruction for initiation to Jesus.

Jesus said 'take up your bed and walk' not only to James, but also to Jonathan Annas. Both of them acted as if the ground where Gentiles walked was unclean, and used a portable bed, a palanquin, from which to teach. It was this practice that Jesus most condemned in Jonathan, who featured in a story in the Synoptics as the 'paralytic', who was incapable of walking. Under his influence both agreed to treat Gentiles as equals.

But then a further problem arose, that of sabbath observance, epitomized by the problem of a Jewish teacher who had to lift up his palanquin on Friday at 6 pm. In the discussion at the council at Qumran that same evening, the different viewpoints on the sabbath and consequent Jewish identity were stated, showing that there were three major parties, with minor differences within each. Some held the strict view, forbidding all work from Friday evening; others allowed exceptions for some purposes such as humanitarian ones; others kept the Julian sabbath so did not forbid work until Friday at midnight. Jesus' view was that he did not observe the sabbath at all.

## 'Feeding the Five Thousand' (John 6:1–15)

The next Sign, the 'feeding of the Five Thousand', was taken up by all the gospels. It is the only narrative, apart from the Passion story, that is found in all four. Yet it is the least believable of all, a mass conjuring trick.

Jesus, apparently, was on the other side of the sea

72

of Galilee, which, in the Synoptic version, was a 'wilderness place', but there was enough grass for 5000 to sit down. Jesus went up into a mountain, sat there with his disciples, and saw the great multitude. It was said to be the Passover, a point that does not seem relevant to a great picnic in the open. There was discussion with Philip about how to find food for them all, for they had brought none with them (why not?). Then Andrew said there was a lad there who had five barley loaves and two fish, 'but what are these among so many?' The 5000 sat down (the actual word is 'fell up', *anepesan*), Jesus took the loaves, blessed them (*eucharistō*), and they and the fish were distributed. Everybody ate their fill, and twelve baskets of pieces left over were collected.

The more improbable the story, the more important is its pesher. This story is found in all four gospels because it is the account of the first ordination of Christian ministers, and from them came the continuing succession up to the present time.

James Niceta and his twin brother John Aquila, the 'sons of Zebedee' of the gospels, were born illegitimate into a family related to the Roman emperors.[8] They had been educated by the Jewish mission after being brought to Judea as boys, and later moved into its Christian form, subsequently being extremely influential in bringing Christianity into the highest circles in Rome and in Ephesus. Both were married men, and their ascetic order was originally the lowest of all in the hierarchy. The imagery associated with their order was that of wheat, from the concept of the Diaspora as the place of sowing seed, Gentiles being one of the kinds of 'harvest'.

73

According to the method of organizing through numbers encouraged by Pythagoreanism, it had been planned that the mission would bring in 12,000 such men, divided into groups of 3000, 4000, and 5000. One man led each group and was called by the number of that group: the Three Thousand being the head of their order, who was Herod himself; the Four Thousand being James Niceta; and the Five Thousand John Aquila. In the 'feeding of the Five Thousand' John Aquila was made a presbyter, equal to a Gershon, a position that had hitherto belonged only to Jews.

In the months following the removal and death of the Baptist, the balance of power in the mission had shifted significantly. Agrippa, still hoping for the friendship of Rome, had found it expedient to hold to Sadducee doctrine, which meant greater liberality to Gentiles, and, moreover, he was now on much better terms with his half-uncle, the tetrarch Antipas. Josephus records that Antipas, after Agrippa's attempt at suicide because of his bankruptcy, came to his aid by giving him the position of controller of markets in Tiberias, the city that Antipas had built and named after the emperor. The first event of the 'feeding of the multitude' was the appointment of Antipas, under the urging of Philip, as Agrippa's deputy, replacing Thomas Herod, another relative, who had previously filled that position. Antipas had Sadducee views and Thomas was a Pharisee.

Antipas was a man of the world who upheld marriage rather than celibacy, so the promotion of married Gentiles became a consequence of the new regime. He was now appointed to be in charge of those Gentiles who paid membership fees, their money coming to him. When it was said in the course of the episode, 'Two hundred denarii worth of loaves are not sufficient, that each one should receive', part of the special meaning was an allusion to Antipas' appetite for both food and money. Josephus notes his 'indolence'.

The episode took place not in a wilderness, but in a building, the building at Ain Feshkha which was the first centre outside the monastery. It was at a meal on a Friday at noon, 21 March, AD 32, an occasion which for calendar reasons was observed by some ascetics as the first meal of unleavened bread at the Passover season. It was a 'wilderness place' because hermits could join in ceremonies there. These were the order of Therapeuts who used only bread, never wine, at their communal meals. In one of the upper rooms of the two-storeyed structure, modelled on the Qumran vestry room, a platform reproduced the one in the Qumran vestry, but extended down to row 10. A table for a noon ceremonial meal was placed here, the higher ministers sitting at its north, the lesser at its south. The podium in the centre of row 7 was preserved, and scripture reading and teaching was now given at the table. Since Law came from the podium, it was thought of as a 'Mount Sinai', or simply 'the Mountain', and this was the place where Jesus sat during the episode.

As the Riddle of the Loaves given in Mark 8:17–21 implies, the treatment of the twelve sacred loaves was the key to many aspects of the hierarchy, and an understanding of it was an essential clue that the pesharist needed. It was the key also to an understanding of the Last Supper. The detail is set out in the section 'More About the Pesher'.

Each of the twelve loaves was numbered. 'Five loaves' meant 'loaf 5', and 'seven loaves' meant 'loaf 7'. At the meals held in the Qumran vestry the principle had been established of breaking and sharing a loaf between two men sitting side by side. The practice was held to give them a common identity and related forms of ministry.

The table at Ain Feshkha was defined as being of common status, equal to a lesser table in the Qumran vestry, and the seating order, which arose from the numbers of the loaves, was that of the common table. This meant that the highest persons present were not those partaking of loaves 1 and 2, but of lesser loaves, which included loaf 4 and loaf 5 (see Figure 7 (ii) on p. 285).

At the west side of the upper row at the table, the Chief Therapeut Theudas sat at the seat numbered 5, holding loaf 5, and when the time came for breaking and sharing the loaves, he shared it with John Aquila, sitting on the outer west beside him. By eating his half loaf and thus sharing in the identity of this man, who acted as a presbyter, John Aquila himself became a presbyter. It was the central moment of his ordination, the receiving of communion that meant entering into the fellowship of ministers.

It was a 'miracle' because it broke established rules to ordain such a man. Theudas would, in the normal course of things, have appointed a Jewish presbyter on this occasion by sharing the loaf with him, but now he appointed a Gentile, and one who was lowest of all in the scale of 'uncleanness', being married.

76

(John Aquila's wife and companion in ministry, Priscilla, is introduced in Acts 18:2.)

The version in John's gospel does not bring out what is more fully shown in Mark, that James Niceta, the Four Thousand, was also involved in the ordination, sitting on the far eastern side and sharing loaf 4 with man 4, thus becoming a bishop. Mark's subsequent 'feeding of the Four Thousand' gives further detail about this part of the history. It was underplayed in John's gospel because James Niceta was personally opposed to Jesus, as is shown in his section of the Book of Revelation, and his Ephesus party remained out of sympathy with those who became Roman Christians.

Twelve baskets of fragments were left over from the five loaves, and in the Markan account of the feeding of the Four Thousand seven baskets of fragments were left over. The kind of ministry that John Aquila received was that of married men who attended meetings on a monthly basis, and their presbyteral leadership was structured in twelve. James Niceta, however, was able to be promoted into an episcopal ministry holding daily services, needing a leadership of seven.

The 'miracle' also involved Titus, who was the second in rank of the individual celibate Gentiles after Philip. He had come to be associated with fish, and ate cooked fish at the common meal, for reasons that will be seen in the next episode. He was given 'Fish 2', and given a promotion at the same time as John Aquila. Both of them would appear as Christian ministers in the history of Acts.

The ruins of the building at Ain Feshkha are still to be seen in the long grass near the beachfront at the

Dead Sea. It was here, according to the real meaning of this story, that the apostolic succession of the Christian ministry began.

### 'Walking On Water' (John 6:16–21)

Probably the best known, and the most ridiculed, 'miracle' of Jesus is the claim that he walked on water. The story is told very exactly, with precise details of time and place, as if demanding belief. It was said to have happened during the night following his multiplying the loaves and fishes. He had stayed in the place where this had happened, while the disciples took the boat and rowed, according to John's gospel, 'twenty-five or thirty stadia' (about 5 or 6 km). The sea became troubled because of a great wind, and then the disciples saw Jesus walking on the water. Mark's version says that it was 3 am, the fourth quarter of the night. Jesus came near the boat and they were afraid; according to Mark they thought it was an apparition (*phantasma*). They received him into the boat, and immediately found themselves at land. Matthew's version adds that Peter asked to be allowed to walk on water too, and Jesus said to him, 'Come'. Peter started walking, approached him, then seeing the wind became afraid and began to sink. Jesus stretched out a hand to him, calling him 'You of little faith'. They went up into the boat and the wind ceased.

Faith is not usually expressed in such a way in the more serious theological parts of the New Testament, although in Mark's gospel it is said that faith will move mountains. This saying, however, is easily seen as a metaphor, whereas the walking on water story is presented as circumstantial fact. Jesus the wonder-worker surpassed himself in this episode.

He did, in fact, 'walk on water' – that is, he walked along a jetty stretched out over water, at 3 am on a Saturday morning, and donned the regalia of a chief priest. That was the 'miracle', that he was claiming to be a priest.

The history of the 'walking on water' had begun some sixty years before, in 31 BC, when 'Noah went into the ark'.[9] Not the original antediluvian Noah, but Herod the Great, who in that year agreed to a further expansion of the mission to the Diaspora, to the Gentiles grouped as the three sons of Noah and the founders of the three ethnic groups of the world according to biblical history: 'Shem', Semites other than the Jews; 'Ham', Egyptians and Ethiopians; and 'Japheth', Greeks and Romans.

The interest of Gentiles in the Jewish religion had begun in the Herod house in Rome, when they came there to dine with the ruling Herod. Those who became seriously interested received instruction in his house, and then sought some form of baptism, which was given to them at another Herod residence on the Tiber Island.

All branches of the mission used imagery drawn from the Old Testament, with a drama of salvation based on that imagery. It was recognized that in the time of Noah there had been no Jewish Covenant, but a worldwide relationship with God that did not require circumcision. A drama using a 'Noah's ark' was developed. The men of 'Shem, Ham and Japheth' were given a baptism and brought on board a boat, which sailed up a water channel to deposit them on the dry land of 'salvation'. It was anticipated, throughout this period, that a great catastrophe would overcome the world in the near future, predicted by the chronology. It could be likened to Noah's flood, and only those Gentiles who had entered the boat would be saved.

Water, like everything else, was graded into three kinds: the still water of an immersion bath being a grade higher than running water, which in turn was a grade higher than sea water, the least pure kind. While the higher kind of Gentile, Shem, closer to the Jews ethnically, was baptized in fresh running water and classed with the 'beasts' that were brought on board Noah's ark, the next two were thought fit only to be baptized in sea water. They were likened to fish, those that must have been caught by the men in Noah's ark. For their baptismal ceremony the men of Ham and Japheth waded through sea water, accompanied by the 'fisherman', a Jewish missionary, before being hoisted on board the boat as if they were fish in a net. It was this practice that developed into fish being used as an emblem for Christians in Rome.

At the Qumran centre all activities of the mission were represented, for the councils of leaders were held there. A Gentile baptismal centre was established in 31 BC at the place called Mazin, the building about 6 km south of Qumran, below the great headland of Ras Feshkha (see Figure 6, p. 142). In terms of stadia (5 stadia are approximately 1 km) it is 30 stadia from Qumran and 25 from an outpost of Qumran, the building called 'the queen's house', just down from Qumran on the plain. The measurements in the miracle story fit it exactly. The ruins of Mazin still stand, and in ancient times it had a waterchannel of about 300 feet leading from a great watergate to the Dead Sea. This is equal to 200 cubits, the distance over which Peter's net of 'fish' was dragged, according to the story of John 21.

From Ain Feshkha it was easier to go to Mazin by boat, for the headland of Ras Feshkha projected into the sea between the two sets of buildings. But it was possible although difficult to walk, three hours being allowed.

On this Friday evening the boat representing Noah's ark left Ain Feshkha at 6 pm, arriving at Mazin by 7 pm,[10] carrying the leaders who were to take part in the Noah's ark drama. But Jesus was not on board. He stayed behind at Ain Feshkha. Midnight came, the start of the sabbath by the Julian calendar, and under the sabbath rule he was now forbidden to travel any distance. But at 3 am he appeared at the watergate at Mazin, joining another leader who was waiting to begin the ceremony. He had walked along the difficult path skirting the Ras, at night. His appearance seemed miraculous, both because of the danger of the journey and because it was forbidden under the sabbath rules.

The Noah's ark drama had an established script. From the watergate a jetty, 100 cubits long, ran to half way down the channel. To the end of the jetty came 'Noah' and 'God'. 'God', the Sadducee priest, told 'Noah' to build the ark and save all life, and 'Noah' told his son 'Shem' to rescue the 'beasts', and his sons 'Ham' and 'Japheth' to catch the 'fish'. The 'sons' did the actual work, rowing the boat and conducting the wading ceremonies. The priest,

81

wearing his full regalia, did not go into the boat, but walked out along the jetty, giving rise to a joke about the privileges of priests; they 'walk on water'.

The actual 'Noah' was the royal Herod, Agrippa, and Jonathan Annas was the actual 'God', but each of them could be represented by another, for the ceremony was repeated in many places. On this occasion, a Saturday morning, neither was present, for only Gentiles could do such work as rowing or lifting up on the sabbath. The levitical minister called Merari, a servant of Agrippa, represented him, and Jesus was due to act as the representative of the priest, for the David was the active head of Gentile schools. But he should act simply in his office of bishop, wearing a simple vestment, receiving Gentiles into membership on behalf of the priest.

At 3 am, when the drama was to begin, one of the actors was missing. Jesus was not there to deputize for 'God'. But then, in the dim light, those in the boat at the end of the jetty saw a figure approaching, dressed in the Chief Priest's full regalia, long white robes and a headdress. It was Jesus, 'walking on water', taking over the role and garments of the priest, expressing as he would do many times his view that a layman could also be a priest. A Christian bishop, the next grade up from a presbyter, should have the power to initiate in his own right.

Peter now saw his opportunity. Merari, the servant of Agrippa, had also 'walked on water', coming out along the jetty, and Peter asked that he should act like Merari for 'Noah', so 'walking on water' himself. In his New Testament epistle, Peter wrote of the Noah story, and of those who were 'saved through water'. Jesus agreed to his request, and Peter was brought up from the boat on to the jetty. But then he had severe doubts, as he always did, about Jesus taking the part of a priest, and about his own ability to act in a levitical role. Jesus called him 'you of little faith', meaning that Peter could not break out of his layman's status. But, as Matthew recorded, writing at a time when Peter was appointed Pope to Gentiles, he overcame his doubts, and became Jesus' true deputy and successor.

## 'Healing the Blind Man' (John 9:1–41)

To heal a blind man, as Jesus did in the sixth Sign, might be considered the most credible of the seven miracles, for the Therapeuts or Healers who were part of the ascetic movement specialized in the medical arts, using natural medical means. In this Sign Jesus did use natural substances, although they are not known to heal blindness. He used his own spittle to moisten clay, put it on the eyes of the blind man, and sent him to wash in the pool of Siloam, the name of which was said to mean 'sent out' (*apestalmenos*, from the verb that gave 'apostle'). When the man came back he was able to see.

There followed a very lengthy and apparently repetitive debate, in which the man took part, about whether the healing was genuine. The man's parents were called to say that he had been born blind, and hostility to Jesus was expressed: 'How can a man who is a sinner do such signs?' At the end of the debate the man said: 'From eternity (*aiōn*) it has not been heard of that anyone should open the eyes of a man born blind'. The debate was far more prominent in the story than the healing itself.

The real event recorded in this way took place on Friday, 19 September, AD 32, on the last day of a period of feasts and councils in which all of the tensions besetting the mission had come to a head. It was at this season that the crises began that led six months later to the crucifixion. The 'healing of the blind man' was a consequence of one of the inter-related events. Its historical meaning was that, following a decisive breach between Jesus and his brother James, Jesus went over James' head and appointed his next brother Joses, who would later be called Barnabas, to the position of his deputy and crown prince.

At the sectarian observance of the Day of Atonement on 12 September of that year, there had been a renewal of the schism between the house of Agrippa and the house of Antipas. Agrippa had allied himself once more with the Pharisees, alienating the Sadducees. Jonathan Annas had been deposed from the position of supreme priest that he had held since the death of the Baptist.

Once more, the question of Jesus' legitimacy arose. Agrippa renounced the decision he had made the previous year, declared James the true David, and Jesus a bastard. Jesus did not help his own case when, in the midst of the Atonement ceremonies, he took a line that was all his own, donning the vestments of the high priest and insisting on enacting a ceremony of atonement himself, again claiming equality with the Aaronite priesthood. But he was quelled by Simon Magus, who himself had seized the position of Pope, as the external literature records.[11] Simon needed Jesus' help and his influence with

Gentiles. He hailed Jesus as his 'Beloved Son', the true David, and from this point there were two men, Jesus and James, both claiming to be the potential Christ.

Jesus could no longer say that James was his deputy and crown prince, as he had done previously. Once again he disregarded protocol and appointed his next brother, Joses, whose opinions agreed with his. This man appears in Acts as 'Joseph called (titled) Barnabas, a levite, from the apostles'. According to the external literature, Barnabas was the Matthias who replaced Judas Iscariot in the Twelve Apostles, having contended for the position with Joseph Barsabbas Justus, a name for James.[12] The name Joseph was a title of the David crown prince, and Joses became a Joseph.

The brothers of Jesus, who were called 'the princes of Judah' in the Scrolls, had received by birth some of the lesser duties, including supervision of the 'Lame and the Blind'. The term, when used metaphorically, meant men whose ascetic rule allowed them to be mendicants, begging for gifts. The first prince, James, taught the higher class, and was himself called 'the Lame Man', and the second prince, Joses, taught the next class and was called the 'the Blind Man'.

The first prince could, on some occasions, stand at the podium, the 'eyes' in the imagery of the Heavenly Man, to give teaching, the enlightenment that came from learning. When the David acted as a priest to Gentiles, the crown prince was his 'levite'. The prince could in this position 'see', for members when they were instructed 'saw the Light'. But if the second prince came up to stand in this position as if he were the first prince, it would be against all the rights of birth. It was as if the blind could see. Jesus' action in making such an appointment was the cause of the intense debate that followed.

Joses was sent to wash in 'Siloam', the pool for 'apostles'. Since all places at Qumran reproduced places in Jerusalem, 'Siloam' was the large cistern in the south-western area which was used by celibates after episodes of uncleanness. To this area belonged those who did not have or had lost their rights in the Qumran monastery. Gentile celibates like John Mark were classed as permanently 'sent out', 'apostles'. Joses-Barnabas was to be appointed head of Gentile communities like those of John Mark, and appeared in the later history with him.

As a teacher Joses-Barnabas would have a lamp, called 'eyes' because it was held at the level of the eyes and used at the podium, to aid in reading the scriptures and teaching. 'To lift up the eyes' meant to hold such a lamp, and if 'the eyes were opened', the shutter of the lamp was opened to let the light shine out. But this kind of lamp was used by Jewish teachers, and it had now been agreed that a different kind of lamp should be used, an oil lamp made from clay or earthenware, probably because it was a more humble one used by the village classes, to whom Gentiles were attached. Such lamps were subsequently used by Christians in the catacombs in Rome. Joses' lamp was 'anointed' on this occasion, filled with oil and given a Christian association.

Jesus used spittle on this and on a clay dish. It was a way of saying that Joses was appointed to the Rome province (where Barnabas taught a few years later, according to the external literature).[13] Christian celibate communities imitated the Jewish ones in many respects, but they did not imitate immersion baths like the 'Siloam' exclusion cistern, which indicated an extreme degree of uncleanness associated with physical functions. They simply washed their hands, and so were said to have 'dry' cleansing. But by the same token, no Jewish 'holy water' was allowed in the Rome province, that of the oppressors. A Jewish leader touched with spittle objects intended for sacred use, to transmit to them his own identity; the action could be secretly interpreted as an expression of hostility to the pagan power.

When the man's 'parents' were called in the story, it was a way of talking about James, who in the role of the David was an 'Adam', the 'first parent'. The debate that followed this event was held on the Friday evening, when Gentiles held their normal evening meal and service, but the Jewish leaders who fasted on Friday evenings stayed in the vestry, holding a council. The detail records an angry interchange between the three brothers – Jesus, James and Joses – and the evening concluded with a further quarrel between Agrippa and Jonathan Annas as to who held the priestly supremacy. The rising tensions were not settled, and the way to the crosses had begun.

### 'The Raising of Lazarus' (John 11:1–53)

The story of the raising of Lazarus, the seventh Sign, is clearly a climax in the structure; it is told at great length, and is openly stated to be one of the main causes of the crucifixion. After Jesus had raised this man from the dead, Pharisees and others decided to destroy both Jesus and Lazarus, for fear that 'the Romans will come and take away our place and our nation'. Why did the Pharisees have such fears? Would the Romans have wiped out the nation simply because Jesus had raised a man from the dead? The absurdities are so great that the political meaning is almost transparent.

In the winter of AD 32 Lazarus, or Simon Magus, or Simon the leper of Bethany, his identity as the most powerful alternative figure in the history concealed by many pseudonyms, had 'died', as he was to do several further times in the history. Since becoming an initiate meant receiving a new spiritual life, being 'born again', then to be expelled from the community was to 'die' spiritually. Later Christian monasticism preserved the same image, and according to both the Scrolls and contemporary writers, the Essenes imposed extreme penalties on a man who was expelled, leading sometimes to actual death. Only a man who had made the total commitment of entering celibate life could be excommunicated.

As the Lazarus story and another story show, an excommunicated monastic was put through a burial rite, dressed in graveclothes, and placed in his own tomb, which in the case of a leader was one of the caves carved out from the ends of the southern cliffs at Qumran. Lazarus' cave was the one now known to archaeologists as Cave 4. It had several levels, the lowest of which would have contained actual burials; but the upper part was a room with openings for windows. The excommunicant was placed there, and on the day that was normally used for his pro-

88

motion he was brought out and sent away into the world, all connection with his previous community severed; unless, during the period of his incarceration, there had been a power struggle and the policy changed. It was then possible for him to be 'raised from the dead', or reinstated.

By late AD 32 Pontius Pilate's trampling on Jewish sensitivities had reached such a pitch that all the leaders of the people were driven together against him. Shortly before, he had done something that invited reprisals. He had ordered his troops to march into the holy city of Jerusalem, carrying banners with the image of the emperor, a pagan god. When a huge crowd of Jews assembled to protest, he ordered soldiers to dress in Jewish garments, under which they carried clubs, and at his signal they set on the crowd, both protesters and bystanders, killing and disabling many.[14]

At the Feast of Dedication, in late November, AD 32, a plan of revenge was conceived by the mission leaders, the prototype of one that actually worked against Pilate a few years later.[15] It might have to become a suicide mission, but should result in the removal of the governor. A demonstration would be staged, provoking Pilate into one of his brutal attempts to put it down, and a complaint would then be laid with Rome by the leaders of the people.

Simon Magus, the Zealot, had been appointed Pope the previous season, and had probably conceived the plan. With him was his deputy in the same order, Judas Iscariot. The two were bound together in the monastic system, although they had opposing views on the restoration of the Herods. Theudas, the Chief Therapeut, saw such danger to the state that he answered the call, despite his age. He could use the title 'Barabbas' in this role. The three of them formalized their structure into a triarchy, an answer to the triumvirate that had once ruled Rome, but saw it in religious terms as Priest (Simon), Levite (Judas) and King (Theudas, in the sense of lay leader).

Each of these acted as representative of one of the three Herods. Simon came into a temporary alliance with Agrippa, whom he normally opposed. (The text makes this clear,[16] for it was a key factor in what followed that the protest took place with the knowledge and approval of Agrippa.) Judas represented Thomas Herod, and Theudas fought for Antipas.

The demonstration, held at the pentecontad, early on Sunday morning, 30 November, failed. Any intention of passive resistance broke down when it got out of hand and the demonstrators themselves killed Roman soldiers, laying themselves open to legitimate punishment and reprisals from Rome. The three leaders fled on horseback to Khirbet Mird (Hyrcania) in the Judean wilderness, where Agrippa had a fortress.

Jonathan Annas, head of the peace party, was with Jesus at Mird. Although they had taken no part in the riot, they understood what had happened, and blamed it on Pilate's misdemeanours. But now Agrippa found himself in a dilemma. He was planning to return to Rome, and needed a good report from Pilate in order to be accepted by the emperor Tiberius, who had long distrusted him. Agrippa was aiming at the restoration of his family's kingship, and knew that he had good prospects through his friendship with Gaius Caligula, the young man who was well on the way to becoming Tiberius' successor. But Agrippa's previous record of bankruptcy meant that he might not even be allowed back into Rome.

It was imperative for Agrippa to gain the favour of Pilate, and the best way to do that was to give the governor, who himself badly needed a recommendation with Rome, the chance to earn credit for rounding up the three zealot leaders. But if Agrippa turned against them and delivered them to Pilate, Jonathan Annas, who himself was free of blame, might well reveal to Pilate Agrippa's involvement in the uprising.

But Agrippa saw that if he waited for a season until March, his plan might work. March was the season when sea voyages were usually undertaken, and if he acted then, gaining Pilate's good report, he could leave quickly before the governor changed his mind. In the meantime, he could have it both ways by excommunicating the leaders for their failure. Simon and Judas would be placed, according to the rules, in the excommunication cave at Qumran, and this would actually protect them from pursuing Romans, for the network of caves around the Qumran buildings were safe hiding places from outsiders. Agrippa would keep their whereabouts secret, pressured by the threat from the peace party. But, in his private plan, only until March.

So 'Lightning fell from Heaven', 'Lightning' being one of Simon's pseudonyms as Pope. He was reduced to the status of 'leper', called Lazarus. 'Satan', Judas Iscariot, was also punished. Jesus said, on the Sunday morning of the demonstration, 'I beheld Satan, as (and) Lightning, fall from Heaven'.[17] Theudas-Barabbas could not be excommunicated but was accused of murder. Jonathan Annas was restored to his position as the Pope who worked for peace.

A monastic excommunicant was sent down through stages, each a day apart. Simon began his descent on Sunday at noon, soon after taking refuge at Mird, and by Tuesday at noon he was 'dead', having been taken by Agrippa to the cave at Qumran. Judas was placed with him, but Agrippa had in mind a different scheme for Judas.

Jesus had taken part in the council at the Feast of Dedication, and had expressed agreement with the doctrines of Simon on questions of priesthood. He shared the peace politics of Jonathan Annas, and had not been one of the demonstrators. But if he continued to show friendship to Simon, who had reverted to his hostile attitude towards Agrippa, Agrippa had good reason for scraping up a case of complicity against him. Jesus, as Agrippa well knew, had influence in the Roman court through his leadership of the Gentile sector of the mission.

There were two possible ways of dealing with the problem of Jesus. The one advocated by Caiaphas at a council later in the season was to take advantage of Jesus' illegitimacy – as the Pharisees held – by defining him as an orphan who had been taken in by the monastery and so was interchangeable with the monastic levite Judas. Judas was Agrippa's man, having been leader of the monarchists for many years, supplying mission funds to advance his cause with the Romans.

The other method, advocated by Jonathan Annas, who had more personal reasons for wanting to get rid of Jesus, was to define him as legitimate, but one who could be proved to be involved with the zealots, and who, as a superior of Theudas, should die in his place.

After Simon and Judas had been taken to the caves, there remained at Mird the leader of the peace party, Jonathan Annas, with Jesus. Jonathan now saw his advantage over Agrippa, with whom he had continually contested the supremacy of the mission. The blame for the uprising should rest with Pilate alone, and the community's ban on the three leaders should be lifted. Annas could deal with any objection from Agrippa by threatening him with exposure to Pilate. Support for this scheme was gained from Antipas, who protected Simon Magus simply because he was an opponent of Agrippa. The order for Simon's release was issued by Jonathan, and Jesus was chosen to deliver the good news to him. Jonathan Annas intended to make sure there was clear evidence of Jesus' friendship with Simon.

The two women, Helena-Martha the mistress of Simon, and Mary Magdalene the wife of Jesus, had been at Mird on the day of demonstration – for the occasion was one when Jesus was again renewing his marriage – and they accompanied Jesus to Qumran and to the cave. Simon was to be released on the Wednesday, the 1st of the solar month in the present position of the calendar, for he was a priest, who used the third and highest of the three council days for his promotions. During the hours of waiting until noon, when the ceremony would take place, Jesus had discussions with Helena, saying 'I am the resurrection and the life'. Although the spiritual symbolism was also intended, the institutional meaning was that Jesus was claiming once more the priestly role of Jonathan, who had the power to promote Gentiles, to 'raise them up' and give them initiation, 'life'.

At noon Jesus stood above Simon's part of the cave, on the opening of which a heavy stone rested, and ordered it to be removed. Helena was quick to point out that Simon should have a cleansing with water before he came out; he would 'stink', not having had the daily monastic bath. The stone was lifted, and Simon climbed out.

With the Sadducees having for the moment gained the upper hand, Jesus was accepted as legitimate, and now had to carry through his marriage. He and Mary Magdalene had been in a trial marriage for more than two years, but no conception had occurred. This December would be the last chance, and with Mary he came to the marriage house on the Mount of Olives in Jerusalem, a place still preserved in tradition by the church of Mary Magdalene standing there. He was personally safe from pursuit by Pilate, for no evidence of zealotry had yet been brought against him. Following the strict form of the marriage rule, unlike his parents, Jesus came together with his wife simply for the sake of continuing his dynasty, and a conception was announced.

# CHAPTER 5

# Jesus' Own Account of His Sufferings

The later chapters of John's gospel were composed by Jesus with the events very fresh in his mind. They give his version of what took place during the terrible days just before and after the March equinox, AD 33. Subsequent gospels would bring out further detail, but he set down the essentials, with the intention of making the actual history as transparent as possible while preserving the outer form of his new scripture. Giving as it does his own emphasis, it is a priceless record.

He began the narrative on Wednesday, 18 March, going straight to the climax, whereas the other gospels filled in detail of what had happened during the previous fortnight when he and other delegates to the equinox council first arrived at Qumran.

On the Wednesday evening, at midnight, the second wedding of Jesus took place at Ain Feshkha, for Mary Magdalene was now three months pregnant and the marriage was to be made binding. The ceremonies continued through the night until early morning, when the couple parted. Only if there were exceptional circumstances would they be permitted to see each other again before their next coming together, which would be after three years if the child born were a girl, or after six years if it were a boy.

When a seasonal council began, it was the right of the royal Herod to enter in state, enacting the traditional ceremony of the coronation of a king, in anticipation of his coming into power in the empire. This was the dream that had been cherished from the foundation of the mission, a Herod as a world power, either a deputy to Caesar in the east in co-operation with Rome, or even a Caesar in his own right over a Jewish world empire, all Gentiles having turned to the Jewish religion.

Although the council was held only in the lowly surroundings of Qumran, and Agrippa had not even become king in his own country, the ceremony was enacted as a drama expressing the hopes of the Herodian party. King David's traditional coronation ceremony used a mule, on which he rode into Jerusalem, the mule being kept at a building 5 stadia away on the Mount of Olives. At Qumran, the reproduction Jerusalem where the council was held, the equivalent of the Mount of Olives building was the 'queen's house' on the plain below the Qumran heights, from which it was possible to ride up the chasm behind the plateau to reach the buildings. Donkeys, still plentiful in the area, were used by the more privileged for transport, while ordinary men had to walk. The building on the plain was called the 'manger', because the animals were kept there.

With Agrippa would ride the heir of David, who had been appointed from the start of the mission to be in charge of Gentiles submitting to the Herodian power. In acknowledgement of the fact that the ceremony of the mule had originally belonged to his family, the David was permitted to ride on a young donkey. As Matthew's gospel shows in recording the earlier triumphal entry, there were two animals, a donkey and a donkey's colt, not, as modern scholars have thought, because Matthew misunderstood a scriptural verse, but because there really were two.

The important point for Jesus was that when, on the Thursday afternoon preceding the Last Supper, Agrippa arrived in style on his donkey, it was Jesus who was chosen to play the part of David, riding on the young animal and receiving the traditional 'Hosanna', the words used to hail the Coming One, the Christ. With the Sadducees in the ascendant at the time, Agrippa had to bow to their will and accept Jesus. But he was biding his time. Within the next twelve hours he intended to carry out his plan of revealing the whereabouts of the three zealots to Pilate. He knew that great hopes for the fulfilment of prophecy were centred by Sadducees on this night, and that when no sign from heaven came, there would be an immediate change in the balance of power.

It was essential to his plans that Jonathan Annas should be silenced, and a failure of the prophecy would result in a lessening of his authority and a rise of the Pharisees, led by Caiaphas the public high priest who was deferred to by Pharisee elements in the mission. These included Judas Iscariot, holding traditional eastern views, to whom Agrippa owed a debt for his longstanding work for the monarchists. To save Judas from execution, Agrippa, with the help of Caiaphas, would apply the Pharisee standard to Jesus, thus having him put to death as a monastic illegitimate in Judas' place. The other two men would be Agrippa's enemy Simon Magus, the undoubted ringleader, and Theudas, who had long been an ally of Antipas.

## The Last Supper

During the evening of Thursday, 19 March, Jesus took part in a communal meal in the vestry room at Qumran, a meal that has passed into tradition as the Last Supper. It was, in fact, one of the regular evening meals of ascetics. It became a midnight vigil, continuing into the later hours in a different room.

It has always been observed that the account of the Last Supper in John's gospel is markedly different from the one in Matthew, Mark and Luke. There is no mention of bread and wine, not a sign of eucharistic symbolism. There is, rather, detail of washing feet, a prediction that one of them would betray Jesus, the giving of the morsel to Judas and his departure, then a long section of teaching occupying several more chapters, after which Jesus is said to have gone across the Kidron to the garden where he was arrested.

John's gospel, moreover, does not call it Passover, as do the Synoptics, but uses that term for the Friday, implying that the climax of the crucifixion, 3 pm on the Friday, was the Passover moment when the paschal lamb was killed.

In fact, the two accounts of the Thursday evening meal are fully reconcilable. The word 'Passover' (*pascha*) has in the pesher the special meaning of the first meal of unleavened bread that went with the Passover, and there were two different views about its date, arising from a conflict in the Old Testament. For those holding the Thursday as the date, the eating of the unleavened bread was a minor part of the evening, taking place in the first hour. It was eaten at the common table set up in the lower part of the vestry room.

In the first hour following, from 7 pm, fermented wine was taken, as an ordinary drink. These first two hours, from 6 pm to 8 pm, were the common part of the evening, and Mark and Matthew do not deal with them at all. It is Luke who deals with them fully, thereby setting a longstanding problem for theologians, that he shows two occasions of drinking wine. The first was in the common part of the meal, the second in the sacred part.

John's gospel deals with the early hours, but in a way that leaves out all mention of the unleavened bread and wine, for according to the calendar behind this gospel the Friday was the day for that event. Instead, John's gospel deals with the 'washing of the feet' that took place in the half-hour preceding the unleavened bread, and for the second hour it records the conversation that took place while the wine was taken, without mentioning the drink.

The 'footwashing' was not altogether what it seemed, although the principle remained in the Christian tradition of Maundy Thursday. The word 'feet', like all words for parts of the body, meant not the part itself but an object used at the part. Placed at the feet of an Essene villager was a bowl into which he put his earnings from working as a craftsman. These Essenes were known for their practice of sharing their income with the indigent,[1] and half the earnings in the bowl went to the Poor Orphan and

Crippled Widow, categories of persons who needed financial help. The Poor had come to include celibates living in their communities, not depending entirely on their common property but on gifts from outsiders. Half of the chief craftsman's money was given at the evening meal to the representative of the Poor, who in turn washed the feet of the villager to allow him to come into the sacred precincts of the monastic vestry. At the same time he washed in a dish of water the coins that were given to him, for coinage coming from the outside world was 'filthy lucre', earned by the married in their 'unclean' way of life. This was the more exact sense of 'washing the feet'.

At 8 pm the sacred two hours began. Seats were taken at the high table, which was placed further up in the room. The order of seating arose from the practice of sharing the sacred loaves (see Figure 7(iv), p. 285). Jonathan Annas sat in the seat of the priest, and beside him in the seat of the 'king' was Jesus, who was now entitled to return to this place, for he was on his way back in to the celibate life. According to the Scrolls, the Messiah of Israel would have the privilege of blessing the bread, while the priestly Messiah would bless the bread and wine, both of them observing the regular custom of the meal.[2]

In addition to the twelve loaves of the Presence that were used for these meals, there was a thirteenth loaf, an especially sacred one. The tribes, who were represented by the loaves, could be numbered as either twelve or thirteen (there being two parts to one of them), and when they were, the priestly tribe of Levi was counted as the thirteenth, for it was different from all the others. Priests being the superiors in the celibate hierarchy, the leading priest was given loaf 13, taking it first, so that it acted as a zero (a concept well known to these Pythagorean mathematicians). The thirteen loaves were then numbered from 0 to 12.

Loaves were shared between two men sitting side by side, and the priest shared his with the 'king', as long as he was in a celibate state. To partake of it made the 'king' a priestly person.

After the eating of each loaf, crumbs or fragments were left over, and these were treated as symbolic of the charity that Essenes extended to the indigent. The principle was illustrated in the story of the feedings of the multitude, in the baskets of fragments that remained. From the priestly loaf also, crumbs were left, and they would have the same power as the loaf itself, bestowing priestliness. They were therefore given only to the higher class of indigent, summed up as the Poor Orphan and Crippled Widow, for these would become celibates. (A 'Poor Orphan' entered a monastery or a community of Therapeuts, and a 'Widow', exemplified by the woman crippled by age in a story in Luke 13:10–17, was given a form of ministry by the Therapeuts.)

All indigent persons were understood to be in the class of the 'unclean', but were permitted to stand on the dais step or its equivalent to receive the crumbs from the table. This was at the same time the place of the 'seed', and an image had developed, expressed in the Scrolls, that celibates were given spiritual fertility.[3] Renouncing marriage, they were led by a celibate whose 'spiritual children' they were, and they themselves would have the power to

101

give such fertility to others through their discipline and learning.

The 'crumbs' from loaf 13, representing seed, were found, then, on row 13, and this row was the beginning of the 'body' in the phallic imagery of the Heavenly Man. It was said that the crumbs from the loaf were 'the body'. When a container of such crumbs, or small pieces of bread, was given to a minister, it was said, 'This is my body', and he took the container away, to distribute derived fragments to others, even at the far corners of the mission field.

Seed imagery for the Eucharist is implicit in the New Testament, and brought out in the document called the Didache, or *Teaching of the Twelve Apostles*, a very early set of rules for Christian communities. In its directions for the blessing of the eucharistic bread, it reads:

> Then (the blessing) over the broken bread: 'We give thanks to thee, our Father, for the life and knowledge thou hast made known to us through thy servant Jesus'. 'Glory be to thee for ever.' 'As this broken bread was scattered over the mountains, but was brought together and became one loaf, so may thy Church be brought together from the ends of the earth into thy kingdom.'[4]

At 9 pm came five minutes' preparation for the most solemn hour, that of the sacred wine, which was the highest privilege. Judas Iscariot, who was sitting in the place of levite in front of the priest, did not drink fermented wine, only new wine. Representing the strictest views of Essene monasteries, he regarded Jesus' party as 'drunkards'.[5] He went out into the night, to prepare for the carrying out of Agrippa's plan.

As in the case of the bread, symbolic meaning had come to be attached to the sacred fermented wine. Being fermented it was equal to common wine, and could be blessed by the king, an addition to the rule of the Scrolls. Given on the west side of the table by the David, one of whose roles was that of the Suffering Servant, the Lamb, it signified 'the blood of the Lamb', whose ascetic practices were believed to be an atonement for sin, substituting for the animal sacrifices of the Old Testament. A smear of his blood was placed on the cup, and those who drank the wine were accepting his atonement, and at the same time declaring their own willingness for martyrdom, the ultimate suffering. In giving the cup, Jesus said, 'This cup is the New Covenant in my blood, which is shed for you'. By the 'New (*kainos*) Covenant' Jesus meant the Christian version of the Herodian New (*neos*) Covenant that had been introduced when the mission first began.

At 10 pm this part of the session closed with the singing of a hymn. They went out, as the Synoptics say, to 'the Mount of Olives'. But John's gospel simply gives Jesus' words 'Arise, let us go hence (*enteuthen*)'. Both mean the same thing, that they went outside the vestry to the area of the pillar bases, then to the east side of the Qumran grounds, through an iron door, and into the great outer hall.

## Gethsemane

When Qumran was built by the first exiles as an imitation or substitute Jerusalem, the west side

103

containing the sanctuary and vestry were thought of as the temple and the city, which lie west of the Kidron, and the outer eastern part corresponded to the Mount of Olives. The literal Mount of Olives contained a building used by dynasts during their marriages, and the outer hall at Qumran, to which married pilgrims came, was considered to be of the same degree of 'uncleanness'. The pilgrims, who came in monthly batches of 120, used this hall for their meals, and slept in tents on the esplanade outside. Selected leaders were permitted to go through the iron door leading into the monastic grounds, for instruction at the pillar bases outside the vestry.

For those students, pilgrims and Gentiles employing the 'Eden' imagery, the west end of this hall near the door leading inwards represented a larger 'Garden'. These Gentiles were celibate like John Mark, and he was told to stay at the west end of the hall during the next two hours until midnight, keeping vigil. The east end, near the door leading outwards on to the esplanade, was for married Gentiles like James Niceta, who would not be entering monastic life. Its preferred name was Gethsemane. During the two hours while they all waited until midnight, Jesus moved from one end of the hall to the other, at the east end saying short prayers to Jonathan Annas, the Abbot, then coming back to the west end, where he gave the extensive teaching that is recorded in John 15–17. Thus the apparently incompatible accounts of John and the Synoptics are both telling the same story.

At midnight Jesus said, 'Father, the hour is come'. The hopes of the Sadducees for an intervention from heaven on this, their preferred date, had failed. They knew that with the failure of the prophecy their political credibility was lost. Political foes could now take advantage of their isolation to destroy their power or put them to death, as had happened to John the Baptist. When all hope for an extension had failed, Judas and the representatives of Agrippa and Caiaphas came through the door. Judas, acting for Agrippa, had sent a message to Pilate in Jerusalem, that the three zealots for whom he was looking were in this building at Qumran, which he had thought was a peaceful monastery. The three men – Simon, Theudas-Barabbas and Jesus – were arrested.

## The Trials

For the next nine hours Jesus must have listened passively while the arguments raged around him. Whatever the outcome, he knew that he, along with Simon, was going to be condemned to death. The issue before the priests and before Pilate was simply whether it would be Theudas-Barabbas or Judas who would be saved. The argument therefore revolved around Jesus' legitimacy. If he were an illegitimate, he would die as the Levite, the second man, to whom an 'orphan' was equal. Judas would then be saved, as Agrippa wanted. If Jesus was legitimate, he should die as the third man, the King, who was guilty of zealotry. Theudas-Barabbas, who had had this role in the uprising, would be saved, and Antipas would have his way.

When Jesus was dressed in purple, given a 'crown of thorns', and set up for mocking, it was a way of dramatizing Agrippa's argument that he was an orphan who had been taken into the monastery. Wearing purple, he could be either the David or a levite. But the David, as an inmate of a Sadducee abbey, wore a metal headband with a star on it. An orphan in the same abbey wore a plaited rope circlet with a thorn in it to indicate his permanent commitment to the harsh ascetic life. This regalia was taken from Jesus when the decision was made that he was legitimate. He was not crucified wearing a wreath of thorns, but with a plain headband over his bare head.

In the end, the issue was solved by bribery, offered by Antipas, the man who had more of the mission's money. Pilate, arriving from Jerusalem at daybreak, and anxious to redeem his shaky reputation with Rome by sending reports of the execution of three zealot insurgents, solved the dispute in a way familiar to all provincial governors.[6]

But appearances had to be maintained, and Antipas made sure that Pilate could legally receive mission money. He made him an initiate, raising him swiftly through the grades until he was at the level of a graduate teacher who could receive fees. When Pilate 'washed his hands', he was performing the ceremony of one who had just been made a minister of the mission, admitted to the vestry.

Once Antipas' bribe had ensured Theudas-Barabbas' release, there was still another alternative before Pilate. Following the Pharisee view again urged by Agrippa, he could still declare Jesus to be illegitimate, and put him in the place of Judas, while James the brother of Jesus as the legitimate David should be crucified as the third man, for he was in a party that condoned militancy. John's gospel brings out the debate on this question, with James, frightened for his life, urging that Jesus should be crucified, and Antipas winning the point by telling Pilate that he ought not to listen to Agrippa, who had ambitions to be a Caesar.

Finally, at 9 am,[7] Pilate gave his decision, with Antipas prompting him. Simon Magus was to be crucified as the main culprit and the Priest; Judas Iscariot as the second man, the Levite; and Jesus the heir of David the third man, the King.


## The Crucifixion

Jesus was crucified, as the New Testament says, 'outside the gate' and 'outside the camp'. To those who knew intimately the layout of Qumran, the headquarters of their mission, an exact spot was being described, through the use of terms with special meanings (see Figure 4). The 'gate' was the southern gate below the area of the pillar bases, down from which ran a long esplanade, ending at the point into which the plateau narrowed. On the west side of the upper esplanade was the row of cubicles that had been used as latrines by priests serving in the original sanctuary. A division of the grounds 12 cubits down from the back gate was made, and within it the visiting pilgrims erected their tents, assigned to this unclean spot because they were married men. This made it a 'camp', and the next division below it 'outside the camp', a euphemism used in the Old Testament for a latrine.[8] In the same area was the exclusion bath used for washing after episodes of uncleanness.

The gospel text indicates that in the first division, that of the 'camp', a skull was placed, to show the priests that they were now on unholy ground, with the uncleanness of a graveyard. A sentence in the Copper Scroll speaks of a grave at a spot that may be identified with this area.[9] For the gospels, it was 'the place of the Skull', or 'Golgotha'. The leaders stood on the borderline, where they read the inscriptions on the crosses, and the men were sent down into the next division to be crucified.

To be crucified meant excommunication, a spiritual death, leading to physical death. The study of the more precise meanings of terms shows that the verb 'crucify' had a special sense. Prior to excommunication a ceremony of cursing was performed, by pushing away the offender with a wooden pole. This action was carried out several times before the actual crucifixion.

Detail in John shows that each wrote his own name down in Aramaic and Greek – for Jesus, it would be the last time that he would use his hands to write – and Pilate wrote each name down in Latin. The names were then copied on to the crossbar of the cross, in the three languages, and John's gospel includes a subtle point for the pesharist: a fine distinction in the titles, that Jonathan Annas wanted to make, was not capable of being rendered in Aramaic.[10]

For each man there was a defrocking ceremony. A celibate wore a white garment that became the Christian surplice. It was of circular shape, the shape of the world circle, with the X marking the divisions enabling sleeves to be formed. In wearing it, the missionary was wearing a map of the world, a

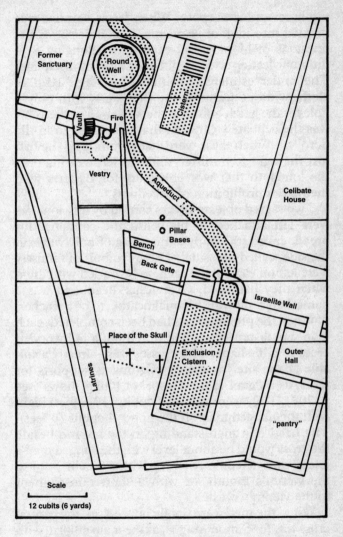

**FIGURE 4 The Place of the Crucifixion**

reminder of his purpose. When Jesus' surplice was divided into its four segments, it stood also for the divisions of his mission, each part belonging to a different leader under a different kind of discipline. The undervestment consisted of a single strip of cloth, without seams at the shoulders, with only a hole for the head, bound at the waist by a girdle. This was the celibate's garment that is referred to in the Scrolls.[11] When these were taken from Jesus, he had lost the right to minister, and was left wearing only the loincloth that was obligatory for Essenes with their strict prohibition of nakedness.[12]

Two sacred objects always carried by missionaries were left attached to his waist: the container for bread, called 'the body', and a bag of holy water at the side, called 'the side'. These symbols of ministry were left on each of the men, to be buried with them when they had died. Over Jesus' headband was a name-band, showing his qualification to be a teacher.

When the preliminaries had been completed, each man was fastened to, then raised on, a tall wooden cross in a T-shape. The crosses were already available at the site for use by pilgrims as supports for tents, as a detail in the Gospel of Philip shows (see p. 208). They were at least 7 cubits (10½ feet) high, with the hanged man on the upper 4 cubits (6 feet). The head of a man standing on the ground beside the cross would be about level with the hanged man's knees, and he could reach up with a 2 cubit reed to the victim's mouth, or with a shorter instrument to the victim's waist.

When the men were finally hoisted up, the central cross was for Simon Magus, as the main culprit, with Judas as second man on the eastern side, and Jesus as third man on the west. The text of all four gospels is carefully worded to make it appear that Jesus was in the centre, as Christian tradition and art has always held, but when the precise meanings of the terms were understood, these were the actual positions. Jesus was crucified as the third and least important man.

The men's hands were nailed, through the lower palm, to the crossbar. They were given sufficient support, possibly under the arms and by a small ledge under the feet, to keep them suspended. It becomes clear that their feet were not nailed, but were linked together by ankle chains.

Crucifixion was the cruellest possible form of capital punishment because it meant prolonged agony, continuing over days or even weeks. A contemporary record shows that it took many days for crucified men to die, and Pilate himself showed amazement when he was told that Jesus was dead after only a matter of hours.[13]

A number of people stood by, including those who would succeed the hanged men in their offices. On the west side of Jesus stood John Mark, the Beloved Disciple. He was also called a 'centurion', the title given to the head of a Gentile monastic community of 100 men, not because he was a guard. Near him, as Jesus recorded, were the four women who were heads of the female orders: Helena, Jesus' mother Mary, Mary Magdalene, now permitted to see her husband again before he died, and the young woman who was betrothed to James, called Mary of Cleopas. Jesus entrusted his mother to the care of John Mark. Mary would continue to live in a convent attached to one of the celibate houses of

Gentiles, as 'the Mother of John Mark'.

Jesus himself records nothing of the next hours. The Synoptics add a calendar point, which they present as an apparent act of sympathy by nature, an eclipse of the sun leading to three hours' darkness. But in fact, they were recording an adjustment that was being made to the measurement of time, correcting it by three hours. The roof of the vestry, usually removed at noon to let the sun shine down, was left on, resulting in darkness where there was usually light.[14]

At the true 3 pm on this Friday, 20 March, AD 33, came the moment to which subsequent history looks back as the central event of Christianity.

# CHAPTER 6

# Jesus' Attempt to Tell the Truth about the 'Resurrection'

If John's gospel only were read, without the other gospels and without the overlay of Christian tradition, its record of events of the next few days would suggest to almost any reader, even one not having special knowledge but with some elementary medical knowledge, that Jesus had undergone a natural if painful experience. Each carefully stated point adds to the evidence that he took poison on the cross, was revived by purgatives left in the tomb, and in the ensuing days came to places where his friends were, showing them the deep wounds that he had suffered in the crucifixion process.

This part of his gospel was made transparent to almost every reader, for Jesus intended, at this stage, to put a stop to the story that had been started in the tomb by Simon Magus for the purpose of his own self-aggrandizement. There are only the most minor supernatural features, such as the two angels in the tomb. Almost all of it reads like a set of natural events.

It simply says, on the surface, that on the Friday

afternoon Jesus saw that all was finished, said 'I thirst', was given a sponge dipped in vinegar (vinegar? for thirst? asks the enquiring reader), received it, said 'It is finished' and 'gave up the Spirit'. There is no statement about a tearing of the veil of the temple, no cry to God.

The Jews then came to Pilate, saying that since the sabbath was beginning the bodies should not remain on the cross (but they knew from the start, surely, that crucifixion took many days). Pilate agreed that the legs of the two thieves should be broken. But when they came to Jesus, and 'saw that he was already dead' (*thnēskō*) they did not break his legs. The verb *thnēskō* is used in other places in the New Testament to mean only an apparent or symbolic death.[1]

One of the soldiers then took a lance and pierced Jesus' side, and there came out blood and water (but a dead body does not usually bleed). There follows a statement in the form of a solemn oath: 'he who saw it bears witness, and his witness is true . . .' The statement draws emphatic attention to the fact of the blood and water, and goes on to emphasize that his bones were not broken.

Joseph of Arimathea then asked for the body of Jesus, and Pilate granted it. Nicodemus joined him, bringing a mixture of myrrh, and aloes weighing about 100 pounds (*litras*). The word means the 12 ounce Roman pound, and 100 pounds is a very large amount – say, half the size of an adult human. Aloes are a plant, the juice of which, when squeezed in large quantities, acts as a purgative, expelling the stomach contents.

The body of Jesus was then placed in a tomb in a

nearby garden. It had to be close at hand because of the rule about not travelling distances once the sabbath had begun.

'On the first of the sevens', apparently meaning the first day of the week, Mary Magdalene came while it was still dark, saw the stone lifted away from the tomb, and ran to fetch Peter and the other disciple. One of them entered the tomb. The *othonia*, cloths in which the body (*sōma*) had been wrapped, were seen with a headcloth close by. The disciple who had entered first 'saw and believed'. Then the disciples went away.

Mary remained at the tomb, stooped down, and saw two angels in white, 'one at the head and one at the feet where the body of Jesus lay (*ekeito*)'. The verb is in the imperfect tense, and means 'was lying', not 'had lain'. They asked her why she was weeping, and she said: 'They have lifted up my lord, and I do not know where they have put him'. She then turned and saw Jesus standing, but at first thought it was the gardener. Jesus said to her, 'Mary'. He told her not to touch him, and to tell his brothers that he was going up to the Father.

That same evening the disciples were gathered, the doors were shut, and 'Jesus came and stood in the midst'. (It does not say he passed through walls; he might have been inside already when the doors where shut.) He showed them his hands and his side. He then breathed on them, (so he had lungs) saying: 'Receive the Holy Spirit', and he gave them the right to forgive sins, one of the functions of a minister.

Thomas was not present at this meeting, and when he heard about it he said: 'Unless I see in his hands the mark of the nails, put my finger into the mark of the nails, and put my hand in his side, I will not believe'. Jesus appeared at a subsequent gathering and invited Thomas to feel his hands and side. Thomas did so, and said 'My Lord and my God'. The more obvious meaning of 'putting my finger into the mark of the nails' was that this was a natural physical action, and that Jesus was simply a man who had been crucified and recovered, and was physically present. Thomas wanted proof that that was all he was, and when he found it treated Jesus with reverence, partly in response to his escaping death.

The ordinary reader, then, coming to this text for the first time, would gain an impression of a very real, physical Jesus, suffering the after-effects of an aborted crucifixion, with only vague suggestions of a supernatural resurrection. And, as may be shown, the reader with an insider's special knowledge would gain complete confirmation of this impression, as well as an exact and detailed account of everything that happened.

The 'vinegar' Jesus drank was wine laced with poison. When he said 'I thirst' it was his signal that after nearly six hours of this anguish, he had had enough, and was prepared to accept the offer that Jonathan Annas had made him the previous night, of a 'cup', wine with extra, lethal ingredients. He had said to Jonathan, as he prayed before him, 'Abba (abbot), let this cup pass from me, nevertheless not my will but thine be done'. It was accepted by all ascetics, and by the Roman world generally, that suicide was a noble way of ending a heroic life, as shown in the account of the final mass suicide of zealots on Masada. The Therapeuts specialized in

116

knowledge of medicines and poisons, including snake poison, giving the Chief Therapeut one of his nicknames, 'the Serpent'. They used a mixture of poisons for political assassinations. Agrippa, subsequently poisoned by his opponents, was 'eaten by worms' (snakes).[2]

The motive of Jonathan Annas was not simply compassion. A man whose priestly superiority had been repeatedly challenged by Jesus, he had seen an opportunity to wreak his personal revenge on him by making quite sure that he died, and that would mean dying quickly, for Antipas had a rescue plan that would include Jesus. In an appearance of sympathy Jesus' enemies offered him a means of escaping the torment, at the same time giving themselves a means of escaping his influence. When the men were first put on the cross they had been offered poison, but had refused it. But by mid-afternoon Jesus was ready to accept it.

He 'gave up the Spirit', meaning simply his own spiritual power, and with it his consciousness, because an anaesthetic drug would have been included in the mix. But a few minutes later a test for death, the piercing of his waist at the side, showed John Mark, who had medical knowledge, that he was not dead. He had chosen the spot at his left side covered by the waterbag, the 'side', both to soften the wound, and to allow the water spurting from the bag to wash away the blood that seeped out. Jesus was taken down from the cross and laid on the ground, apparently close to death.[3]

Pilate was susceptible to almost any pressure, not only from bribes but also from threats to report him to Rome for his flagrant acts of disrespect for Jewish law. He had already learned to his cost that the ritual law forbade many things, and the primary ritual law concerned the sabbath. Antipas, who was intent on saving Simon Magus, came to him and persuaded him that the Jewish law forbidding a hanged man to stay on his gibbet overnight was applicable to crucifixion (although he had not previously raised the point), and was especially applicable to the sabbath, which in the strict sense began on the Friday afternoon. Would Pilate change the method of execution to the method of being buried alive, which would not transgress any law?

They had nearby, Antipas explained, a cave that was very suitable for the purpose, capable of being a dungeon, with a heavy stone closing its top. At 6 pm it would be sealed, having no windows, and men placed inside it would eventually suffocate. To go to it, just down at the end of the esplanade, would not break the sabbath law which forbade travelling. They could carry Simon and Judas there, for only after 6 pm was it forbidden to lift up any kind of burden.

This prohibition also meant that no Jew would lift the heavy stone after the sabbath had begun, even if he wanted to rescue the men. They might try to push it up themselves from inside, although it would be difficult, and to prevent this or any other attempt to escape, their ankles should be broken, by pulling tight their ankle chains and snapping the bones.

Antipas' plan of rescue depended on the fact that some of their members did not begin their sabbath until Friday at midnight or even at 1 am. Once Pilate had returned to Jerusalem, deceived into thinking that the ritual law was on his side, there would still be time to rescue Simon before he suffocated. Judas might or might not be rescued; that was another question.

The ankle bones of Simon and Judas were broken, and they were carried to the south end of the esplanade, down a short path, then down steps to the top of the eastern cave.[4] They were lowered into its opening and left to sit on the floor.

There was no need to break Jesus' ankles, for it was believed that he would not recover consciousness. He was carried down to a cave adjoining the other one on the west, of a different shape and serving a different purpose (see Figure 5). One purpose was to be a sabbath latrine, used on Friday afternoons, when the sabbath law forbade walking the usual distance away. It consequently had openings for windows, looking both west and south.[5] It and the adjoining dungeon, where money was stored, were under the authority of the David prince, as one of the Scrolls indicates.[6] This was James the brother of Jesus, who used as one of his titles the name 'Joseph of Arimathea'. It was his duty to open the western cave at 4 pm on Fridays, and he helped to lay Jesus there. At the time James left him he was still alive, but unless he was given help Jesus would die before morning.

For the next two hours James kept Pilate occupied, by ministering with him at a Gentile worship service in the vestry. Pilate's rapid promotion to the ministry of the vestry was turned to advantage by the friends of Jesus, who thus ensured that the coast was clear for them to leave certain objects in the cave. It was James' duty to conduct the Gentile service for Pilate in the absence of Jesus, offering the communion bread kept in the container, called the 'body' of Jesus. The container had been taken by James from his brother when he helped carry him down, for at this point James was simply a substitute for Jesus while he was ill. Once he had finished the service he brought the container back to the cave, reaching it a few minutes before 6 pm.[7]

The objects placed in the cave were the container for the medicines, a very large quantity of aloes, and myrrh, a soothing ingredient. They were placed near the head of Jesus as he lay on a ledge. His head would have been placed to the south, as all Qumran burials were, so that the containers would not be seen by Pilate when he made his last inspection of the cave.

At 6 pm Pilate, at the cave, understood John Mark to say that Jesus was dead, although he was actually being deceived by the double meaning of the word

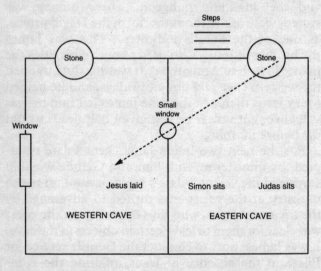

**FIGURE 5  The Burial Caves**

120

'to die'. At 5 minutes past 6 James closed the cave with the stone used to block its opening at the top. He had to roll it rather than lift it, for it was now technically his sabbath.

The two adjoined caves were thought of as having the level of uncleanness of the dais step, that of the 'seed' and 'stones' of the Heavenly Man. The two actual stones, closing the openings in the outer part of the roof of each cave, were consciously likened to the testicles. Phallic symbolism also gave these caves the association of seed, making them another 'garden'. The pagan word 'Paradise' could be used, as in the saying on the cross, 'Today you will be with me in Paradise', which meant, 'We will be in the burial caves by 6 pm'.

It did not take long for Agrippa's party to work out Antipas' plan, for all actual members knew of the variation of the sabbath rule observed in the Diaspora, and knew that Gentiles such as John Mark did not keep the sabbath at all. It was possible that he would enlist the aid of others who did not begin their sabbath until 1 am, removing Simon and setting him up as a man of great power who had escaped death.

Coming to Pilate, they asked for permission to place their own man on duty as a guard, one who also could work up to 1 am but would prevent any attempt at escape. This was the levitical deacon, whose title was Merari, one who performed such lowly duties as guarding a latrine. He was the servant and representative of Agrippa, so would be vigilant against Agrippa's enemy, Simon Magus. His own name was Ananus the Younger, the youngest of the Annas brothers. He belonged to a nationalist branch of the Sadducees, a man who would play an important part later in the history. With him was placed another guard, Theudas, who was hostile to Judas and would see that he did not escape.

By the time darkness fell, all seemed to be quiet. Both stones were now in place, and the guards patrolled the top. At 9 pm Pilate and his men returned to Jerusalem, relying on the sabbath rule to finish the execution.

Now, Theudas, instructed by Antipas who was trying to help Jesus, played his part, telling the other guard that Jesus would be still alive and could be revived with the medicines. Merari had no objection, for he had not been assigned to guard Jesus, and he agreed to help on compassionate grounds. They lifted both stones, as their sabbath rule entitled them to do, and went down into the eastern cave, knowing that Simon Magus had the medical knowledge to administer the drugs and other means of resuscitation. They lifted Simon out and lowered him into the western cave. Sitting beside Jesus' head, where he could reach him despite his broken ankles, Simon squeezed the juice of the aloes into Jesus' mouth and brought about an expulsion of the poison. Slowly Jesus regained consciousness.

At midnight the guards carried Simon back to his place in the dungeon. There was a chance that he might be needed again, and both stones were left off until the final limit of the time.

Early in the evening Mary Magdalene and Mary the mother of Jesus had gone down to the queen's house on the plain. As Luke shows, it was in a direct line from the end of the esplanade, and from there Mary Magdalene saw the light of an oil lamp through the south window of the western cave, where she knew that her husband was buried. Taking her own lamp, she came quietly up the chasm, across the neck of land, down past the buildings to the end of the esplanade, then down the path and steps to the cave, arriving at midnight. She saw that the stones had been lifted off. Peter and John Mark were quickly at the scene, and with them came Antipas, alerted to a means of helping both Jesus and Simon.

The three men went into the western cave and found Jesus alive, but weak. In his own account, Jesus records that the first thing he said to Antipas was that Simon had been with him and had now been taken back into the east cave; he made no claims about a miraculous recovery.

Peter saw that a means of carrying Jesus out would be needed, and he went to the top of the caves. Antipas, with John Mark, had been with Jesus for less than half an hour when another plan was devised. Although the common wall between the two caves, carved out of rock, appeared to have no opening, it contained, in fact, a small window into which a stone was jammed. It was used when it was necessary to check on the treasure in the dungeon, the property of the 'Rich Man', James, that was stored there. Too high up to be reached by the men with broken legs, it would still not affect the plan for suffocation – unless it was removed from the western cave side. But there had been no prospect of that while Jesus was thought to be dead in the cave.

On Antipas' orders, and in the brief time while the patrolling guards were changing sides, as they did every half-hour, John Mark removed the small blocking stone and allowed air to come through. It

123

was not needed now, while the eastern cave was open, but would be when the stone was put back at 1 am.

John Mark then came out of the western cave and across to the top of the eastern one. Under the guise of saying a prayer he knelt down and was able to see through the small hole straight into the western cave, assuring himself that air was coming in. He saw the cloth wrapping Jesus' bread container lying in the western cave.

Shortly before 1 am John Mark went down into the eastern cave to check on the airhole again, and to carry out Simon's orders on another matter. Simon's headcloth, worn attached to his headband when he was in the outside world, had been left in the western cave. It was a cloth that could be used to wrap Gentile money, as another story in Luke shows,[8] and it was now agreed by James, who had just arrived on the scene, that Simon could have access to the Gentile fees stored in this cave. The headcloth was passed through the opening, and money wrapped in it ready for the next stage of Simon's plan.

At 1 am there were five minutes to go before the stones were put back, and in those few minutes it would be permitted to bring Jesus out of the western cave. James, now come to help, was aware of a sabbath law, given in Luke's gospel,[9] that in the five minutes at the beginning of an hour, counted as a zero time, it was permitted on the sabbath to lift up a beast that had fallen into a well. He would apply this law to allow Jesus to be lifted out, then would ensure that the stones were rolled back into place.

When James had gone down into the western cave,

124

Mary Magdalene stood at the top, on the far eastern side. Kneeling to say her prayer, and at the same time looking down through the eastern opening, she saw Simon and Judas, the 'two angels'. She explained that she wished, as a wife, to go into the western cave, but needed priestly permission, because she was in the state of separation. Simon gave it to her, and she went down into the western cave where, in the dim light, she saw two figures, both standing, both of about the same height and with a similar appearance. Not expecting to see Jesus standing, she confused him for a moment with James, who, taking the role of the David as an 'Adam', could be called the Gardener.

Just before 1.05 (the minutes marked on the oil lamp carried by James), Jesus was sufficiently recovered to make a characteristic humorous attack on James' subservience to the sabbath law. Jesus was supposed to say a prayer during these minutes, the same kind of silent prayer that he had said during his trials, when he 'did not answer'. Saying it, as if with an excess of fervour,[10] he continued after 1.05, and James, well aware of the passing of the minutes, was caught: he now could not lift Jesus up to carry him out. Mary, understanding his dilemma and permitted as a woman to lift burdens on the sabbath, offered to lift up Jesus herself – possibly an indication that he was of small stature. Jesus spoke to Mary, simply using her title, 'Miriam'. One of its meanings was that she was not a working woman who should lift burdens. He could walk of his own accord.

With the help of Peter and John Mark, Jesus was brought out of the cave. He was weak, but able to walk, as his feet had not been nailed. He leaned on the two men as they went up the steps and the path to the edge of the esplanade. In the words of the later Gospel of Peter,[11] which included some of the traditions of what had actually happened, two men (here said to be supernatural) had gone down into the cave, and three came out, 'two of them sustaining the other'.

It was this departure that the guard Merari later referred to when he said of Jesus, 'His disciples came and stole him away while we slept'. The guard was not sleeping, but was observing the sabbath, and therefore 'resting'. To take advantage of the sabbath law in this way was to 'steal', something that a Gentile 'thief' would do if he took treasure from the dungeon during the sabbath. The same story shows that Merari was willing to take money to say nothing, not for himself, but for his master Agrippa, who was still in need of funds to enable him to pay his debts and return to Rome.

Jesus was taken down to the women's house on the plain, where he received nursing attention from the women, including his mother Mary, and was able to rest for the remainder of the day.

But there were still two men in the caves needing similar attention. There should be no objection to the women coming to give such help; Mary Magdalene returned to the caves and brought with her Mother Mary and Helena. At 3 am, having made the one hour walk up from the queen's house, they found the heavy stone already removed, and went down into the eastern cave to attend to Simon and Judas. Simon at once told them the story he had ready, using the double meaning of 'to arise'. Jesus was either resurrected, or simply restored to be Chief

Initiate, according to different kinds of under-standing of the term.

At the same time Simon's roll of money was produced, and a substantial donation made to Agrippa through his servant Merari. The guard consequently raised no objection, knowing his master's need of money. With the willing agreement of Theudas, the other guard, Simon Magus was lifted up out of the cave and set on the heavy stone that had now been rolled to the centre, adopting a grand style, as 'Pope Lightning'. Theudas, appointed his deputy instead of Judas, was in the role of 'Earthquake', a name often given to the Chief Therapeut. Simon again repeated his ambiguous message to the women. The women were intended to repeat it to the Gentiles whom they taught, and through the Gentiles it would go out to the whole world.

## The 'Appearances'

John's gospel goes straight from the scene in the cave to the Saturday evening, at the Ain Feshkha building a little further down the coast, where the regular evening meal was held. Jesus had been able to make the two hour walk down from the women's house. At every meal, the doors were closed at five minutes past the hour when everyone had taken their place at the table. Antipas was present, and Jesus took his place at the podium, opening both the common and sacred part with the Sadducee formula, 'Peace to you'. He showed them, not his literal hands and side, but the bread paten that he would have held in his

127

hand, and the waterbag containing holy water that was used as a drink by some Therapeuts in place of wine. They saw that his hands were so damaged that he would never be able to hold the bread paten himself again. But he used the opportunity to ordain John Mark as a bishop, giving him 'the holy spirit'.

Thomas, from the royal Herods, was not present on this occasion, but the following day he was at the noon meal of Herodian celibates at Mird. Jesus, aided by a lifetime of ascetic discipline, had made the walk with friends from Ain Feshkha to the inland.

The exchange with Thomas about seeing the hands and side meant, more exactly, that Jesus was rebuking him for using the eastern zealot symbol on his communion vessels. The 'type of the nails' meant the X sign, standing for a severe ascetic discipline, and Thomas had it engraved on his bread paten. Jesus – who spoke the words to Thomas, not the reverse – would not admit him to the Christian form of communion until he ceased to use this sign, or modified it with a superimposed circle. Thomas, a Pharisee, now expressed his willingness to adopt some Sadducee practices, allying himself with Jesus, calling him 'Lord' (simply meaning a superior of Gentiles), and with Jonathan Annas, calling him 'God'.

It was at this point that the gospel of John in its original form, Chapters 1 to 20, concluded its account. Other gospels would continue with the events of the next two days, bringing Jesus to the day when he was 'taken up to heaven' – that is, returned within the walls of the monastery. Years later, when Peter was rising in favour, Chapter 21 was added, recording the occasion in June of AD 33 when Jesus was permitted to make a brief visit to Mazin, since he would not become entirely enclosed in monastic life until after the birth of his child. In contrast with his very limited appearances in the earlier form of the gospel, Peter was here given great prominence, being told by Jesus to 'feed my sheep'.

In the last few chapters of John there are more frequent references to James Niceta. It is shown in the other books with which this Gentile was concerned that he had reached the same rank as John Mark, although under a different discipline, that of married Nazirites, and at the time in AD 43 and 44 when John Mark fell out of favour, James Niceta took his place. The gospel of John was re-assigned to him, the name of John Mark being removed from it. He relates this himself picturesquely in Revelation, in his account of 'eating the little book'.

The main part of the gospel of John was begun between March and June of AD 33, with John Mark playing some part in it. As the head of celibate Gentiles he was named as its author, for Jesus necessarily had to remain anonymous. In June, Agrippa finally found the means to set out for Rome, helped financially by members of the mission. He took John Mark, his charioteer Eutychus in public life, with him. A replacement was then needed for the Chief Gentile, and under pressure from Jonathan Annas, James Niceta was chosen.

A device parallel to the use of 'We' in narrative was introduced to refer to him. Just as John Mark was designated by 'We', James Niceta was referred to as 'You', in the plural, in narrative. In the crucifixion story the words 'that You (pronoun) might believe' appear in a third person narrative, the meaning being that James Niceta should believe in the legitimacy of Jesus, for he had previously doubted it. At the conclusion of Chapter 20 the words were added, 'Jesus did many other signs in the presence of the disciples, which are not written in this book; but these are written that you might believe that Jesus is the Christ, the son of God, and that believing you may have life in his name'. On the surface, the reader is being addressed, but in terms of strict grammatical form 'you' is being used in narrative, which means that it is a name. The addition comes from the time when the book was re-assigned, and James Niceta, who had previously not accepted that Jesus was the legitimate David, 'the Christ the Son of God', had changed his mind.

The 'further signs' which Jesus did, mentioned in this verse, came a few hours after the meeting with Thomas, at a different place, when James Niceta was the leading Gentile present and entered into discussion about the status of Jesus. Luke records this meeting fully in his 'road to Emmaus' story, but the part of the New Testament ('This Book') that was John's gospel would not give James Niceta such prominence, and did not record this episode, or those of the next day.

In the very last verse of the added Chapter 21, the first person singular 'I' appears, in narrative. When not in speech, 'I' means Luke, the successor of John Mark, before he took over as 'eunuch'. He introduces himself in this way in the opening paragraph of Acts, in verses 1 and 4. Luke, the head of the 'sons of Japheth', had had to act as substitute 'eunuch' and medical adviser for Mary Magdalene when John Mark left for Rome, attending the birth of a daughter in September AD 33. In AD 44 he succeeded to the position of 'eunuch' after John Mark quarrelled with Paul. His words in the final verse of John 21 were written in AD 43, and indicate that the growing New Testament had been taken over by the 'world', the married classes, so despised by John Mark.

Jesus finished the composition of John 1–20 himself, between AD 33 and 37. In the latter year, everything changed. The news reached Judea late in the year that Tiberius had died, Gaius Caligula had become emperor, and as had been hoped, had given his friend Agrippa the rule of the country, at first in a limited way, but preparing for the full monarchy that he was to receive a few years later. Simon Magus' plans to prevent the restoration of the monarchy were defeated, and Simon was driven to the east, to the centre for mission in Damascus.

A schism opened up, the party of Jesus under Peter and Paul becoming dominant among Gentiles. Jesus, now formally declared to be legitimate by Sadducee high priests, had no alternative but to ally himself with the party that advocated peace with Rome, especially when the tolerant Claudius succeeded the savage and unprincipled Caligula. The gospel that had championed Simon Magus as the Lazarus of the seventh and greatest Sign was seen as hardly representative of the Christians' views. It sank down in status, and when the four gospels were canonized at a ceremony in Ephesus in AD 49, John was treated as the fourth and least gospel, associated with 'the green horse whose rider's name is Death', the Magian system.[12]

But the genre had been established. Peter himself

131

would produce his version next, then Jesus would have another chance in a new alliance with Luke. Finally Matthew would fill in what had been seen as missing. The book that had sprung from Jesus' suffering proved to be fertile seed, bearing many offspring.

# CHAPTER 7

# What Peter Did with Jesus' Book: Mark's Gospel

Peter had always been rather doubtful about Jesus. Connected with the village Essenes, Peter was a conscientious, honest man, whose religious scrupulousness attracted the notice of even the external historian Josephus. It was Peter who in AD 43 confronted the fickle Agrippa I, attacking him for compromising the Jewish religion, but who was once more won over by the charm of the charismatic Herod.[1]

Peter's order, based in Capernaum in Galilee, had been drawn into the Herodian mission from its foundation, and was always monarchist. Those men in it who were Diaspora oriented and spoke Greek had the special task of evangelization of Gentiles, Peter being the 'fisherman' of the Herodian Noah mission. As the Gentile side of the mission grew, so did Peter's authority. He was answerable ultimately to the Agrippas, but under them to Jesus, directly in charge of mission to the uncircumcised.

But Jesus kept breaking the bounds that had been set for him. It was acceptable for him to be called 'the

Christ', the heir of David who would come into power as a spiritual head of Gentiles when the Kingdom came. The name 'the Christ' was used for Jesus publicly, among others by Josephus, a supporter of the Herods.[2] Peter, taught by Sadducee priests, accepted that Jesus was the legitimate descendant of David. But the Messiah of Israel, the Christ, had to be subordinate to a Messiah of Aaron, as a passage in the Scrolls clearly states,[3] and this for Peter was a Sadducee priest. In Peter's view, Judaism, especially the hellenized kind practised in the Diaspora, needed its priests to lead worship and speak with the authority of God. No layman should usurp the authority of a priest, and Gentiles must be baptized by both a layman and a priest, although the latter was too holy to actually touch them. It was for this reason that an 'unclean' married man had to make the physical contact, wading through the baptismal waters with them.[4] But Jesus constantly attempted to take over the functions of a priest, and this would mean that any layman could do so through ordination, even Gentile laymen, and the distinctive core of Judaism would be lost.

When Peter said to Jesus 'You are the Christ',[5] he was not revealing a 'messianic secret', as has been thought by modern theologians. Speaking in September, AD 32, Peter was aware that Jesus was planning to take over the functions of the high priest and himself perform the act of atonement on the communal Day of Atonement. But Agrippa had just changed his alliance back to the Pharisees and had declared Jesus to be illegitimate. Although Peter was affirming his support of Jesus as the David, so taking a stand at the schism, he reminded Jesus of the illegality of claiming the high priesthood.

At the time of Jesus' trial before the Jewish high priests, Peter suspected that Jesus was getting what he deserved, and made his own position clear by saying his prayers towards the east, and by denying to the female doorkeeper that Jesus was a priest. But when Jesus was in the cave, he hastened with John Mark to his side, and supported him as he came out of the tomb. The 'young man in the tomb', Simon Magus, particularly specified that Peter should be told of Jesus' whereabouts.

From the time Agrippa's appointment to the Herodian monarchy was known, late in AD 37, Peter and all that he represented began to come into his own. By AD 41 the Sadducee high priest and head of the mission was Matthew Annas, a man of great wisdom who was respected far more than his brother Jonathan, and both he and Peter accepted uncircumcised Gentiles and gave them ministry. It had by now become clear that Jesus, believed to have been resurrected, was an immensely influential figure for Gentiles, and Peter built his party around his name, while still insisting that he was merely a Christ, hence using the name 'Christian', which is found in his Epistle. (It would only be through Paul that the necessity for Jewish priesthood was abandoned, and Jesus given the combined roles of Priest, Prophet and King. Paul does not use the term 'Christian'.)

As a married man, Peter had not been given a monastic education. He was one of the *idiotai*, a word actually meaning married men with private property, but also of a lesser degree of education. Men in this category were taught only during the month they spent in the outer hall at Qumran, and special priestly knowledge was kept from them. The heir of David was one of their teachers, and Jesus had again crossed bounds by giving them more learning than they were entitled to. Peter was partly suspicious, partly impressed, and only later, when he himself, as a widower, entered a celibate order, did he gain the learning that made him eventually a teacher.[6]

The upshot of this was that Peter found it necessary to produce a gospel that both continued the work of Jesus, and yet put him more in his place by showing a negative side. Mark's gospel, which is clearly stated by a Christian historian to have been written under the influence of Peter independently of Jesus,[7] was that gospel.

All sources, including Christian sources outside the New Testament, converge to show that in late AD 44 or early AD 45 Peter arrived in Rome.[8] He had, in fact, played a minor part in the assassination of Agrippa I, driven to it by conscience when the megalomaniac Agrippa, imitating his mentor Caligula, declared himself not only a Caesar in the east, but a god. For a time Peter fled with the other conspirators to Antioch, where he appeared as 'Simon Niger', 'Simon the Black'. Peter was by now a widower and had begun his higher education. In Rome, where he met with Gentiles at the building called the Forum of Appius,[9] he acted as a lay priest and a lay equivalent of the Father, in effect a Pope to Gentiles, but side by side with a Sadducee priest.

For a short time he was independent of Jesus, who came to Rome in late AD 45. From Peter's point of view Jesus was under a cloud, for his marriage to Mary Magdalene had now ended. Early in AD 45 Peter found himself a scribe, one who would do for him the work that Philip had done for Jesus, recording the document and helping him with Greek. Philip had been the head of the 'sons of Shem', but had separated from the Herodian Noah mission to follow the Magus, so it was necessary to appoint another in his place. This was the man called Mark, who borrowed part of the title of the Gentile superior John Mark. Peter called him his 'son' – that is, deputy – when he wrote of him in his Epistle. Mark, according to the Christian historian, had never met Jesus, so wrote without consultation with him. By the time Jesus came to Rome Mark had left for Alexandria.

The source of the new gospel would be the gospel of John, a copy of which Peter had with him. It gave the information and set down the ground rules for a composition intended for a pesher. But the information would be put in a quite different setting, so that it would not be apparent that John's gospel was the source. It, and the subsequent two gospels that built on Mark, appear to be very different from John. They are grouped together as the Synoptics.

The spine of John's gospel had been the seven Signs, in most of which Jesus appeared, on the surface, as a good humoured thaumaturge, transforming nature for the benefit of his friends. Peter added more of the same, nature 'miracles'. But in each of them Jesus is shown in a more negative light than the one in which he had presented himself. The most striking is the story that, shortly before the crucifixion, Jesus had felt hungry and had gone up to a fig-tree, demanding that it give him fruit. But it was not the season for figs, which would not be until September, and the tree had only leaves. Nevertheless, Jesus cursed it, saying 'Let no-one eat fruit from you for evermore'. Next morning the fig-tree was found to have withered up and died, and Peter commented on it. Jesus' reply was to tell him to have faith in God, and if he had faith he could say to 'this mountain', 'Be lifted up and thrown into the sea', and it would happen.

This was an image of a petulant, irrational Jesus. Those who knew better of him would have to look for another explanation, and it would readily be found when it was understood that the Fig-tree was the emblem of the zealots. In the mission, they were not producing legitimate 'fruit', but giving false doctrine, preaching subversion against Rome. At the time when Jesus was about to be crucified for being an associate of the Magian zealots he had, according to this story, denounced them, withdrawn their rights, taught that the Sadducee priest had the more correct doctrine, and added that the centre of the Gentile mission could well be transferred to Rome, 'the Mountain (Jerusalem, and its reproduction at Qumran) will be thrown into the Sea (Rome)', where Jewish political issues would be avoided. Peter thus blurs the point that Jesus was crucified for Magian sympathies, but he had good reason for drawing out Jesus' political attitudes, which were anti-zealot. It was only on the question of lay priesthood and gnostic learning that Jesus was a comrade of the Magus.

Since, according to John's gospel, Jesus could 'walk on water', Peter added another aquatic feat. At the time of a storm, when the boat was in danger of sinking, Jesus was in the stern, calmly asleep on a cushion. The disciples had to rouse him, accusing him of not caring that they perished. He woke up, rebuked the wind, and said to the sea, 'Be silent, be muzzled' (the literal translation). The wind abated, and there was a great calm. Jesus then told them that they should have faith.

A closer study of the text about this apparently uncaring Jesus yields a different story. It was at the time of one of the expectations of fulfilment of the prophecy, when its non-appearance led to a political crisis. Jesus' part had simply been to solve the calendar problem, as he did on several other occasions, by giving good reasons why the expectation should be deferred.

In the next story, he landed at Gerasa, a place that was actually some 40 miles inland on the east side of the sea of Galilee. However, he was immediately there as soon as he stepped out of the boat, and he was met by the demoniac called Legion, who engaged in wild behaviour, 'in the tombs and in the mountains, crying out and cutting himself with stones'. He was not able to be controlled with chains or with foot shackles. He ran and 'worshipped' Jesus, at the same time saying, 'What have I to do with you, Jesus son of God Most High? I adjure you by God, do not torment me'. The unclean spirits were ordered to come out of him, but then Jesus went further. There was a herd of pigs nearby, and the demons begged Jesus to send them into the pigs. Jesus agreed, and the whole herd, 2000 of them, rushed down the cliff into the sea and were drowned. The owners made some demur, but their attention was mainly directed at Legion, who was now clothed and in his right mind. He begged to stay with Jesus, but he was sent away to Decapolis, where he was told to become a preacher.

This story depicts a rather destructive Jesus, as well as one who communicated freely with demons. It is, moreover, a very long narrative, the longest of Mark's twelve healings, and on the analogy of Lazarus it ought to have some importance. Pigs are an obvious enough indication of Gentiles, swine being the most unclean of foods to Jews, and this raised the question of a political meaning. When the language is understood, it is seen by the pesharist that this is the record of a turning point in the gospel period. 'Legion' was Theudas-Barabbas, the Chief Therapeut, whose order of Therapeuts lived in Egypt but whose elders and married members had a centre in Rome, so living in both the 'Tombs' (the Egyptian pyramids) and the 'Mountains' (the seven hills of Rome). Their ecstatic communal meals, lasting all night, are described by Philo, and account for the image of frenzy. Even when they lived in Rome they could be zealous, having 'demons'. But in this year, AD 31, that of Agrippa's change of allegiance, Theudas was also changing to Sadducee views, less hostile to Rome, and the spirits of zealotry went into other members of his mission, those led by a man called the 'Two Thousand', a title with similar meaning to the 'Five Thousand'.[10]

Peter enjoyed little puzzles about locations, of the kind Jesus had set up with his notes of distances in stadia away from 'Jerusalem', distances that fitted exactly Qumran and its outposts. Peter added more

140

of them, but with an element of absurdity that even Jesus did not resort to. He must have perplexed casual readers who had a knowledge of the Judean homeland, while inviting those who were already convinced of the authority of the book to look further. In his new introduction to the feeding of the Five Thousand, he seemed to say that Jesus was on the west side of the sea of Galilee, and from there set out by boat for a desert place on the east side. The crowds saw him set out, and went on foot to the same place, arriving there before him. To get there on foot they would have had to go up north, around the northern shore of the sea, and down part of the east side, while Jesus went by boat the shorter distance across. They could not have arrived there before him.

But when it was known that the places were all in the region of the Dead Sea, and that the 'wilderness place' was Ain Feshkha, it made perfect sense. Everyone had started at the inland meeting place at the Mird wady, from which it was eight hours due east to Ain Feshkha and eight hours south-east to Mazin (see Figure 6). They left at 3 am on a Friday morning, and some, those who were not with Jesus, had gone due east, arriving at Ain Feshkha at 11 am, the time when a purification ceremony took place. Jesus and those with him had gone south-east, arriving at Mazin at 11 am, then had taken the boat for another hour up to Ain Feshkha, doing so because they avoided the 11 am purification. They joined the others, who had arrived an hour before them, at noon for the meal at which the 'feeding of the multitude' took place.

For the same reason, when Jesus arrived at 'Gerasa'

141

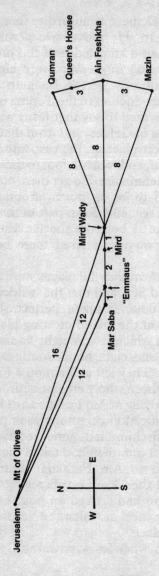

FIGURE 6  Scheme of Distance – Hours  Wilderness of Judea

Distance in hours between the settlements in the Wilderness of Judea

2000 cubits ≈ 1 kilometre ≈ 1 hour's walk

5 stadia ≈

142

in the Legion story, he did not miraculously cover 40 miles in a moment, but was arriving by boat at the same place, Ain Feshkha, which became 'Gerasa' when the bishop of Gerasa was there for council. The literal Gerasa was in the ancient tribal territory of Gad, and this accounts for it being called the country of the Gadarenes in another gospel. All the names for the ancient twelve tribes were used for the ascetic orders, and the order of Gad, that of Therapeuts when in the married state, played an important part in the history.

Using the same methods, Peter gave Jesus an incredible journey shortly afterwards, when he took him to the regions of Tyre, which is on the far northern seacoast of the country, through Sidon, even further north, then to the sea of Galilee, which is south of Tyre. He then added that he was 'in the midst of the regions of Decapolis', a district on the east side of the sea of Galilee. But, in fact, Jesus had begun at Mird, at the women's cells he had just been visiting to see Helena and Mary Magdalene (the 'Syrophoenician woman' and her 'daughter'). Helena was head of the female order of Asher, the tribal territory of which was in Phoenicia, with its two main centres Tyre and Sidon. These names were transferred to Mird when the female leader came there. Jesus then took the south-east route to Mazin, which was 'the sea of Galilee', the place to which the bishop of Capernaum came. He was there at the 'limits' (the precise meaning of 'regions') of 'Decapolis', meaning that he was now eight hours from the Mird wady, one function of which was to act as a meeting place for ascetics coming from Decapolis.

Peter and Mark did, however, contribute a new and important element to the gospel genre, the historical parable. Different kinds of symbolic sayings are called parables in all the Synoptics, but one kind is quite distinctive, telling a story in the past rather than giving generalized sayings about moral truths. Mark's gospel contains the parable of the Sower and the parable of the Vineyard, both stories about a farmer. The form was derived from earlier Jewish literature, but it was now used to tell the history of the previous mission, from the first century BC, out of which the Church came. If it were not for these stories and their successors, the history of Jesus' reforms recorded in John's gospel would be unaccounted for; it would not be known why there was a need to reform.

The parable of the Sower tells the story of a farmer who scattered his seed, mostly on land where it could not grow. There were four different kinds of soil: 'beside the way', where the birds came and ate it up; on stony ground where there was no depth of soil and where seed sprang up quickly and was withered when the sun rose and scorched it; on thorns, which choked it; and finally on good soil, where it bore fruit. Exact figures are then added about the increase: thirtyfold, sixtyfold and a hundredfold.

Following this there is an interpretation of the parable, thus stating openly that it does contain another meaning. The interpretation says that it concerns four kinds of Christians, with different kinds of reception of the gospel. In the interpretation there is sometimes inconsistency, with the original imagery repeated rather than explained, and the figures about increase are repeated without any explanation. The reader is still left wondering about some points, and about phrases in the interpretation that themselves seem to need further explanation, such as 'the cares of the age, the deception of riches, and lust concerning other things', all of which are found in the 'thorns'.

This interpretation is essentially allegorical, giving moral meanings. Later Christian writers who saw deeper meanings in scripture, as was common in Alexandria, spoke of a threefold level, which they called the 'body, mind and soul' of scripture.[11] An allegorical meaning, especially one that does not satisfy all the detail, does not preclude a further meaning, one that was not to be made public for moral edification, but was accessible to those with specialized knowledge.

When Luke adopted the genre for twelve historical parables which, with other material, gave a complete history of the mission, the meaning and place of the parable of the Sower was made clear. This full history is given below (see Chapter 12). It may be briefly stated here that the two parables in Mark concern the history of mission to the two Gentile orders. The order of Asher contained married men headed by James Niceta and John Aquila, likened to wheat, the subject of the Sower parable; and the order of Dan contained individual celibates, using wine, so giving the parable of the Vineyard. The two parables drew on the two elements in the sacred meal.

## The Twelve 'Healings'

Mark's gospel has a spine consisting of twelve healing miracles, in the same way that John has the seven Signs. Peter would have seen the value of the structure as a way of giving a unified account of the history, and he made his own modifications. The main one was that the numbered series were all healings, not nature miracles, and most came closer to being credible on the surface, for spiritual healing, with associated physical healing, was one of the arts practised by the Therapeuts. Further, there were twelve, not seven. The numbers themselves said a great deal, that his gospel was a product of the married branch, men living in villages who counted their times for pilgrimages and meetings in terms of months of the year, not days. Only celibates living in a community counted in terms of the seven days of the week.

One of the healings is a double event, placing the story of the menstruous woman within the two parts of the raising of Jairus' daughter. That is because two women alternated in the same function, to allow for one being absent at the time of menstruation. The inclusion of one story within the other shows that it is to be counted as one, giving a total of twelve healings of individuals.

The twelve healings were: a demoniac in a synagogue, the mother-in-law of Peter, a leper, a paralytic, a man with a withered hand, Legion, the menstruous woman with Jairus' daughter, the Syrophoenician woman, the deaf-mute, the blind man of Bethsaida, the epileptic, and the blind beggar Bartimaeus.[12] All described the response of particular people to Jesus.

To a pesharist familiar with the seating arrangements for twelve at a village common table, the subjects reflected the twelve positions, the order of the episodes indicating status (see Figure 7(iii), p. 285). At the centre was normally to be found an elder and his wife, whose superiors were a levite and a Widow, who had a form of ministry. The demoniac in the synagogue, with the adjoined story of the 'mother-in-law' of Peter, held these two offices.

At each side of the centre were seats for a bishop like Kohath, and a presbyter like Gershon. The third story, that of a leper, concerned Simon Magus, who when excluded from the monastery could still hold the office of a village bishop. The fourth story, of the 'paralytic', drew on Jonathan Annas' habit of using a palanquin when he came into the unclean world of the married. When he came to the village as visiting priest he sat at the table in the levite's seat. The levite moved to the Widow's seat, and she went aside into that of the presbyter. Thus the first four healings concern the occupants of the leaders' seats.

On the opposite side of the table, in the centre, was normally to be found a lesser person, a deacon, who looked after the occupants of the four seats in the remainder of this row, all of them indigents who were invited to the village table. The fifth healing concerns such a deacon, while the last four concern men who were in charge of the categories of the 'blind and lame'. Detail in the story supplies their identities, as is the case with all the healings.

The central seat on the south could also be used by a levitical figure acting as a head of the congregation, facing southwards and directing their worship. The Chief Therapeut acted in such a role, and his importance is shown in the long story of Legion.

Therapeuts gave ministry to women, and the episodes concerning women show additional female ministries besides that of the 'Widow', permitted to women sitting on the outer corners of the upper side of the table. The two women concerned were Helena (the 'menstruous woman' and the 'Syrophoenician woman') and Mary Magdalene ('the daughter of Jairus' and 'the demoniac daughter').

For his treatment of the crucifixion, Peter used the information given in John, but put his own slant on it. The most striking feature of the ending of his gospel is that he gave no 'resurrection' appearances at all. The original ending showed the women fleeing from the tomb, then it stopped. Only in much later years were the appearances of the last dozen verses added. This was Peter's way of dealing with the ethical question, for he knew very well what had actually happened. But in his Epistle, he adopted the policy that was coming to be accepted, of speaking to the 'babes' of a real resurrection. 'We have been born anew to a living hope through the resurrection of Jesus Christ from the dead'.[13] It was already clear in Peter's mind that only to an elect few was there given 'the mystery of the Kingdom of God'.

# CHAPTER 8

# Luke and Jesus Improve Peter's Book

As soon as the reader turns to Luke's gospel, a quite different atmosphere is sensed. Now, for the first time, we have a virgin birth, something of which there is not the slightest hint in John and Mark. Two chapters at the beginning of Luke show the angel Gabriel, Mary and Elizabeth, the birth in the manger, the shepherds in the fields, most of the Christmas story. Then, throughout the narrative, there are twelve parables in historical form, including the Sower and the Vineyard, but with many more, containing considerable detail, yet each with only a very simple moral point. Other sayings also appear, such as the extended teaching of John the Baptist, and these are recognized when they appear again in Matthew. At the end of the book, there are longer accounts of resurrection appearances than are found in any of the other gospels.

Scholars have long had an explanation for these features. Leaving aside John, which they thought was written late and quite independently of the rest, they saw Mark as written first, then a collection of sayings they called Q, then Luke and Matthew incorporating Mark and Q. These two then independently added their versions of the birth stories and other material.

There can be no doubt that these stages for Luke are correctly observed. But the background history available from the pesher shows the personalities involved, the motives behind the composition, and makes the whole process much earlier than has been supposed.

From the pesher of Acts comes the history of Luke, whose personal name was Cornelius. He was almost certainly the Cornelius son of Ceron who is named in a letter of the emperor Claudius written in AD 45.[1] The Acts story introduces him earlier, in June, AD 43. He was at that time in Caesarea, on the Judean coastline, the Roman administrative centre. According to the surface story, he was a centurion of the Italian band, a devout man who said prayers and gave alms. He was praying one day at 3 pm – the time is particularly emphasized – when an angel appeared and told him to send to Joppa, where Peter was.

Peter in Joppa received a similar divine message, this time from Jesus himself. Peter was praying on the roof at noon, and heard the voice of Jesus above him. A cloth was sent down to him, containing various beasts, and he was told by Jesus to rise and eat them, despite Peter's protestations that they were unclean. Soon after he received Cornelius' message and went to Caesarea where, following his preaching, the Holy Spirit fell on Gentiles (*ethnē*, meaning 'nations', translating Hebrew *goiim*).

In June, AD 43, the time of the 'visions' to Cornelius and Peter, Jesus also was in public life in Caesarea. A son and heir had been born to him in June, AD 37, and six years later, according to the dynastic rule, he and Mary Magdalene must try again for a third child. He left the enclosed life and came out to meet Mary in the women's house at Joppa. The Mother Superior there was his mother Mary, also called Dorcas the Widow, who at this time 'died', but not literally, undergoing a change of doctrine under the teaching of Peter, who 'raised her from the dead'.

When Jesus appeared in a 'vision' to Peter, he was no higher than the third storey of the building. Following the model of the building at Ain Feshkha, prayers were said on a platform corresponding to the platform in the Qumran vestry, called a 'roof' (*dōma*) because in the vestry it was an actual roof. But at Ain Feshkha the real roof was above it, and was used for noon prayers by priests, and called a 'third storey'. It had developed into a tiered arrangement, so that from the third storey Jesus let down to Peter a table-cloth, containing not real birds and beasts, but the cloth to be spread on the common table, embroidered with emblems of Herodian ministers derived from the Calf, the Man and the Eagle. Such a cloth was used at the Herodian common meal, and Jesus was giving Peter an important message, that now, in the peaceful reign of Claudius, even Roman Gentiles of Luke's order were to be admitted to communion. Agrippa was currently on their side, in favour with Claudius, and Peter was to renew his fellowship with Agrippa through his servant Cornelius.

Peter went to the house of Cornelius in Caesarea, and the one on whom the Holy Spirit fell was not Luke, as appears on the surface, but Agrippa, the 'Noah' who was designated the 'nations' (Gentiles), the father of the three ethnic divisions of the world.

The story occupies more than a chapter in Acts, telling as it does a very important piece of the history. Following it, 'the Gentiles received the Word of God'. Jesus in Caesarea was in fellowship with Agrippa, and this meant that he met with Luke, who represented Agrippa in this role. Luke was to replace John Mark, becoming Jesus' 'eunuch' and 'Beloved Physician'. Once again Jesus was able to collaborate in authorship with his close associate.

It would be during these months that the parts of Luke's gospel that show the influence of Jesus most clearly were prepared. The birth stories are characterized by the style of the Signs in John – incredible stories involving angels and visions and a virginal conception, in which the critical and informed reader would recognize the genre of myth, for there were many such stories in the Greco-Roman world. Such a reader, however, understanding the gospel genre, would look further, discovering a major segment of Jesus' history that had not yet been recorded.

A myth was being deliberately composed, one that they all knew would be powerful in the Greek world, the story of a virginal conception that answered very well the Greek longing for freedom from the body and from sex. Jesus must have begun the composition of these stories very soon after he had finished John, and he took the first opportunity he could to have them written down, intending a gospel directed wholly at Gentile readers.

It had been perceived that a myth required a drama. It was at about this time, as the Book of Revelation shows, that a dramatic re-enactment of the crucifixion was being developed, using the actual Qumran site, 'the city called Sodom . . . where their Lord was crucified'.[2] The idea of a liturgical drama had been borrowed from the Therapeuts, who celebrated the Exodus as a drama of salvation. But now the new Christian version of the doctrine called for new dramas. One kind of religious emphasis preferred the theme of suffering and renewal expressed through the Passion, but another, less Jewish, found hope in the idea of incarnation, a divine man.

The Christmas drama was conceived, ready for acting at a Christian festival. From the actual circumstances of Jesus' birth, plays on words gave a story to which many people in the Greek world would respond. A pure woman, a virgin, a simple village maiden, betrothed to a humble man, although one who was 'of the house of David'; the woman chosen to be impregnated by the Holy Spirit, giving birth without intercourse; and informed of this by a visionary appearance of the angel Gabriel. When the time for the birth came, it happened to be the time when Joseph had to enrol in the census imposed by Quirinius, the governor of Syria. The pair came to 'a city of David which is called Bethlehem', but found no room at the inn (*katalyma*), and the child was born, amidst animals in a manger. Nearby shepherds received another heavenly visitation, including the message 'Peace on earth', and went to honour the mother and the child.

So every human, no matter how lowly, is capable of being touched by the divine. There is hope for the most oppressed. Any ordinary woman may be chosen for union with God; her son, from the most humble beginnings, may himself be God in human flesh. The story was conceived by a mind very much aware of the role of religion in the lives of the poor and alienated.

But the more privileged, who had received an education, would be given food for thought. One point would at once attract their attention: the census of Quirinius, a well-known event because it had meant the removal of the Herodian monarchy and the beginning of the zealot movement, had taken place in AD 6. As this was said to be the year of the birth of Jesus, he must have been twenty-three years old in AD 29, when Luke says that his ministry began. But the very same Luke says that he was 'about thirty years old' at this time. Twenty-three is not really 'about thirty', and Luke seems to have gone out of his way to expose his faulty mathematics.

The critical reader, sure that the record was reliable, was intended to suspect that the 'birth' Jesus had undergone in AD 6 was in fact his first initiation at the age of twelve, the age of the Bar Mitzvah for Jewish boys. It was a symbolic 'bringing forth', the boy being formally separated from his mother at that age. In that case, Jesus had been born in 7 BC. It would then follow that further suspect points of the chronology were in fact accurate. The opening story, in which the angel Gabriel instructed Zechariah, the father of John the Baptist, about the birth of his son to the barren Elizabeth, was set during the reign of Herod the Great, who had died in 4 BC. Yet it says that Jesus was born only six months after John, apparently in AD 6. But if Jesus' birth was in 7 BC, the problem was removed.

A further study of special meanings shows that Jesus was born in March. Luke's birth story was set in March, at the same season as the Passover, and would have been intended for a single Christian drama played at that season, designed to replace the Jewish Passover. It was only later that this part of the story was transferred to December, the season when there were no traditional Jewish feasts, and which was already celebrated by the Therapeuts as a season of 'joy', when sex was permitted.

Actual events had made possible the plays on words. Mary was an Essene Virgin, a woman bound by the marriage rules of this ascetic sect which preferred to avoid sex as far as possible. Joseph was indeed 'of the house of David', a descendant of David who was of the highest status within the community, aiming at a restoration of the David monarchy. Following the dynastic way of life, he lived most of the time in the monastery at Qumran, but came out when it was necessary to continue his dynasty. While outside he lived like the village Essenes, based in Galilean villages and working at crafts, including carpentry.

Mary and Joseph, caught up in the stirring political events towards the end of the reign of Herod the Great, came together while they were still betrothed, and their son Jesus was conceived six months before the rule laid down, but after their binding betrothal. Following the idea of incarnation of divine beings by humans, Joseph could be called 'Holy Spirit' (in the form *pneuma hagion*; other forms of the name mean different persons). Thus Mary, legally but not physically still a Virgin, or nun, had 'conceived by the Holy Spirit'. The 'angel Gabriel' was the priest called Simon the Essene, the heir of the Abiathar priesthood.

Jesus was counted as illegitimate when there was a Pharisee in the office of high priest, as legitimate when there was a Sadducee. At the time of his birth the country was under the Pharisee Boethus, and Mary had to go to the building near Qumran called 'the queen's house', which was used for many purposes, including as an orphanage. Another of its purposes was to house the pack animals used for the climb up the chasm to the plateau, so it was a 'manger'. Mary and Joseph were excluded from the *katalyma*, the word that is also used for the 'upper room' in the Last Supper story, because being regarded as sinners they were excluded from the communal meal.

In March, AD 6, the family came together to celebrate Jesus' Bar Mitzvah in the building in which he had been born. At this season, when the Romans had taken government and the census of Quirinius had been imposed, there was a political crisis, leading to the zealot uprising. When it failed, Ananus the Elder, a Sadducee, was appointed the public high priest, with a policy of co-operation with Rome. The immediate effect was that Jesus became officially legitimate, and the ceremony became that of his appointment as the next in line after Joseph to the throne of David. Moreover, the liturgy in services now began with the words 'Peace be to you', meaning peace with Rome, so the hymns sung by the 'shepherds' (pastors of the Therapeuts meeting at the Ain Feshkha building) included the words 'Peace on earth'.

In another new story, Jesus was said to have been in Jerusalem 'when he/it became twelve years'. The story's outer form was intended for the education of children, as the birth story also was; a further expansion of the purpose of the gospel. But the actual story was set in the year AD 17, 'year 12' of the dating from AD 5, as two stories in Mark had been. The dating from AD 5 was an early version, for good calendar reasons,[3] of the dating that finally settled for AD 1 as the beginning of the Christian era, an era that Luke recognizes with his note about Jesus being 'about thirty years old' when his ministry began. In AD 17 Jesus was twenty-three years old, and it was the year of his full initiation, an important step always made at that age. The story of his staying behind in Jerusalem after his parents left because he must be 'about his father's business' concerns the initiation ceremony and the political stance that he took at that time, supporting the pro-Gentile peace policy of the current high priest Eleazar Annas against Joseph's more nationalist views.

The next stage of the composition of Luke's gospel was when he incorporated Matthew's Sayings collection and much of Mark's gospel. In a history that will be shown in more detail in the account of Matthew, the Sayings collection, called by the ancient fathers Matthew's Logia, and by modern scholars Q, became available, and Luke incorporated a shortened version of the material, some of which may have been preserved from a very early period. It included the teachings of the Baptist and some of the sayings from the Sermon on the Mount.

The assassination of Agrippa took place in March, AD 44, and Peter, who had played a small part in it, fled to Antioch and the protection of Matthew Annas. Luke, now called Lucius of Cyrene, joined them. At the end of the June council season of that year Peter and Luke went to Rome where, in the first part of the following year, Peter with Mark wrote his gospel, using John as a source but not using Matthew's Logia. Luke obtained a copy of the gospel of Mark.

Claudius was now the emperor, and the younger Agrippa was in Rome. Claudius was very friendly to him, saying that he had 'brought him up', and he was 'of the greatest piety'. On 28 June, AD 45, a letter marked with that date was written by Claudius, declaring friendship for the Jews, whose envoys had been brought before him.[4] The envoys spoke of 'the tender care' of Claudius for their nation, and asked for his help in the matter of the guardianship of holy vestments and the crown. He authorized a letter granting their requests, designed to bring about good relations, and sent the letter back to Judea in the care of several bearers, one of whom was Cornelius son of Ceron.

Jesus arrived in Rome later in the year 45, but Luke-Cornelius, on this indication, had already returned to Caesarea. He saw that he had the task of composing a gospel acceptable to Gentiles, but at the same time acceptable in Judea, at the Council of Jerusalem which would take place in AD 46. The basis on to which he grafted some of the Sayings and much of Mark was the gospel for Gentiles that he and Jesus had begun a few years before, but by incorporating material acceptable to Jewish Christians he was more sure of having his gospel accepted in both west and east. John's gospel was already in the process of being rejected, revised and re-assigned, and Luke's formula for Jesus' work was likely to be more successful.

Luke, with Peter, returned to Rome after the Council, and they were reunited with Jesus, the 'Beloved Son' who had come to the 'Vineyard'. All worked there, in fellowship with the younger Agrippa, whose inheritance of the Herodian crown was now assured. But in early AD 49 tensions between the Tiber Island mission of Simon Magus and the Christians led to the latter being expelled,[5] and they were forced to go to Greece and then to Ephesus. It was not until Pentecost, AD 49, when a coronation of Agrippa II was held in Ephesus, that they and Matthew Annas were accepted again. Matthew's gospel had by now been completed, and the four gospels were canonized at the ceremony in Ephesus described in the Book of Revelation as a 'vision in heaven'. Jesus, 'the Lamb', was present, 'opening the seven seals' – that is, dedicating the New Testament in the form that it had by then reached, four gospels and some epistles. It was the culmination of Jesus' literary career, the creative period that had begun in the dark days following the crucifixion.

**Twelve Historical Parables**

During the periods when Jesus was working with Luke, he may well have contributed much of the substance of the twelve historical parables that are woven through the gospel. The content of these parables, which include a full pre-history of the movement before the time of Jesus, is given in Chapter 12.

The structure of twelve arises from the same

scheme as Mark's twelve healings, the seats at the tables, for twelve ministers of a mission. These parables, however, reflect the ministers at the village high table (see Figure 7(ii) and (iii), p. 285). The first four (the Sower, the Good Samaritan, the Rich Fool and the Fig-tree) give the history of the offices of those entitled to sit in the seats of king and priest with their guests; the next four (the Banquet, the Prodigal Son, the Steward, and the Rich Man and Lazarus) the offices of those entitled to sit at the table itself, in row 7; while the Importunate Widow and the Tax-Collector corresponded to the presbyter and bishop on the south side, being also leaders at the low table. The last two (the Pounds and the Vineyard), placed in the final and most important part of the history, concerned the levite and the priest who could occupy either the highest two places or come as visitors to the low table.

## Further 'Resurrection' Appearances

One of the motives of Jesus in writing John, and in collaborating with Luke, was to make as transparent as possible the actual facts about the 'resurrection'. The further 'appearance' stories in Luke show Jesus acting in a normal fashion, with just a touch of mystery, such as his not being recognized when he joined the group on the road to Emmaus, and his 'disappearing' at the end of their meal. In the subsequent story, when he appeared again to a group, the surface story is emphatic that he was in a normal physical body. 'See my hands and feet, that it is I myself; handle me and see; for a spirit has not flesh

160

and bones as you see that I have . . . They gave him a piece of cooked fish, and he took it and ate it before them.' The influence of Jesus himself is clearly to be seen in these chapters.

In this final part of Luke, enough is given, in the course of an apparent repetition of the story of the women at the tomb, to make the pesharist suspect that Judas had been disposed of on the Sunday morning, after the rise of Simon Magus' influence and the defeat of Judas' Pharisee supporters. When Luke came to write Acts, he was able to tell the story openly, that Judas had 'fallen headlong' and his 'bowels had gushed out', but without showing, except to the pesharist, that he had been hurled from the caves high above the plain.

The movements of Jesus from 4 pm on the Sunday after Good Friday are described, first in the 'Emmaus' story. One of its main purposes was to show that James Niceta, about to succeed John Mark, came round sufficiently to acknowledge Jesus as the true David, even if he did not believe the resurrection story.

The 'village' of the Emmaus story was at the site now known as Mar Saba, where a Greek Orthodox monastery, reconstructed in the nineteenth century, runs in spectacular fashion in a series of terraces down the cliff. It is at the spot where it is possible to climb down to the wady Kidron below. A track wanders along the low hills on the north of the wady between this site and the building at Khirbet Mird or Hyrcania. The pesher indicates that pilgrims came to a building at Mar Saba after a twelve hour walk along the wady from Jerusalem, stayed overnight at the building, then continued to Mird and thence to Qumran.

After an evening communion meal at Mar Saba, where Jesus was 'recognized' politically, not physically, the party made their way along the wady, arriving for the noon meal on the Monday at the Essene Gate in Jerusalem. Ascetic discipline, still practised by Jesus even after what he had suffered, enabled him and others to go without sleep, and to walk rather than ride, as lay celibates were normally required to do.

The building, on the south flank of the city of Jerusalem overlooking the valley of Hinnom, was the place to which Essenes had first gone when they had been expelled from the temple. Their small pools for bathing have recently been uncovered, and the Cenacle building, said to be the traditional place of the Last Supper, stands in the vicinity. The surface story of the gospels is intended to make it appear that all events happened in this area and on the Mount of Olives on the east across the Kidron. In fact, this building was now the place for a Herodian school, with the attached Gentile school on the Mount of Olives at the site of the Mary Magdalene church. Some of the events took place here, but Qumran, the 'New Jerusalem', indicated by the plural form of the word, was the council centre and the place where all the great political events happened.

A noon meal of the kind held at Ain Feshkha was observed in the Essene gate building. It was at this meal that Jesus made it quite plain that he was present in the flesh. When he said, 'Behold my hands and my feet', the exact meaning was that he was indicating the bread paten, which he could no longer handle himself, and must be lifted for him by another, and indicating also the dish for shared property that was placed at the feet of a village bishop. An ascetic in the world, following the rules of village Essenes, carried both a bread paten for giving the charity loaf, and a bowl for property to be shared with the indigent. When the piece of dedicated fish, held by a Gentile minister, was blessed, as at the 'feeding of the multitude', Jesus received it and ate it on behalf of Gentiles.

Agrippa in Jerusalem had several reasons for protecting Jesus from the notice of Pilate. He knew already that Jesus had great influence with Gentiles, who in Rome, could make or break his chances of monarchy, and now that it was believed that he had undergone a resurrection, Jesus' influence would be enormously increased. Simon Magus' gift of money through Merari also smoothed the way. Jesus was permitted to be present for the noon meal, and to teach in the afternoon.

Monday was the literal third day from Good Friday, and it would have been this occasion in Jerusalem, known to many Jews but not to Pilate, that gave rise to the Testimonium Flavianum, the account of Jesus' appearance on the third day that is found in Josephus. As the text stands, it reads:

> About this time there lived Jesus, a wise man, if indeed one ought to call him a man. For he was one who wrought surprising feats (*paradoxon ergon*) and was a teacher of such people as accept the truth gladly. He won over many Jews and many of the Greeks. This man was the Christ. When Pilate, upon hearing him accused by men of the highest

standing amongst us, had condemned him to be crucified, those who had in the first place come to love him did not give up their affection for him. On the third day he appeared to them living, for the prophets of God had prophesied these and countless other marvellous things about him. And the tribe of Christians, so called after him, has still to this day (late first century AD) not disappeared.[6]

After finishing his teaching of Gentiles, Jesus began the long walk back to Qumran for his delayed re-entry within its walls. He would be semi-enclosed until the birth of his child, then fully enclosed for either three years or six, depending on the gender of the child.

The first chapter of Acts records his last conversation with John Mark, James Niceta and Peter, who had accompanied him on the walk back. Luke himself was present on the premises, giving medical attention to Simon Magus, who would be protected for a time, for the same reason as Jesus. Then 'a Cloud received him (Jesus) from their sight'. The 'Cloud' was yet another title of a levite, similar to 'Thunder', 'Lightning' and 'Earthquake'. Jesus was escorted by the levite from the outer hall through the iron gate into the monastery grounds. The 'two men in white' who spoke to the disciples, promising Jesus' return, simply reiterated the marriage rule.

Luke's gospel is characterized by the same desire to communicate, within the set limits, as is John's. It is Luke who supplies most detail of chronology enabling reconstruction of the calendar, and makes many points about persons and places almost transparent. If it were not for Luke, in the gospel and the later book of Acts, the task would be impossible for the modern pesharist. His books serve to educate, whereas Mark's gospel would be understood only within a very tight circle determined to keep its secret safe. One senses the personality of Jesus, at ease with Luke, a cultivated Gentile, one who enjoyed Jesus' bitter wit, giving him his services as physician and close companion.

Their creative collaboration must have lasted for twenty years, from AD 43 in Caesarea to AD 63 in Rome. When Paul wrote his last letter from Rome, he spoke of the departure of other associates, adding, 'Only Luke is with me'. Paul was shortly to stand trial for his part in the misdemeanours of the governor Felix, and was to be beheaded at the same time as Peter, who died in Nero's persecution. Luke left his book of Acts unfinished, and it seems probable that he suffered the same fate as Paul. Jesus was left alone, his literary work done, the books leaving their authors far behind as they became the scripture of the new era.

# CHAPTER 9

# Matthew Adds the Finishing Touches

'Thou art Peter, and on this rock I will build my church, and the gates of Hades will not prevail against it.'

With these words, attributed to Jesus – and actually said by him, but in a less solemn context – Matthew Annas, sponsor and part-author of Matthew's gospel, declared his support for the man who at the time he was writing, about AD 46, was a candidate for the position of Pope to the Gentiles.

Peter had never been so prominent before. He was studiously overlooked in John's gospel, appeared humbly in his own gospel with his failings admitted, and was simply included in Luke. But now both he and the word *ekklesia*, 'church', came forward for the first time. 'Hades', which the church would overcome, was a way of talking about Rome, and it was being affirmed that Peter was appointed to Rome as the head of the mission to Gentiles. This would achieve the purposes of the original Herodian mission by introducing a form of the Jewish religion into the capital of the empire.

Matthew Annas was one of the five Annas brothers who filled the office of high priest in

Jerusalem in the first century AD, all of them holding the Sadducee view of priesthood and a Diaspora oriented culture which put little importance on Jerusalem as the true place for worship, and advocated amiable relations with Rome. Josephus records that Matthew was the most highly respected of the brothers. Jonathan Annas, having refused a renewal of his own high priesthood from Agrippa I, recommended Matthew with the words: 'I have a brother, pure of all sin against God and against you, O king. Him I recommend as suitable for the honour'.[1]

Matthew was the most hellenized of the brothers, the most welcoming to Gentiles, allowing them to join the mission simply by assenting to the spiritual aspects of Judaism, without its ritual practices. It was he who in Antioch authorized the word 'Christian' to describe those Gentiles for whom Jesus the Christ was a spiritual king, who were not bound to any loyalty to a Herod, and to whom only the priest was higher than Jesus.

But that was the sticking point – the necessity of a priest. The Christian party had arisen among Diaspora Jews, whose priests were as hellenized as the members themselves, and who had many friends among Gentiles. But the priests were still the centre of their communities, and were revered by them. Their charisma was expressed through the belief that they, more than others, had incarnated divinity, and this gave them a needed personal authority in the absence of a temple. Even when they did become high priests in Jerusalem out of the political necessity of co-operation with Rome, it was as a focus for world Judaism rather than as servants of the temple.

The hidden figure behind Matthew's gospel was

James Niceta, brother of John Aquila. The two, although both within the Christian fold, took different directions, John Aquila eventually becoming an associate of Paul, and James Niceta staying closer to the Jewish origins. His western limit was Ephesus, and his attitudes are found in the Book of Revelation, which he initiated, writing its original first section. Both brothers, handed over to a school of the mission in Caesarea, had first been taught by Simon Magus and then had turned away from him to the Sadducees, but James Niceta stayed with the Sadducee doctrine of Jonathan Annas. From him he learned a distrust of Jesus, whose views about priesthood were far too advanced for him. For James, the two poles were political, between Simon Magus, the zealot 'Beast 666', from whom he had turned away, and the Annas brothers, friendly to Rome.

In a chapter in his section of Revelation, James Niceta gave an account of his part in the writing of Matthew's gospel. His words may be understood with the help of the patristic tradition that Matthew first wrote the Logia, a sayings collection, in Hebrew, and later a full gospel in Greek.[2] James speaks, in a disguised way, of a ceremony that took place in Ephesus in September, AD 43, at the time of the sixteenth birthday of Agrippa II. Matthew Annas was present as the 'Seven Thunders', and when he spoke, 'I was about to write', said James. But he heard a voice from heaven saying, 'Seal what the Seven Thunders have said, and do not write it'. But soon after, 'in the days of the voice of the seventh angel . . . the mystery of God was completed, as he preached (*euangelisen*) to the servants . . . the prophets'.[3]

Matthew Annas had been appointed high priest by Agrippa I in AD 41, and for two triumphant years the Christian version of the Gentile mission flourished. But in September AD 43 the capricious Agrippa changed his mind again and dismissed him. As Revelation shows, Matthew went first to Ephesus, where he had some influence over the younger Agrippa, who was being educated in Rome but came there for his birthday ceremony. Matthew now began or continued a sayings collection, in Hebrew, the Logia. They were sayings only, including the teachings of the Baptist and other teachings on laws and ethics, some probably going back to an early period in the mission, for they show the influence of Hillel the Great, the Jewish sage who taught at the time of the foundation of the mission under Herod the Great. James Niceta, a leading Gentile in his party, was appointed as Matthew's scribe and told to write the sayings down and publish them. But then an edict from Agrippa I, a 'voice from heaven' came, banning the book, for Agrippa had become anti-Sadducee and hostile to Rome again.

By the following season, however, Matthew had gone to Antioch, where he acted independently of Agrippa, knowing that he had the support of most of the Diaspora against the erratic king. The plot to assassinate Agrippa was under way. Now, 'the mystery of God was completed'. A 'mystery' was a gospel with a pesher, and Matthew saw his opportunity to complete the set of gospels. The Logia were published, and in this year and in the next few he included them in the Greek gospel called after him, with the help of James Niceta. Because of Matthew's considerable influence, the final book was placed first in the list. In June, AD 49, all four gospels were canonized at a ceremony in Ephesus at which Jesus, 'the Lamb', was present, and 'the Lamb opened the seven seals'.[4]

## The Sermon on the Mount

For many people the Sermon on the Mount, in Matthew 5–7, represents the essence of Christian teaching, which is perceived as primarily ethical. It is quite apparent that it is intended to set out a new Law, going beyond the Law of Moses given on Mount Sinai. Even the 'mountain' underlines that point.

With the discovery of a fragment of the Dead Sea Scrolls, it becomes clear that the form the Beatitudes took was a very familiar one at Qumran. The piece called 4QBeatitudes sets out a series of sayings, all beginning with 'Blessed':

> [Blessed is the man] with a pure heart, who does not slander with his tongue.
> Blessed are those who adhere to her (Wisdom's) precepts, and do not adhere to the ways of wrong-doing.
> Blessed are those who rejoice in her, and do not join in ways of folly.
> Blessed are the ones who seek her with pure hands, not pursuing her with a deceitful heart.
> Blessed is the man who has achieved Wisdom, and who walks in the law of the Most High . . .

171

But the content of these Blessings is little different from the Wisdom literature of the Old Testament, whereas those in Matthew speak about people who appear not to be of high status, but are promised rewards nevertheless:

Blessed are the poor in spirit, for theirs is the kingdom of the heavens.
Blessed are the mourners, for they will be comforted.
Blessed are the meek, for they shall inherit the earth . . .

These sayings, part of Matthew's Logia, retain the balance between an outer form immediately available, of the greatest spiritual benefit, and an inner historical and institutional sense. Their surface teaching on ethics is of permanent value, and their pesher is of historical value as a description of the different types of ascetic discipline. Each kind of virtue listed means a form of the ascetic life, from the 'Poor' (the 'Poor Orphans' in a celibate community), the 'Mourners' (those equivalent to a 'Crippled Widow'), through the different rules for the married: the 'Meek' (pilgrim 'Sheep'), 'Hungering and Thirsting for Righteousness' (moderate fasting of the Righteous, the next grade below 'Holy Ones' or 'Saints'), 'Merciful and obtaining Mercy' (giving alms and at times living as mendicants); then the kinds of higher celibates: 'Pure in heart' ('Virgins', equal to an Essene monastic), and 'Peacemakers' (members of a Sadducee abbey).

When it came to the lesson 'Love your enemies'

(Matthew 5:43–44), the political views of Jesus were being expressed. The words were: 'You have heard that it was said, "You shall love (*agapēseis*) your neighbour and hate your enemy". But I say to you, "Love your enemies".' It has always been assumed that the contrast is between Old Testament teaching of revenge, and the New Testament teaching of love, but in fact the Old Testament is never as specific as this about one person's duty to hate another. But there is a direct background to it in the Scrolls, in the opening paragraph of the Manual of Discipline, which states that the Sons of Light, the members of the Qumran community, are to love one another, but hate the Sons of Darkness. Moreover, the same work uses for the members who are to be loved a Hebrew word for 'each other' that can also be translated 'neighbour', in the sense of 'fellow'. The Sons of Darkness were the Romans, the Kittim, who were to be overcome by the Sons of Light in a great battle in the near future. Against this background the teaching meant: 'You have been told by the Qumran zealots that you are to share the sacred meal (the Agape feast) with Jewish celibates only, but exclude from it any Roman, with whom you are at war. But my teaching is: "Admit Romans to the Agape feast, as a sign of political friendship".'

## Matthew's Christmas Story

It is from Matthew that the much loved tradition of the Wise Men and the Star originates. In this gospel also the story of the Virgin Birth is given in more detail, appearing to say that before Mary and Joseph came together sexually, Mary was found pregnant by the Holy Spirit. Joseph was a righteous man, and considered whether to put her away, but was advised in a dream by an angel of the Lord, who told him not to be afraid to take Mary as his wife. The birth would fulfil Isaiah's prophecy of a virgin birth. Joseph married her, and 'knew her not until she brought forth a son'. After this, Herod set out to destroy the child, who was being hailed as a future king of the Jews, issuing an order to kill all children of two years of age.

Matthew, in fact, is telling the same story as Luke, but whereas Luke, when he arrives at the actual 'birth', is recording events of AD 6 when Jesus was already twelve years old, Matthew is telling more of what happened in 7 BC, the year of Jesus' actual birth. In the course of his account he supplies useful information on chronology, a subject that was of special interest to a priest. Matthew's gospel is a major source of information on all such questions.

The opening genealogy of Jesus has appeared to the critical scholar to be mere invention, especially when it is compared with the genealogy in Luke, which differs from it. Both genealogies say that Jesus was descended from King David through his father Joseph, a point that at once makes the careful reader question the virgin birth. Yet it is the same two gospels containing this story that supply the genealogies.

According to Luke, Jesus was descended from Nathan, a younger son of Kind David. According to Matthew, Joseph came through the royal line, from Solomon who reigned after David. In fact, both are giving true information. The pesharist, accepting both as correct, discerns from this and from the history that the family of Jesus was actually a junior line, from Nathan, and would not have been distinguished but for the initiative taken by the man named Heli, the grandfather of Jesus. In the forties BC he had joined in the mission to the Diaspora, becoming its 'patriarch Jacob', under its 'patriarch Isaac' (Menahem the Essene) and its 'Abraham' (Hillel the Great). The royal line either died out or became inactive, but the junior line carried to the Diaspora and to Gentiles the traditions of sacred kingship that clung to the Davids, claiming the title 'the Christ'. Heli was the father of Joseph, called by this name in Luke's list, but grafted into the royal line in Matthew's list, where he is called by his patriarchal name 'Jacob'.

Matthew gives the date of Jesus' birth through his story of the arrival of the Magians who, accepting Jesus as legitimate, came to hail a new member of the David dynasty to work with them in mission. Through the complexities of the solar calendar, different parties kept different versions of the year date. It was agreed that the next heir was to be born in the generation year 3930 from creation, and for the Magians this was 7 BC. For Herod, however, it was 5 BC, so he waited two further years before looking for the child, by which time Jesus was two years old.

In Matthew's version, Mary was found with child by 'the Holy Spirit' (*pneuma hagion*), a title of Joseph in the celibate state, during his betrothal period. If Joseph followed the stricter rule, he should admit his own sin and break off the betrothal, leaving the child to be brought up as one of the orphans adopted by

Essenes. He was advised by 'an angel of the Lord' ('Gabriel', or Simon the Essene), to take the intermediate way, to marry Mary, leaving both of them in an honourable state, but to treat the child as the son of Mary, not his son. Drawing on a contemporary understanding of a verse in Isaiah, the child would be given at birth the name 'Immanuel'.

Joseph went through with a wedding ceremony, combining both weddings of the Essenes, the first one allowing sex, the second one when the woman was three months pregnant. Since there was a rule that there must be no intercourse during pregnancy, 'he knew her not' after the wedding.

The Magians, (the 'Wise Men') taking the liberal view that a child conceived after the binding betrothal was legitimate, came to hail Jesus at 'the queen's house', just below Qumran, where Jesus was still being looked after by his mother. They were led there by Joseph, who used the emblem of the Star of David, and for this reason was called 'the Star'. The Magians paid the child the reverence due to a future David, with traditional gifts. Not trusting Herod, they did not return to him, for their breach was now opening up with him.

Two years later, in March, 5 BC, events took a turn that set Herod on a path of vengeance, not only against the infant but also against one of his own sons. He had run into trouble with the Pharisees because he had increased his friendship with Rome to a point that seemed to them to compromise the nation's independence. It was from their protest that the subsequent zealot movement emerged. Joseph the father of Jesus, very much involved in the politics as any loyal Jew had to be at this time, sided with the Pharisees. At that time there was a Pharisee high priest, Simon Boethus, whose daughter Herod had married, and with her Herod had had a son, the man to appear later as Thomas Herod. Boethus with the Pharisees took part in a plot to poison Herod, who was becoming more and more irrational; he had previously put to death his two sons by his favourite wife. The plot was discovered, Boethus was dismissed, his daughter divorced, and Thomas Herod disinherited.[5]

Now Herod learned that the two-year-old son of Joseph was accepted as legitimate by the Sadducee who had replaced Boethus, and that he had misunderstood the meaning of the generation year. He issued an order to destroy Joseph and his family, who were forced to flee into hiding. During the year 5 to 4 BC all lived in terror of Herod until his death brought an end to his own physical agonies and to the current political tensions.

## Matthew's New Parables: Ten Virgins, Sheep and Goats, Workers in the Vineyard

Matthew added further parables, like those of Luke, giving detail of the actual history of the mission.

The story of the Ten Virgins is found in Matthew alone. It concerns the question of female ministry, dealt with in the context of the schism of AD 44, in which one of the issues was the divorce of Jesus from Mary Magdalene.

On the surface, the story tells of ten virgins, of whom five were foolish and five were wise. Going to meet the bridegroom at midnight, the five foolish ones found that their lamps were quenched because they did not have oil. They asked the wise ones for oil, but were told to go and buy some. When the bridegroom came, the wise ones were admitted but the foolish ones shut out, the door closed.

One of the rules of pesher is that a term like 'ten virgins' means 'Virgin 10', an individual, of grade 10 in the system of grades. 'Five wise ones (fem.)' means 'wise female 5', a woman at grade 5. The story concerns individual women at these grades: Mary Magdalene, Helena, and Mary the mother of Jesus, with a brief mention of Bernice the sister of Agrippa II.

The occasion was the great 'wedding feast' in Antioch in June AD 44, at which Matthew Annas declared the separate identity of the Gentile party and their adoption of a new name, 'Christian'. The same occasion is the subject of part of the Book of Revelation, the 'sounding of the seventh trumpet' (Revelation 11:15–19). It was held by the Christians to be the fulfilment of the mission, the messianic feast which had always been expected when the time appointed by Heaven for the end of mission came. The 'doors would be shut', and there would be no more chance for the unsaved to come in. But to some inside it would be a 'wedding feast', their time for entering into union with the priestly head of the mission. This was the image used for uncircumcised Gentiles, who were likened to women.

Women could join the communities of the Therapeuts, 'aged virgins' as Philo called them. They took part in the all-night banquet and Exodus liturgy, led by a woman who took the title of Miriam (Mary) the sister of Moses. This meant that they had a form of ministry, for all who took part in these meals became teachers and missionaries. In the New Testament, an ordained ministry for widows of the age of sixty was permitted.[6]

In AD 44 Mary the mother of Jesus had this form of ministry, and was given a seat at the common table. Previously doubtful about the methods of Jesus, she had come over to his point of view when, as 'the Widow Dorcas', she was 'raised from the dead' by Peter. It would normally be the case for the wife of the David to play the part of 'Miriam' in the liturgy of the banquets, hence she was called 'Mary', but since Mary Magdalene had separated from Jesus in March AD 44 after the birth of her third child, his mother took her place at the banquets, returning to the title 'Mary' that she had held as the wife of Joseph. It was Mary Mother who 'had oil' and was admitted into the feast, but Mary Magdalene's 'lamp was quenched', and she was excluded from a place, and from membership of the Christian party, when the doors were shut.

The meaning for women's ministry was that a woman, even though 'wise', should have 'oil' – that is, she should regard herself as a lay minister, not a priestly one. According to Josephus, the highest Essene celibates did not use oil on their skins, indicating that oil was a sign of being a non-monastic member who followed normal cleansing practices and did not use immersion baths.[7] A woman teacher used an oil lamp, as village elders did, placing it at the centre of the common table for use when reading, and the oil had the additional significance of indicating a lay presbyter, a 'Five', one who corresponded to a presbyter whose number was 5. Mary

Mother had the duty of teaching, so was a 'wise 5'.

But Mary Magdalene preferred the views of Helena, the chief woman of the Magian party, who held that women could be priests, rising to cardinals and bishops, so 'clothed in scarlet and purple'. (Mary Mother, as lay, wore blue, the third of the levitical colours, the colour always associated with her in tradition.) Acting like male ministers, the women carried a lantern, a different kind of light, which did not use oil. After her divorce Mary persisted in Helena's doctrine, remaining with the eastern party. Mary the mother of Jesus, now the chief woman in her place, refused her membership of the newly formed Christian party, and she was left on the Damascus side of the schism.

Writing of events in June, AD 44, Matthew Annas (who was himself the 'Bridegroom', the Chief Priest admitting Gentiles), could include a brief reference to Bernice, the twin sister of Agrippa II, aged sixteen at this season. She was not admitted to the new party. Later she would succeed Helena as the 'Scarlet Woman' of the Book of Revelation, not only claiming priesthood but also trying to wrest the monarchy from her brother.

Another parable unique to Matthew describes the fate of the 'sheep and goats', when they were finally separated from each other. It is not, as it appears, about the Last Judgement, but about an occasion that was taken to foreshadow it, in this same year of fulfilment. In September, AD 44, at Salamis on the island of Cyprus, there was an eventful meeting between the younger Agrippa, who was to become Agrippa II, and Matthew Annas, who for the moment had supreme power in the mission. He had gained influence over the younger Herod a year before, and now used it to determine a number of appointments. The active work of mission to Gentiles was done by a representative of the David, and for Jesus this was Peter, who was head of the 'sheep', the village Essene pilgrims. Peter had been told to 'feed my sheep'. But for traditionalists it should be done by James the brother of Jesus, head of the 'goats', a term used to describe the proselytes taught by James. A separation was now made between Christians led by Peter, and Jewish Christians led by James.

Matthew gives more useful chronological information in his additional parable of the Workers in the Vineyard, added after his gospel had been canonized, since it brings the history up to AD 60. It is like the earlier parable of the Vineyard, concerning the mission set up in the royal Herods' house in Rome, but tells more of its history. It had been founded in 1 BC, as a branch of the Diaspora mission, one of its purposes being to give advice and a nominal kind of membership of Judaism to Romans visiting Judea. In AD 6, when the country came under the rule of Roman governors, it served the useful purpose of preparing them for their term. It developed as an instruction centre for Romans who were seriously interested in the liberal Herodian form of the Jewish religion.

As their interest developed, 'workers in the Vineyard' – teachers and missionaries – were needed. They were sent from Judea, and, since Rome was so far away, appointed for periods of five years, with new leaders being appointed every fifteen years. This mission drew on a chronological scheme which was derived from a Sadducee version of the chronology, one that counted history in periods of 480 years (unlike the solarists' reckoning in sets of 490 years). The 480 years were sub-divided into eight sets of 60 years, and each one of these was called a 'day'. There had, in the past, been seven 'days' for mission to Diaspora Jews, but now there was to be an 'eighth day' for Gentiles, the sixty years from 1 BC to AD 60. In that latter year, the crisis of the year 4000 from creation would come, the Eschaton. This last sixty years was, therefore, a time of great tension.

Since sixty years was a 'day', it was divided into twelve parts, as the daylight day was, each division of five years being counted as an 'hour'. (The correspondences of different units of time was a favourite device of calendrists.) When a worker was appointed to Rome after five years, he was sent out at 'the first hour', AD 5, and when new leaders were appointed every fifteen years, in AD 15, 30 and 45, they were sent out at the 'third', 'sixth' and 'ninth' hours, respectively, as the parable shows. The leader sent in AD 45 was Peter. On this reckoning, the 'eleventh hour' was AD 55. In that year, a serious problem arose for the mission. The governor Felix, procurator in Judea at that time, received more than a token membership, becoming an active member in order to marry Agrippa's younger sister Drusilla, and so was qualified as a 'worker'. He proved to be an embarrassment, and was soon to give the order for the assassination of Jonathan Annas. There was much grumbling about this worker who had been appointed 'at the eleventh hour', and in AD 60, when it was believed that the Eschaton was about to come, his membership was opposed by the Jewish

Christians, but defended by Paul, who had instructed him. In this way Matthew gives not only information about the organization, but an account of the events leading up to the trial of Felix in Rome which also led to the arrest of Paul and his final execution.

Matthew's Logia and gospel were written in the interests of the Ephesus party of James Niceta, intermediate between Peter's Roman Christians and James' Jewish Christians. For James Niceta and for Matthew, Jesus was formally the head of Gentile mission, but they regretted many of his attitudes, and in the gospel preferred to use him simply as a mouthpiece for their own views, which were still close to a Jewish structure of thought. Since this gospel represented the New Law, it had to be placed first in an arrangement that reflected the divisions of the Old Testament. But, like Mark, it does not really reflect the personality and the distinctive emphases of Jesus, and, once its history is known, it gives no support to any claim that the essence of Christianity is the ethical teaching of the Sermon on the Mount.

# CHAPTER 10

# Behind the 'Visions': Jesus in the Acts of the Apostles

In the book called the Acts of the Apostles, the wit and wisdom of Luke speaking for Jesus is again apparent.

No New Testament book is more historical in its form. The first main episode of Acts is set in Jerusalem, in the month of June following the crucifixion. The replacement of Judas in the Twelve Apostles is described, followed by an account of great excitement on the Day of Pentecost, in which the speeches of Peter are given verbatim. The organization of the church in Jerusalem is detailed, including community of property and the daily common meal. Conflicts and tensions in the church, all quite natural, are recorded, including the appointment of a new ministry of seven men and the martyrdom of Stephen.

The conversion of Saul is described, and he becomes increasingly the central figure, a factual account being given of the expansion of the church through his mission from Antioch, through Asia Minor, to Ephesus, and, after a return to Judea, to

Rome, to which Paul was taken as a prisoner. Enough dates are given in the book, or are available, to know that the history ends shortly after AD 60. During its course it refers to the emperor Claudius (AD 41–54), and to his edict expelling the Christians from Rome, independently attested for the year AD 49. Acts has always been hailed with relief as a fairly reliable source for the history of the early Church.

What, then, is the historian to make of the less credible stories, sometimes with a humorous twist, that take up quite a large part of its space? For example, in the lengthy record of events in Ephesus in the late fifties, it is reported in the same factual way as the rest, that there were some Jewish exorcists, seven sons of Sceva, a Jewish high priest, who treated people with an evil spirit by saying, 'I adjure you by Jesus whom Paul preaches'. The evil spirit (now acting independently of the man) answered them, 'Jesus I know and Paul I understand, but who are you?' The man in whom this evil spirit was found then leapt on the seven exorcists, mastered 'both of them' (the translation alters this to 'all of them', obscuring the error) and overpowered them, so that they fled naked and wounded out of the house. As a result, fear fell on all, the name of the Lord Jesus was magnified, and the books of those practising magical arts were burned, their value amounting to 50,000 pieces of silver, the figure carefully noted (Acts 19:11–20).

In another example, earlier in the book (Acts 12), Peter had been put in prison by Herod Agrippa I, in the season, March, AD 44, that was to see the king's death. That night Peter was sleeping between guards, when an angel of the Lord stood over him, and a light shone in his cell. Peter was struck on the side and told to rise up. The chains fell from his hands. The angel told him to gird himself, put on his sandals, then, when he had done so, to put on his garment and follow him. Peter obeyed, not knowing whether it was true, went past the guards, came to an iron gate which opened of its own accord, and went into the city. The angel left him, and Peter said to himself, 'Now I know truly that the Lord has sent his angel and has delivered me out of the hand of Herod and all the expectation of the people of the Jews'. He then went to the house of Mary, the mother of John Mark, and knocked, but on hearing his voice Rhoda the doorkeeper did not open the door for joy. She went and told the others inside that it was Peter, but they said 'You are mad', or 'It is his angel'. Peter kept knocking and was admitted, and subsequently 'went to another place'.

Far from confining to Jesus the power to raise from the dead – as its theology of the significance of his resurrection would seem to imply – the book also attests that power for Peter and for Paul, in narratives who's extraneous detail is given as much attention as the revival. In Joppa, Peter was called to the bier of a widow named Dorcas. He was led into an upper room, where all the widows stood weeping, showing Peter the coats and garments that Dorcas had made while she was alive. Peter 'threw them out', knelt and prayed, and turned towards the body, saying 'Tabitha, arise'. The woman opened her eyes, and seeing Peter, sat up. Peter gave her a hand, raised her up, presented her alive to the saints and widows (Acts 9:36–43).

187

Paul had the same power, apparently. On his journey back to Judea in the late fifties, he came to Troas, where he stood in an upper room with many lamps. He was due to leave the next day, and he preached all night. A young man named Eutychus was sitting at a window on the third storey, and being overcome by sleep he fell down and was 'taken up dead (*nekros*)'. Paul came down, 'fell on him', and said, 'Do not be disturbed, for his soul (*psychē*) is in him'. The night's proceedings continued, with the breaking of bread, and Paul departed next morning. The lad was alive, and they were comforted (Acts 20:7–12).

Most striking of all, Jesus continually appears in visions to Peter and Paul, at vital points in the narrative where they needed to change their policy or plans. In Damascus he was seen by Paul in the Way (*hodos*, the same word that is used as the name for Christians in Damascus and elsewhere), his rebuke leading to Paul's conversion (Acts 9:1–30). In Joppa, he appeared above Peter, who was on the roof (*dōma*), and Jesus sent down a cloth to him, containing unclean creatures, with the instruction to Peter that he was to call nothing common or unclean (Acts 10:1–48).

In Corinth, in the early fifties, Paul suffered attacks from the Jews, and after moving to the house of a Gentile saw a vision of Jesus in the night, saying to him, 'Do not fear, but speak and do not be silent, for I am with you, and no-one will oppose you to harm you, for I have many people in this city' (Acts 18:9–10). Some years later, in Jerusalem, Paul was in even more trouble, and the Lord appeared to him at night, saying, 'Take courage, for as you witness for

me in Jerusalem, so you must bear witness in Rome'
(Acts 23:11).

The 'visions' are the most transparent device that
Jesus with Luke could employ to show to critical
readers, who were taking the whole book seriously
but did not believe in miracles, that he was still alive
during the years after the crucifixion, and that
behind the scenes he was directing and guiding his
executives Peter and Paul.

From AD 50, the year of Jesus' second marriage,
Luke would have remained close to him. The writing
of Acts would have begun during this association,
and continued during the whole period until the
arrival in Rome. Jesus was with Luke on the journey
to Judea in AD 58, and on the ship journey to Rome
in AD 60, as the use of 'we' shows. The book ends
abruptly, with its story unfinished, in AD 63. There
can be little doubt that Luke intended to finish it, still
hoping for a conclusion to the mission history in the
form of the Gentile party being accepted in Rome.
But in the following year there was only a defeat,
with Nero's persecution and cruel destruction of
Christians.

When Paul and his party sailed to Rome in AD 60,
Paul was not, at this stage, a prisoner. The prisoner
was the governor Felix who, on the arrival of his
successor Festus, had been recalled to Rome to face
trial for his mismanagement of Judea. One of his
inadvisable actions included giving the order to stab
Jonathan Annas simply because he kept interfering
in affairs of state. But Paul had recently been
instructing Felix, who had married into the
Herodian family, so as to make him an active initiate.
He travelled with Felix to help him, at the same time

taking advantage of the opportunity to bring the whole party of Christians, including Peter, Luke and Jesus, to re-establish their base in Rome.

Felix, at this point, was confident of acquittal in Rome, for his brother Pallas was the richest and one of the most influential men in the court. But a year after their arrival the capricious Nero turned against Pallas. Felix lost his case, and Paul, who went through a series of trials, not for being a Christian but because of accusations of complicity with Felix (Jonathan Annas was a long-standing enemy of Paul), was condemned to execution.

The Felix history is the actual subject of the incredible story about the man with the evil spirit. Such stories, which were likely to be disregarded by an outsider, were used to record the most secret political facts. The 'man with the evil spirit' was Felix. As an initiate he had become a 'man' , but he had not been initiated by a Jewish priest and was opposed to their priests, so he had an 'evil spirit'. At a council in Ephesus in June AD 57, he came into conflict with James Niceta, who as a bishop of Ephesus was 'Son 7' of Jonathan Annas, called Sceva. James Niceta insisted on the necessity of a Sadducee priest for valid membership. He was himself initiating ('exorcizing') Gentiles in the name of Jesus, and referring to Paul as a fellow missionary with whom he disagreed. Felix affirmed that he accepted Jesus, but that he agreed with Paul. Felix's side won in the council, and when he went back to Judea the following season, he issued an order for the death of Jonathan Annas, who had become isolated from the rest of the mission and was doing it damage. Thus the side of the 'exorcists' had been overcome.

It was 'both' (*amphoteroi*) who were overpowered and forced to flee out of the house naked and wounded. Yet there were 'seven sons' of Sceva. An apparent slip is one of Luke's favourite ways of giving important information. The pesharist would know that missionaries like James Niceta, 'Son 7', worked in pairs – either two men, or a husband and wife (like Aquila and Priscilla). James Niceta and John Mark, linked together during the gospel period, were the chief Pair, the leading Gentiles, for whom the term 'both' was used. Each was opposed to Paul, for different reasons, John Mark because Paul was a servant of the royal Herods.

James Niceta, always the opponent of Beast 666, Simon Magus, saw at this time the necessity for a public show of anti-zealot sentiment, and organized a burning of Magian books. (It was very probably at this period, back at Qumran, which had been taken over by Jewish Christians, that books representing Magian opinion, including multiple copies of the Damascus Document, were stowed in Cave 4, a cave defined as unclean, to show that they were heretical.)

With another item of apparently irrelevant information, that the Magian books were worth 50,000 pieces of silver, Luke gives a further vital piece of the history. There were 500 men in the Samaritan Magian order of West Manasseh. The whole order of Manasseh contained 1000 men in the homeland, but they were divided into western and eastern branches as the original tribe had been, the Samaritans of the west being hellenized. All, however, paid an annual fee for promotion and forgiveness of sins, in the form of silver, as they were levites (gold for priests, silver for levites, copper for

191

laity). Over 100 years, this would have amounted to 50,000 pieces, used for purchase of their library. Thus, the figure told the pesharist that they had been founded 100 years before AD 57 – that is, in 44 BC (in calculating from BC to AD, the BC date less 1 must be used, as no zero year was allowed). This was the year after the promulgation of the Julian calendar, and these hellenized Essenes of the Diaspora had adopted it, splitting from their eastern branch, and beginning in that year, under the leadership of Menahem, the mission that by now had become Christian.

The story of the 'raising of Eutychus', occurring the following year, gives a development in the history consequent on this one. Eutychus was the personal name of John Mark, as is seen from a comparison of his history with Josephus' account of a man named Eutychus, the charioteer of Agrippa I.[1] He had been at Qumran since early in AD 45 when, after the death of his employer Agrippa I, he retreated into full monastic life and at the same time separated from the newly formed Christian party.[2] For John Mark, the Christians were in the 'world', the *kosmos*, meaning public, married life. They used the word in the account of their celebration in June, AD 44: they were 'the kingdom of the world of our Lord, and of his Christ' (Revelation 11:15).

After developing his celibate Gentile community at Qumran for a number of years, with still some link with the Damascus Magians, John Mark would have become increasingly alarmed about rising zealotry following the accession of Nero. Damascus was its centre, out of reach of the Roman procurators. By early AD 57 he had reason to break all links with

Damascus and Judea and to move his community to Ephesus, where he again came into an alliance with James Niceta. James Niceta had taken over his 'little book' (John's gospel) and opposed his Magian, monastic sympathies. John Mark now came closer to James Niceta, their two kinds of mission joining. John Mark's community was established in Troas, in the same province as Ephesus. Meanwhile, John Aquila had succeeded his brother in Ephesus, and he had a much friendlier attitude to Paul. Tradition says that the graves of both Johns are found in Ephesus.[3]

In Troas in March, AD 58, Paul and Jesus, on their way back to Judea, spent an evening teaching and preaching. The 'young man' Eutychus (reduced to a novice in the eyes of the Christians) was listening on the 'third storey', and as Paul's preaching went on during the night, he 'fell down from the height, and was taken up dead'. Paul restored him to life – that is, lifted a ban of excommunication. It was a way of recording the reunion of Jesus and his old friend John Mark-Eutychus, so long separated. From this time John Mark acted as the superior of Christian monasteries in the Rome province.[4]

Similarly important history that should be kept secret was told in the story of Peter's 'miraculous' escape from prison brought about by an 'angel of the Lord', in March AD 44. This was the same 'angel of the Lord', who 'smote' Agrippa I in the following episode, so that he was 'eaten by worms' and died, five days later. The reason, according to Acts, was that Agrippa 'did not give the glory to God'. It was shown on the surface, and recorded in Josephus, that he had declared himself to be a 'god', like

Caesar, but the additional meaning was that he had dismissed Matthew Annas, called 'God' as all Sadducees were. He was the high priest who had brought about great advances. Agrippa was such a danger to the state that at this point both parties, the peace party of Matthew and the zealots of Simon Magus, combined together against him, and Simon organized the administration of snake poison, using Agrippa's eunuch, Blastus. Even Peter, and Jesus, played a part in the plot. Peter was imprisoned because Agrippa had got wind that his chief missionary to Gentiles was against him, and Jesus, who was 'the Light' who appeared in Peter's cell, had to agree on the only method available to get rid of a tyrant. (The assassination of the mad emperor Caligula, a friend of Agrippa's, had been brought about by the noblest men in Rome.)

Peter's 'prison' was in the Qumran monastery, in the outer hall which was the meeting place of pilgrims. Qumran on the night in question had been taken over by the anti-Herod faction, as had happened previously in the history. Simon Magus and Jesus came to free Peter, and he was led through the iron door that separated the outer hall from the inner monastery. It appeared to open of its own accord because it could only be opened from the inside.

Peter then went across the open space to the vestry room, which had been taken over by John Mark's celibate Gentiles, and with them their 'Miriam', the 'Mother of John Mark', the mother of Jesus who had been entrusted to John Mark at the crucifixion. Her deputy at this point was still Mary Magdalene, using the name 'Rhoda' because leading females were heads of the women's convents located on islands in the Mediterranean. She was acting as doorkeeper, and details of the story illustrate her as the 'foolish one'. It was shortly before the birth of her third child, but a pregnant woman in the hellenized orders could appear in public, although a woman in the eastern tradition had to hide herself.

The last appearance of Jesus was recorded, not by Acts, but by the Book of Revelation. Using his title 'the Lamb', the book shows that he was present at a council in Ephesus in AD 70, the year of the fall of Jerusalem to the Romans, at the age of seventy-six. Agrippa II and his twin sister Bernice had fled their city and established a court in Ephesus, and the brother and sister were in conflict about both the monarchy and national identity. Jesus came to the council to give support to Agrippa, helping him to regain his authority. Having been taught by Paul, he had come very close to a Christian point of view, favouring the downplaying of Jewish identity and the adoption of a Greco-Roman style. At the council, nationalists putting forward another viewpoint 'fought with the Lamb', but 'the Lamb conquered them'.

No more is heard of Jesus. A few years later, in AD 73, the wedding in Rome of his son Jesus Justus at the age of thirty-six was accompanied by a 'coronation', showing that his father had died. Jesus would have died in Rome, in the seclusion into which he had been forced, probably in the catacombs. But no record was made of the death of the man who, to his outer circle of followers, had entered heaven forty years before.

# CHAPTER 11

# The Gospels of Thomas and Philip

In 1945, a few years before the discovery of the Dead Sea Scrolls, a find of equal importance was made in Upper Egypt, at a place now called Nag Hammadi. A jar containing twelve flat, bound codices (the early form of a book) was uncovered under rocks, just below a cliff face in which the caves had been used for monastic retreats. In the vicinity were the sites of the ancient Christian monasteries of Pachomius, and there is good reason to suppose that the documents came from their libraries.

The books contain fifty-two tractates, short works reflecting Christian gnosticism in the form that flourished in this district in the early centuries AD. They are in the Coptic language (ancient Egyptian written in Greek letters), but had originally been composed in Greek. Their titles are given on the well preserved documents, and several of them are called gospels. Of these, two called by the names of followers of Jesus – the gospel of Thomas and the gospel of Philip – are of special interest in the present context.

Biblical scholars have had every reason to suppose that some biblical and para-biblical writings bearing the names of great authorities are productions from a much later period, using the name of the authority to give them the weight of tradition. One famous case is the book of Daniel, which was written in the second century BC to encourage Jews suffering under persecution, but purported to have come from the sixth century BC when a hero had stood up to similar persecution. The book gives itself away because its history of the sixth century is hopelessly confused. Another example is the Temple Scroll from the Dead Sea Scrolls, which claimed to have been dictated by God on Mount Sinai to reveal the plan of the true temple. It also gives itself away by the thoroughly Hellenistic nature of its plan. Such books are called pseudepigrapha, false writings.

It was at once assumed that the gospels of Thomas and Philip were examples of this genre, derived from the New Testament writings in the second or third centuries AD when, it was believed, Christian gnosticism first arose. A hidden assumption behind this and many such judgements was that the New Testament represented the pure and original form of Christianity, and that all related works were to be judged by it. If such works were different, they must be derivative or the products of later developments. That was a theological assumption, but not a sound historical one.

From the start, another opinion was urged: that earliest Christianity, first century Christianity, was a great deal more diverse than has been supposed, and the New Testament was the expression of only one of its streams of thought.[1] There was no such thing as a 'pure and original form of Christianity', but it was, rather, the many-sided product of complex social forces. To that side of the debate the present analysis of the gospels adds evidence, but with the additional point that the New Testament gospels themselves contain the gnostic-monastic tradition.

It may be seen, in the light of the pesher of the gospels, that Thomas and Philip are not pseudepigrapha. They are products of the same impulse and of the same years that produced the four gospels, but they come from parties that did not succeed in gaining power in the Roman church. Each comes from a losing side, Thomas from Herodians in the east; and Philip from anti-Herodians in the west.

## The Gospel of Thomas

The gospel of Thomas begins: 'These are the secret sayings which the living Jesus spoke and which Didymos Judas Thomas wrote down'. It goes on: 'Whoever finds the interpretation of these sayings will not experience death'.

The theme of seeking after something that is accessible only to privileged people continues: 'Let him who seeks continue seeking until he finds. When he finds, he will become troubled. When he becomes troubled, he will be astonished, and he will rule over the all'. The theory of mystery, of something that is capable of being discovered but not immediately seen, is plainly set out, and there follow more than a hundred sayings in enigmatic form, of which a considerable number are found in the Synoptic gospels and have been shown in the foregoing to be capable of a pesher. Here we have a book openly inviting a solution to a mystery that is of such an objective nature that it will trouble and astonish the seeker, and make him an authority. It both supports the view that the canonical gospels are capable of such treatment, and sets itself in the same class.

It contains sayings only, no narrative, and most are new and hauntingly beautiful, such as: 'There are five trees for you in Paradise which remain undisturbed summer and winter and whose leaves do not fall. Whoever becomes acquainted with them will not experience death.'[2] But frequently there are familiar sayings, directly parallel to the gospels, and with variations that seem to require an explanation. Most striking of all, the parable of the Sower is found in Saying 9, and after a repetition of the four kinds of soil, the rate of increase is altered: 'It bore sixty per measure and a hundred and twenty per measure'.

Numerical differences like this are hardly likely to be the product of an imitated version of the parable. In the gospel parables of the Sower, the Ten Pounds and the Dishonest Steward, such calculations all come from a single system, the educational sets given to Gentiles (see Chapter 12). They were tied either to a generation of forty years, or a period of thirty years, the periods themselves being determined by the chronological theory. The length of the period is shown by the fact that the figures fit that period only ($10 \times 4$ and $5 \times 8$ for forty years; $10 \times 3$, $6 \times 5$, $3 \times 10$ for thirty years). Now, in Thomas, the figures given indicate a period of sixty years for the education of Gentiles, six sets of ten years and twelve sets of five years, the sets multiplied by ten for the ten fee-paying provinces.

These figures give a date for the composition of the work. Thomas, a Pharisee ascetic, belonged to a branch of the Therapeuts who drank wine, meeting at Mird, whereas the Therapeuts using bread only for their sacred meal met at Ain Feshkha. Thomas was Agrippa's deputy, and could associate with Sadducees of the Vineyard mission. The plans for the Vineyard, set out in Matthew's gospel, built on a period of sixty years, originally extending from AD 1 to AD 60, when the year 4000 from creation would fall. But one of the adjustments to the calendar, done in order to eliminate Herod the Great from the history, was to declare a zero generation of forty years, so that the year 3900 which had originally fallen in 41 BC now fell in 1 BC, and that meant that the year 4000 fell in AD 100. The plan for the Vineyard was correspondingly adjusted, its revised sixty years being from AD 40 to 100. AD 40 was the year from which Thomas' calculations began, and the year of writing the gospel.

By this time the Vineyard had accepted Christian doctrine, so the sayings are attributed to Jesus. But it was an eastern form of Christianity, favouring the views of James the brother of Jesus. Saying 12 reads, 'Jesus said to them, "Wherever you are, go to James the Just, for whose sake heaven and earth came into being"'.

Two Lukan parables, the Rich Fool (Saying 63) and the Banquet (64) appear in a different form. It was around the year AD 40 that Jesus was beginning to compose the parables that found their way into

Luke's gospel. The versions in Thomas may well be their first draft.

In several sayings Thomas makes plain the true form of doctrine for Gentiles, in his view. He was the head of a class of sub-proselytes, who were not circumcised but adopted other aspects of Jewish identity. They observed the sabbath, as Saying 27 shows: 'If you do not observe the sabbath as a sabbath, you will not see the father'. But in Saying 53 Jesus was asked: 'Is circumcision beneficial or not?' and he was said to reply: 'If it were beneficial, their father would beget them already circumcised from their mother. Rather, the true circumcision in spirit has become completely profitable'.

All the persons named in this gospel belonged, historically, to the party lying between the Jewish Christians and Paul's Romans: Simon Peter (13, 114) and Matthew (13), both of whom upheld the necessity of Jewish priests; Mary (21) who agreed with James; and Salome (61) – that is, Helena – who was the head of the order of married Gentiles.

As given through the pesher of the gospels and of Revelation, Thomas' sub-proselytes formed a monastic community, based at Qumran; the members of this community were accused of sodomy. Their higher member, the Chief Proselyte, was the eunuch of the royal Herods. It is in this gospel that the celebrated passage on the loss of gender in the truly spiritual life is found:

When you make the two one, and when you make the inside like the outside and the outside like the inside, and the above like the below, and when you make the male and the female one and the same, so

that the male not be male nor the female female; and
when you fashion eyes in place of an eye, and a
hand in place of a hand, and a foot in place of a foot,
and a likeness in place of a likeness; then you will
enter the kingdom. (Saying 22)

It has been thought that in the final saying in the
book this ideal has been overruled, when it quotes
Jesus as saying that Mary will be made male, 'so that
she too may become a living spirit resembling you
males. For every woman who will make herself male
will enter the kingdom of heaven'. But the word
'male' is used in the special sense of 'minister', for
higher initiates were the only true 'men', and the
passage actually advocates the ordination of Mary,
the Widow, to the presbyteral ministry. In a community where gender was of no account, a woman
who had ceased to be sexually active was treated as
an equal of male ministers.

Thomas' celibates remained in the Qumran
region, in touch with the west, but thrusting their
way in the eastern mission through Magian opposition. The apostle Thomas remained associated
with the east in Christian tradition, his mission
reaching as far as India. Far from being late and
derivative, his gospel is an independent source,
preceding the Synoptic gospels, and showing the
direct influence of Jesus.

## The Gospel of Philip

With the gospel of Philip, we are back in the atmosphere of John's gospel. Its series of meditations arise

from some of the favourite themes of John: light and darkness, the heavenly man, the bread of heaven, the bridal imagery, the emphasis on women. The unity of its poetry with its special meanings is perfect: it speaks directly to the spiritual person without the sense of a barrier that the intellect must pass. A typical passage is:

> The chrism (anointing oil) is superior to baptism, for it is from the word 'chrism' that we have been called 'Christians', certainly not because of the word 'baptism'. And it is because of the chrism that 'the Christ' has his name. For the father anointed the son, and the son anointed the apostles, and the apostles anointed us. He who has been anointed possesses everything. He possesses the resurrection, the light, the cross, the holy spirit. The father gave him this in the bridal chamber; he merely accepted the gift. The father was in the son and the son in the father. This is the kingdom of heaven.[3]

As with the gospel of Thomas, it has been taken for granted by modern scholars that Philip is late, coming from new developments unknown to earliest Christianity. A date in the late third century AD has been given to it.

But there is direct evidence, in the plain meaning of the text, that it comes from the very earliest period. Throughout, it uses the word 'Hebrew' in contrast to 'Christian', and shows that Hebrews were Jewish missionaries making proselytes to the Jewish faith. They insisted on a Jewish identity and birth for the missionary. Its opening sentence is: 'A Hebrew makes another Hebrew, and such a person is called "proselyte". But a proselyte does not make another proselyte.' Moreover, this was in the same generation as the writer, who had changed from being a Hebrew to a Christian. 'When we were Hebrews we were orphans and had only our mother, but when we became Christians we had both father and mother.'[4] (Pesher: Gentiles instructed by Jewish missionaries were baptized by a woman, since a priest, a 'father', was too holy to touch them. But in the Christian party they were baptized by a male, a priest or celibate called 'father'.)

Such a situation existed only in the period of transition from the Jewish to the Christian form of the mission, in the forties and fifties AD. It was in no way relevant to the third century, when the Church had left its Jewish origins far behind.

The writer is clearly upholding the values of a celibate community, in which sex is sublimated through marriage imagery. Members are called 'sons of the bridal chamber'. They are part of the 'heavenly man', who 'has many more sons than the earthly man'. 'For it is by a kiss that the perfect conceive and give birth. For this reason we also kiss one another.'[5]

Having adopted monastic imagery, members are 'born' and can 'die' – that is, be excommunicated. These members consider that they have ceased to be Gentile, using that word for uncircumcised men living in the world. Both these points account for the saying: 'A Gentile does not die, for he has never lived in order that he might die'. A non-monastic cannot be excommunicated, for he has never received monastic initiation likened to life. As has been seen, the second Sign of John's gospel records the giving of this higher status to Philip in AD 31.

The thought of Philip would, then, have been directly derived from Jesus, with whom he was closely associated as amanuensis up to AD 37. Something of Jesus' desire to overcome ideological rigidities, while himself remaining hidden, is seen in the saying:

> Jesus took them all by stealth, for he did not appear as he was, but in the manner in which they would be able to see him. He appeared to them all. He appeared to the great as great. He appeared to the small as small. He appeared to the angels as an angel, and to men as a man. Because of this his word hid itself from everyone. Some indeed saw him, thinking that they were seeing themselves, but when he appeared to his disciples in glory on the mount he was not small. He became great, but he made the disciples great, that they might be able to see him in his greatness.[6]

In Caesarea in AD 58, Philip had 'four virgin daughters' – that is, 'Virgin Daughter 4', a nun who had the status of a bishop of grade 4.[7] Attached to his monastery was a convent, for female celibates, continuing the Essene tradition. In such a tradition females were given status as ministers, and this accounts for the many passages on women in Philip's gospel. It speaks quite frankly of the relationship between Jesus and the three leading women, in a way that would not have been possible in subsequent centuries. 'There were three who always walked with the lord: Mary his mother and her sister Magdalene, the one who was called his companion. His sister and his mother and his companion were each a Mary' (because each used the title 'Miriam' in the Exodus liturgy). In another passage it speaks of Jesus kissing Mary Magdalene.[8]

The virginity of Jesus' mother Mary is affirmed, and there is only a very indirect hint of a natural explanation of Jesus' conception. 'Some said, "Mary conceived by the holy spirit." They are in error. They do not know what they are saying. When did a woman ever conceive by a woman? Mary is the virgin whom no power defiled.'[9] It could be said that the 'holy spirit' was a woman because this term simply meant a bishop.

Similarly in error, this gospel says, are those who use the term 'resurrection' in the wrong way. It is made plain that 'resurrection' means initiation of a dynast into the monastic life, and to 'die' means not only to be excommunicated, but also to leave temporarily for marriage (a sense also found in the canonical gospels). Only the dynastic kind of marriage is permitted, that followed by Jesus; a man must not first marry and then enter the enclosed life. So, 'those who say that the lord died first (married first) and then rose up (entered the monastery) are in error, for he rose up first (entered a monastery as a dynast) and then died (left temporarily for marriage). If one does not first attain the resurrection he will not die (only a man who has entered at the dynastic level or above can be excommunicated)'.[10] The saying shows a purely symbolic sense for 'resurrection', and a formulation that could be used against any notion of a literal death being followed by a literal resurrection.

An intriguing saying in this gospel is the only one directly attributed to Philip. 'Philip the apostle said,

"Joseph the carpenter planted a garden because he needed wood for his trade. It was he who made the cross from the trees which he planted. His own offspring hung on that which he planted. His offspring was Jesus and the planting was the cross. But the tree of life is in the middle of the garden".[11]

This is both poetry and history. Joseph the father of Jesus was, indeed, a carpenter during the periods when he was out in the world for marriage, for Essene villagers worked at trades.[12] When he was inside the monastery, he as 'Adam' taught pilgrims who came to Qumran and received instruction in their 'Eden'. These laymen were called 'trees', a theme developed in the Scrolls.[13] The learning they were given was derived from the 'tree of life', and the higher 'tree of knowledge'.

While staying at Qumran they slept in tents on the esplanade, the same area in which Jesus was crucified. The wooden tent-poles were made under the direction of Joseph, in a T-shape, likened to trees, their base driven into the ground with cloth stretched over the tops. Being easily available, three of these were used for the crosses, one of them for Jesus. His father had indeed made the cross on which he hung.

# CHAPTER 12

# The Unrecognized History of the Church in Luke's Parables

In twelve historical parables scattered through his gospel, Luke is not simply telling stories with a moral point, but giving the history of the mission from the time of Herod the Great up to the schism when the Christian party separated. All persons in the parables – the Sower, the Prodigal Son, the Good Samaritan – were real people, leaders appearing at vital points of the mission history. The simple moral point that emerged from their histories was a valid one, but far more than that was being told.

By studying the structure and grouping of the twelve parables, the pesharist was able to see that each corresponded to a seat at the table for twelve, and the parable would have been told at that seat. They were intended for entertainment, imitating the manners of Greco-Roman society.

On the pesharist's assumption that there was a real history and that all details were specific, figures appearing in the parables were known to be the same as those with the same designation in the main narrative. The Lazarus of the parable was the same as the

Lazarus of John's seventh Sign, the Rich Man of two parables the same in both, and the same as the rich man who encountered Jesus in Mark 10. Consequently the history in the parables is continuous with that of the main narrative, and time expressions relate to the same period. It proves to be the case that whereas the 'miracles' explain the changes of rule that Jesus made in the gospel period, the parables deal with the history before and after that time.

An understanding of the chronological theory and terminology gives a date to each parable. They fall into three groups: first the Sower, the Good Samaritan, the Rich Fool, the Fig-tree in the Vineyard, covering the jubilee from 21 BC and its extensions; next the Banquet, the Prodigal Son, the Dishonest Steward, the Rich Man and Lazarus, the Importunate Widow, the Pharisee and the Tax-collector, covering the two generations from the start of the Herodian millennium in 44–41 BC; and third, the Ten Pounds and the Vineyard, both beginning in AD 1 when a new dating was adopted. All three sets end in the forties AD, as these were the years when the schism took place, leading to the separation of Christians. The history in the form of parables would have been composed at this time.

It is possible, then, to set out a consecutive history, as given through these parables, of the main events in the mission. Other events are given through Luke's typological histories in Acts, and in other passages in his gospel, but these twelve stories give the turning points.

## 44 BC: Parable of the Banquet
## (Luke 14:15–24)

According to the parable, a man gave a banquet, and sent his slave to invite three people. All made excuses, the first saying: 'I have bought a field and I have necessity to go out to see it'; the next, 'I have bought five yoke of oxen and I go to examine them'; and the next, 'I have married a wife and because of this I cannot come'. The householder then became wrathful (*orgistheis*), and told his slave to go out into the open places and streets of the city and bring in the poor, crippled, blind and lame. The slave did so, and said there was still a place. The slave was told, 'Go out into the ways and hedges and make it necessary to come in, so that my house will be full'.

In January, 44 BC, Menahem, leader of westernized Diaspora Essenes, the Magians of West Manasseh, adopted the Julian calendar promulgated the previous year, with its year starting in January. This practice gave his ascetic order an opening to the Greco-Roman world. He allied with the Pharisee Hillel, the great sage. They saw the need for a mission to the Diaspora, to bring Jews into a modernized form of the Jewish faith, a New Covenant, a New Israel. A Babylonian priest named Ananel, a Sadducee, joined with them.[1] Menahem persuaded the rising star Herod, on his way to the kingship, to co-operate with them, especially as admission fees would be charged and would give Herod revenue from Diaspora Jews for his ambitious plans. Herod was also told that he would be inaugurating the last millennium of world history, as 41 BC would, they believed, be the year 3900 from creation, and from a prophecy in the books of Enoch they held that the world was to last 4900 years. The last thousand years would see Judaism triumphant in the world.

Another man joined with them, Heli, a descendant of a junior David line, who was to become the grandfather of Jesus. In January, 44 BC, he was following the Essene marriage rule, calling marriage a 'necessity', requiring him as a dynast to go out into the world and earn his living during his marriage period. His son Joseph was conceived at this season, and would be born in September, 44 BC (so was aged thirty-six in 8 BC, the year of the conception of Jesus). While in the world Heli was to be especially responsible for mission to proselytes, Gentiles who wished to adopt the Jewish faith. They were the 'field' that Heli was to 'buy', using their fees to pay other missionaries.

Forming a New Israel, Hillel was its 'Abraham', the Father, Menahem its 'Isaac', patriarch of the east, and Heli its 'Jacob', patriarch of the west. Menahem was the dominant figure, using mission income to support, or 'buy', Hillel, whose ascetic order (later that of Paul) used the emblem of a yoke of oxen, and whose status was that of a presbyter at grade 5.

It was Ananel who 'called the banquet', following the custom of the Essene sacred meal. However, soon after appointing Ananel as his high priest Herod dismissed him, and the mission leadership was divided. Herod himself could not attend an Essene sacred meal because it was for celibates, and he had married the first of his nine wives.[2]

But in 31 BC Herod, the 'householder', the nominal head of the mission, became an ally of Augustus after the battle of Actium. He became the representative of the Wrath, a name used for Rome in both the gospels and the Scrolls. A new, pro-Roman start was made, and uncircumcised Gentiles were admitted in addition to proselytes. They were attached, not to monastic Essenes for whom they were unclean, but to the communities who lived like married village Essenes, those who cared for the indigent, classed as the Poor, Crippled, Blind and Lame. These Gentiles attended their synagogues and were instructed there in the spiritual principles of Judaism. A Gentile could become an extra person at the table, 'still a place', on the dais step where lay the thirteenth loaf, now shared with him as he was classed with the indigents.

This development is told in a different way in Luke 17, where, in the year of the 'cataclysm', the earthquake at Qumran in 31 BC, 'Noah went into the ark', baptizing uncircumcised Gentiles. Their admission was a direct consequence of Herod's pro-Roman politics.

## 21 BC: Parable of the Sower (Luke 8:4–15)

The Sower, who was said in the interpretation to sow seed that was the Word of God, scattered his seed first beside the way (*hodos*), and the birds of heaven came and ate it up. Next on the rock (*petra*), and it became withered. Next on thorns, which choked it. Next on good soil, where it bore fruit a hundredfold (and, as Mark gives it, sixtyfold and thirtyfold). The allergorical interpretation adds detail, such as that the 'birds' were 'the devil', the seed sown on rocks did not have a root and fell away in time of temptation, and that the thorny phase was accompanied by divisions, troubles about wealth, pleasures of life.

In 21 BC there was a great crisis in the mission. Relying on the prophecy of Enoch, the ascetics, following the north solar version of their year dating, believed that this was the year 3920 from creation, and that meant that it was the eighth period of 490 years, a date when, they were convinced, their Restoration to the temple should take place. Herod had announced plans to rebuild the temple using the money their mission brought him, Menahem was still friendly with Herod, and they had every reason to hope that he would build the temple according to their plan, set out in the Temple Scroll. But Herod rejected their plan. From that time on, Menahem's party, the Magians, established an anti-Herodian version of the mission, based in Damascus.

A way out of the disappointment about the prophecy was found, by declaring a Last Jubilee, on the reasoning that a zero jubilee of forty-nine years should have been allowed from creation. The expression 'Last Jubilee' is found in the Scrolls (11Q Melch). It would end in AD 29, and this calculation was responsible for many of the tensions of the time of Jesus. The parable of the Sower takes the history of the mission, in brief form, through these forty-nine years until it reached the 'good soil', the time of Jesus.

Jacob-Heli, sowing 'the Word of God', a name for

214

the Davids, was now with the anti-Herodians, who continued mission to the Diaspora. Celibate Gentiles who had joined, permitted to remain uncircumcised by the Magians, called themselves 'the Way', in Damascus. (This was 'the Way' which Paul later persecuted, and from which the Damascus Document of the Scrolls came, after the final schism.) Being patriarch of the west, Jacob-Heli continued a parallel mission, 'by the Way', in Ephesus, regarded as the western counterpart of Damascus on the world map. His subjects were now men like James Niceta, married Gentiles who adopted the Nazirite rule. The imagery of their mission continued to use wheat, for as Nazirites they did not use wine.

Some years after this came 'the affair of the Eagle', when Herod, so enamoured of Rome that he adopted their emblem, set up a golden eagle on the Jerusalem temple.[3] The 'birds came and ate up the seed'. He was bitterly opposed by the ascetics, who were respected among the people as the 'exegetes', teaching the ancient laws. At the same time Jacob-Heli's mission was criticized by 'the devil', in Damascus, the missionary who insisted on circumcision for all Gentiles and who would go on to become zealot.

The next main division of the jubilee was in AD 1, and in that year another party was founded. Sadducees linked with village Essenes, men who would later be led by Peter, the 'Rock'. 'The seed was sown on the rock'. They were opposed to the zealot organization formed at that time, called the 'Plant-root', so 'did not have a root', but when the zealot crisis ('temptation') came, their leader weakened and joined in the uprising.

Fourteen years later in AD 15 came the next quartodecimal division of the jubilee, and in that year Eleazar Annas became high priest, a pro-Roman Sadducee.[4] (He was the 'Father' whose opinions the twenty-three-year-old Jesus adopted in AD 17, according to the story in Luke 2.) The emblem of his abbeys was the thorn. (It was his younger brother, Jonathan Annas, who became the 'thorn in the flesh' to Paul.) This was the period of the financial troubles of the young Agrippa I in Rome, after he spent his large fortune on entertaining Romans in his house, and Pharisees rather than Sadducees helped him and became dominant in the mission. When Caiaphas the Pharisee became high priest in AD 18 he declared Jesus illegitimate and worthy only of wearing the thorn emblem in place of the star in a Sadducee abbey, so 'the thorns choked the seed (of David)'.

The end of the jubilee came in AD 29, when the mission to Gentiles fell on the 'good soil' of Jesus' teaching. Great changes were now made, giving them more privileges, including a revision of their educational system leading to a new method of increase. The year AD 30 was 3970 from creation, they believed, and there were only thirty years left until 4000, when a dramatic event was expected, the Eschaton, ending the present order of human affairs. In these thirty years, some Gentiles in the schools would be given ten sets of three years' instruction, others given five sets of six years, others still three sets of ten years. This was a modification of a previous scheme based on a forty year period, shown in the parable of the Pounds (see below). At the end of each educational set Gentiles like James Niceta paid fees, yielding the 'increase' of the seed. When applied to all ten of the fee-paying provinces into which the mission had divided the world, this would be a hundredfold, sixtyfold or thirtyfold increase.

## 4 BC: The Prodigal Son (Luke 15:11-32)

The record of mission found in the Sower had at first been the only one, used in Mark, and it took the history up to the gospel period. But subsequently composed parables filled in the intervening history. The next in chronological order was the Prodigal Son.

The younger of two sons of a father demanded that he divide his property between them, and went off to a distant region, where he wasted his property in 'riotous living'. There came a famine, and he was forced to join a citizen of that region, who sent him into the fields to feed swine. Coming to himself, he resolved to return to his father in repentance. The father had mercy on him, embraced him, and received him back, giving him 'the first robe', a ring on his finger, and sandals on his feet. He killed the fatted calf, and gave a celebration with music and dancing. The elder brother, however, who had stayed with the father, complained of this, saying that the father had never given him a kid (a young goat, not a calf), and that the younger son had wasted his living with harlots. The father replied, however, that the son had been dead and was now alive, had been lost and now was found.

217

In 4 BC Herod the Great died, and the mission was beset by schisms. The anti-Herodian faction persisted, led by Simon the Essene (the Simeon of Luke 2). After a dispute in the Roman courts Archelaus, one of the surviving sons of Herod, became the ruler, as ethnarch only, not king.[5] Within the mission hierarchy he used the title the Calf, one of the 'Living Creatures'.[6]

The Therapeuts of Egypt were always torn between the different factions of the mission, for their meeting place in Alexandria stood on the border of east and west. Their leader at this time was Theudas, who was to survive into the time of Jesus as Barabbas, and who was associated with Joseph. He appears in this story as the Prodigal Son. At first he supported Archelaus, and it was for this reason that he came to Simon the Essene, then the 'Father' (Pope), and demanded a split in the mission property, for his party was in schism. Influenced by Judas the Galilean, he believed that the objectives of the mission, to gain power in the Roman empire, could only be obtained by force of arms, not by the peaceful evangelism that Simon the Father and Jacob-Heli the Elder Brother upheld.[7]

Qumran had been reoccupied some years after the earthquake of 31 BC, and it was now, in the first few years of the first century AD, further fortified and made a centre for zealots. It was the 'distant region' to which the Prodigal Son, Theudas, departed. A triarchy was formed, in rivalry with Rome, called by colourful pseudonyms: Joazar Boethus the Pharisee high priest, the 'Dragon' (Priest); Archelaus the 'Calf' (Levite); and Judas the Galilean the 'Beast' (king figure, like the Lion). Joseph and Theudas named themselves separately, as 'the Star (of David)' and the 'Sceptre'.

Theudas 'wasted his property in riotous living', both because he agreed to spend the mission money on buying arms, and because the zealots, in opposition to the strict celibate discipline of monastic Essenes, allowed marriage, and at times sexual licence in the ecstatic banquets of the Therapeuts. They had women ministers whom their opponents called 'harlots'. When in the married state, the Therapeuts had a centre in Rome, from which they conducted mission to the 'swine', the Romans.

By AD 4, however, Theudas changed his political views, reverting to support Antipas the tetrarch who had lost in the battle for the Herodian succession. Opposed to the royal Herods, Antipas associated with the anti-Herodians including Simon the Essene. Theudas brought his Therapeuts back to Simon's side. The Prodigal Son returned.

Two years later, according to Josephus, some leading men of the country banded together to demand the dismissal of Archelaus, and their appeal succeeded. Simon the Essene was among those who 'killed the fatted Calf', Archelaus. At the same time Simon made some compromises in order to gain the support of Therapeuts. He allowed Theudas to act as a lay levite, wearing a priestly robe, but it was only the first of several worn by a priest. He also wore a ring on his finger as a bishop, and sandals on his feet to indicate that he was lay, not like the priests who had bare feet in the sanctuary. He permitted the use of music and singing in meetings, the choral dances of the Therapeuts.

Jacob-Heli the Elder Brother had retained half the

property at the schism, for as the patriarch of
Ephesus he led the five provinces of Asia Minor, half
of the ten fee-paying provinces. He and the members
in Asia Minor had remained anti-Herodian and anti-
zealot, and he objected to the standards of the
Therapeuts. But his objections were overruled, for
the return of the Therapeuts meant an alliance with
Ananus the Elder, a Diaspora Sadducee priest
agreeing with their views. He and Simon now came
together as a powerful faction. In AD 6, after Judas
the Galilean's zealot uprising failed, Ananus was
appointed high priest by the Roman governor.[8]

## AD1: The Ten Pounds (Luke 19:11–27)

A man of noble birth, expecting to receive a
kingdom, called ten slaves and gave them ten
pounds (pound, Hebrew *mna*, or *minah*, 100 half-
shekels) telling them to work with them until he
came. His citizens hated him and sent elders after
him, saying 'We do not wish this one to be king over
us'. He received the kingdom, however, and called
the slaves to account. The first said that his pound
had made ten pounds more, and was rewarded with
authority over ten cities. The next said that his
pound had made five pounds, and he was given five
cities. But the next said that he had hidden his
pound in a headcloth (*soudarion*), for he was afraid
of the master, who was an 'austere man', 'you reap
what you have not sown'. The master accepted this
description of himself, but said the servant should
have put the silver 'on a table' (*trapeza*), and he
would have worked with it. The servant's pound was

220

taken from him, and given to the one who had ten pounds. The judgement was given that to the one who had, would be given, and from the one who did not have, would be taken away. The order was further given that the enemies who did not want the master to reign over them should be slain.

In AD 1 the anti-Herodian mission that fled to Damascus in 21 BC was able to return to Jerusalem, and they began again their mission to Gentiles, treating the date as the start of a new generation for evangelism. This was the time when, in the Sower parable, 'the seed fell upon rock'. Allied with Simon the Essene and Jacob-Heli was the Sadducee priest, Ananus the Elder, whose following included village Essenes.

Ananus was aiming at the high priesthood, and would soon attain it, for he co-operated with the Romans who occupied the country after the uprising. Forty years later in AD 41 his son Matthew Annas would become high priest,[9] and for the Christians who saw him as their vindicator, it was the end of a successful generation. The time when the man 'obtained the kingship' (headship of the Gentile mission) was in AD 41, the successor being treated as having the identity of the originator, and the missionaries called before Matthew were the successors of the original ones, including Peter, Apollos (an alternative Chief Therapeut) and Simon Magus.

The renewed mission followed the pattern that had originally been conceived for the Herodian mission to Diaspora Jews, who paid fees of a half-shekel for admission to the New Covenant. Some initiates would be given four years' instruction, with ten sets of initiates in the forty years. Grouped in hundreds as Essenes normally were, a hundred men paid a half-shekel each at the end of the instruction period, making a pound, and after ten sets there was a yield of ten pounds. The original missionary had been given a pound to pay his travel expenses to the Diaspora, so his pound had made ten pounds more. This scheme was applied to the renewed mission to Gentiles like James Niceta, who paid fees, and at the end of the forty years the head of mission to his kind was Peter. His order had done their work well, and Peter was appointed by Matthew Annas to 'City 10', Rome, which was province 10 in the system.

A second kind of missionary gave eight years of instruction to Gentiles like John Mark, preparing them for a monastic type of discipline. There were five instruction periods in the forty years, and, since they still paid the initiation fee, the pound had made five pounds. Apollos, serving with Matthew Annas in AD 41, was appointed to 'City 5', province 5, Pontus.[10]

But Simon Magus, who led a mission on the Tiber island in Rome (as external historical records confirm)[11] was unwilling to give the yield of his mission to Matthew Annas, for they were political opposites, even though allied for some purposes. Nor did he want to send money to Jerusalem as part of the project of regaining the temple (the original purpose of the revenue-raising scheme), for he held that the temple should be on Mount Gerizim in Samaria. He, and missionaries like him, obtained money from Gentiles, ostensibly for the temple, but kept it for themselves, as a contemporary account shows.[12] Simon stored the money in a vault in his own province, wrapped in his headcloth that was used for 'unclean' contents. But if the mission rules were followed he should have brought it to the main council and placed it on the table for the sacred meal.

The schism of Christians was in the making, and Matthew Annas ordered that the mission in Rome should be taken over by Peter. Simon's 'pound' was given to 'him who had ten pounds'. Moreover, Matthew had enough power to bring about a further political coup – his 'enemies' (a word always meaning the Roman governor), who had opposed him, were 'slain'. As Josephus records in the context of the appointment of Matthew to the high priesthood, the Roman governor Petronius was at this time dismissed, and Marsus put in his place.[13] Petronius was an appointee of Caligula and a friend of Agrippa, and would have resisted the appointment of Matthew which was approved by the peaceful emperor Claudius. Marsus, on the contrary, became an ally of Matthew when he was forced to oppose Agrippa.

## AD 1: The Vineyard (Luke 20:9–19)

A man planted a vineyard and went away, leaving it to farmers. At the season (*kairos*) he sent a slave to collect the fruits, but the farmers beat him and sent him away, 'empty'. He sent another slave, but they beat that one, dishonoured him, and sent him away, 'empty'. He sent a third, but they wounded this one and threw him out. The lord of the vineyard then said, 'I will send my Beloved Son, they may respect him'. But the farmers said, 'This is the heir, let us kill him, so that the vineyard is ours'. They threw the heir out of the vineyard and killed him. So the lord of the vineyard would come, destroy the farmers, and give the vineyard to others.

Agrippa, who was to become Agrippa I, was the grandson of Herod the Great. Born in 11 BC, he was sent to Rome for his education while still a child. While he was there the split between the houses of Archelaus and Antipas took place.[14] Archelaus went back to Judea to lead anti-Roman forces, but the young Agrippa in Rome was a close friend of the imperial family, and on reaching adolescence entertained leading Romans in his house. His mentor was a Sadducee priest, possibly the Matthias who had been the high priest in Judea during the last year of Herod the Great's life. The priest took the opportunity to instruct interested Romans in the Jewish religion, giving them a form of initiation marked by the drinking of wine. Such instruction continued, mixed with conviviality, and Agrippa's house became known as 'Tavern Three' and the mission there 'the Vineyard'.

As in all forms of the mission, those joining it paid fees, the 'fruits of the Vineyard', which were made part of the mission property and could be used to support Agrippa's growing ambition to regain the Herodian kingship, which had been abolished in AD 6. The Gentiles who joined were of the kind who had once joined the 'Noah' mission, receiving baptism in 'Noah's ark' on the Tiber Island. It was possible, in biblical terms, to make the missions continuous, for the original Noah had, after the Flood, 'planted

224

a vineyard'. In 31 BC, there had been co-operation between the royal Herods and their lesser members on Tiber Island, but now, with the split between the royal Herods and Antipas, the missionaries of Antipas, led by the Magian 'farmers', did not co-operate with Agrippa. Any initiation fees they received were not handed over to him. His expenses, incurred through sumptuous entertaining, increased, and at one of the regular payment periods, in AD 15, he asked for money, but was refused it. In AD 23 Agrippa was bankrupt, 'empty', and had to leave Rome in disgrace, returning to Judea.

Agrippa eventually gained the kingship, becoming the third Herod to rule, counting Archelaus. But when he overreached himself, claiming godship, the Magians took part in his assassination. They now thought they would have the Rome mission to themselves, using it for covert political activity against Rome. But in AD 45 'the Beloved Son', Jesus, was sent to Rome, following the appointment of Peter. He was accepted in the house of the youthful Agrippa II, still the 'Vineyard', where peaceful instruction of Gentiles continued in the reign of Claudius. A building outside the walls of the city, called the Forum of Appius, was used as Peter's school.

However, Peter's followers caused some disturbance when they thought that fulfilments of their prophecies were about to come. They 'rioted at the instigation of Chrestus', as a Roman historian says, having misheard the name of Christus, their leader.[15] Claudius, who had issued an edict of tolerance towards the Jews, was not sure what to make of this

225

new sect, and was advised by the Tiber Island missionaries, declaring their Jewishness, to expel them. He did so, and in AD 49 the 'Beloved Son' was excommunicated from the Rome province, and with his friends Peter, Luke and John Aquila, forced back to Ephesus, thence to Macedonia and Achaia. However, in the same year, AD 49, Agrippa II, now of age, was crowned king, 'the Vineyard was given to others', and the Magian political ambitions were defeated.

The question of chronology was a pressing one through the whole of this period, because of anxiety about the fulfilment of the Enoch prophecies. In 1 BC the anti-Herodians had abolished the Herodian millennium, 3900 in 41 BC, and started it again by declaring a zero generation of forty years from creation, with 1 BC as its year 3900. It was this manoeuvre that established the dating of the Christian era. There had always been two different ways of dividing time, into generations and jubilees, and one group, priests like Ananus, counting in generations of forty years, calculated the first generation of the millennium as being from 1 AD to 41 AD, as in the parable of the Ten Pounds. Another group counted in jubilees of forty-nine years, and revised the jubilee system in a way that is demonstrated in the Book of Revelation. The parable of the Vineyard uses their jubilee dating, ending in AD 49, and shows that it was because of their belief that the end of the jubilee would bring a fulfilment of the prophecies that the Christians in Rome 'rioted at the instigation of Chrestus'.

# AD 17: The Dishonest Steward (Luke 16:1–8)

A steward was accused by his master of wasting his goods, and was asked to give the account of his stewardship. He wondered what he should do: 'I do not have strength to dig, and to beg I am ashamed'. Then he thought what he should do, so that when he was put out of his stewardship he would be 'received into their houses'. He called each of the debtors of the lord, and asked how much they owed. The first said that he owed one hundred measures of oil, and the steward told him to 'receive the letters' and write fifty. Another said that he owed a hundred measures of wheat, and the steward told him to 'receive the letters' and write eighty. The steward was commended for this, told he had done wisely, and the comment was added: 'The sons of this aeon (*aiōn*) are wiser on behalf of the sons of light to the generation of themselves' (literal translation).

In AD 17, as several other stories show, there was a further change of policy towards Gentiles, under the leadership of Antipas, who had received favourable treatment from the emperor Tiberius and had built and named the Galilean city of Tiberias in his honour.[16] Now pro-Roman, he allied with the Sadducee high priest, Eleazar Annas, to give Gentiles longer periods of instruction.

Some celibate Gentiles used oil as their emblem, indicating that they were lay, like women. They had been given four years of instruction, so there were ten sets in the forty years, each owing fees amounting to a 'measure of oil', and in the ten provinces a hundred measures of oil were owed by this kind. But they were now given four extra years, a total of eight years, bringing them to the graduate level of monastics, so there were only five sets in the forty years and only fifty measures of oil were owed.

Other Gentiles, such as James Niceta, used wheat as their emblem, and were normally given four years of instruction, so on the same principle a hundred measures of wheat were owed. Some of these were given an extra year, making eight sets of five years in the forty years, so in ten provinces eighty measures were owed.

The 'steward' was Theudas, the Chief Therapeut, still active in the mission, who while out in the world for periods of marriage instructed Gentiles and collected their fees. He had had a lapse back into zealotry, accused of wasting the money on arms, as he had done as the Prodigal Son. But now he and the Egyptian Therapeuts had become pro-Roman again under Tiberius, and he agreed with the reforms. Theudas had to give the account of his stewardship because he was about to return to the celibate community, be 'received into the houses', not as a coenobitic acolyte who would do labouring work in the monastery, but as one following the easier rule.

The enigmatic saying concluding the story introduces the phrase 'Sons of Light', one of the clear signs of a link with the Dead Sea Scrolls, in which at one stage members were called 'Sons of Light'. The term appears also in John's gospel, in the mouth of Jesus.[17] It means the Judean coenobitic community, as opposed to the Therapeuts. The Therapeuts were merely 'wise' (*phronimos*), as women also could be, whereas the Sons of Light had a higher standard of learning. Theudas on re-entering was 'wise', and in this year, AD 17, Antipas ('Themselves', see the Lexicon) was appointed Herodian deputy in the east, so was 'wiser', a grade higher. He had reached the age of forty in this year, as the term 'generation' (*genea*) shows. But Agrippa, now allied with Judas Iscariot and the 'Sons of Light', had declared his hopes for kingship in this year, which in one version of the chronology should be that of the Restoration, the 'aeon'. Antipas merely acted on his behalf in the east.

## AD 29: The Good Samaritan (Luke 10:30–7)

A man went down from Jerusalem (singular form) to Jericho, and fell among thieves. They stripped him, struck him with blows, and went away, leaving him half dead. A priest passed by on the other side, as did a levite. But a Samaritan had compassion on him, bound his wounds, pouring on oil and wine, put him on his own donkey, brought him to an inn, and took care of him. The next day (literally 'tomorrow'), he gave two denarii (two days' keep, according to Matthew 20:2) to the innkeeper, and said 'Care for him, and whatever is lacking I will give you when I come'. It was the Samaritan who was neighbour to the man who fell among thieves.

In September, AD 29, came the end of the Last Jubilee that had been declared in 21 BC. Now, surely, the Restoration prophesied by Enoch would come. Agrippa, rescued from a suicide attempt after his return as a bankrupt to Judea, renewed his hopes for

229

kingship in alliance with John the Baptist, Judas
Iscariot and Caiaphas, the reigning Pharisee high
priest. The latter two were the 'Scribes and
Pharisees' of the gospels.

Now Simon Magus came forward as the magnetic
leader of the anti-Herodian party, the Magians. He
claimed the position of a Priest of Diaspora communities. With him was Antipas, preferring that
there should be no royal Herods and that he should
be left in his comfortable position holding the
Herodian wealth in Judea. Still supporting Antipas
was Theudas, now ageing. He acted as deputy or
levite to Simon as priest. Simon was leading his
faction into a greater sympathy with zealotry to
oppose the insensitive rule of Pontius Pilate, 'the
Young Lion of Wrath', who had arrived in AD 26.

At a council held at Mar Saba, the intermediate
place between Jerusalem and the celibate communities in the Wilderness of Judea, an intense dispute
broke out between the two Herodian factions. John
the Baptist had come forward as a candidate for the
papacy, but his claims were defeated by Theudas.
He 'fell among thieves' (Theudas as a zealot), was
defrocked, and reduced down to the grade just
before excommunication, 'half-dead'.

The priest, Simon Magus, and the levite,
Theudas, would not support him. But Jonathan
Annas, 'the Good Samaritan' because he held
Diaspora views, now with his eye on the high priesthood, held an intermediate position as Sadducee,
between the Pharisees and the Magians. He represented Diaspora celibate communities, and was 'a
neighbour' in their terms. Although earlier in the
year he had sided with the Magians, he now

distanced himself from their increasing militancy. Holding the casting vote, and knowing that the Baptist taught reliance on the intervention of heaven rather than on force of arms, Jonathan voted for him, restoring him and giving him the papacy.

Whereas lay celibates walked the paths through the barren region of the Wilderness of Judea, priests were entitled to use donkeys, and Jonathan ceded his donkey to the Baptist, thereby becoming his deputy. Jonathan brought the Baptist to Mird, the Herodian council centre and sanctuary. The Baptist's 'wounds' had been 'healed with oil and wine', meaning that Jonathan had brought to his support the Gentiles whose emblem was oil (Titus, head of the 'sons of Ham'), and wine (Philip, head of Shem, for whom 'water was turned to wine'). The 'innkeeper' was Agrippa at Mird, and on the 1st of the solar month ('Tomorrow') Jonathan paid him his annual promotion fee of a denarius, adding also another denarius for the Baptist, since a man with money could pay on behalf of another (as Peter did when he paid the half-shekel temple tax for both himself and Jesus).

## AD 36: The Rich Fool (Luke 12:16–21)

A rich man's land prospered, and he said to himself that he did not have a place to put his produce, so he would pull down his barns and build bigger ones, where he would put his wheat and good things. He would say to his soul, 'Soul, pause, eat, drink and be merry'. But God said to him, 'Fool, this night your

231

soul will be required of you, and what you have prepared, to whom will it be?' Thus is he who lays up treasure to himself and is not rich to God.

When Agrippa returned to Rome in September AD 36, he was close to restoring the monarchy through his influence with the rising star Caligula. After a temporary setback when his plotting was betrayed by the ailing Tiberius, Agrippa succeeded in gaining rule in March AD 37 when Tiberius died. The chronology counts his accession from the double date September 36, seven years from the jubilee (a 'Woe') and January 37, the Julian year. Although the news of his success did not reach the country until late in 37, it was known the previous year that he was likely to succeed, and this would mean that the deposits of treasure stored in the vaults at Qumran would be seized by him, in his constant need for money. The fees from the Herodian mission had long been stored at Qumran and its surrounds, the record kept in the Copper Scroll.

The 'barn' of James the brother of Jesus was the vault where Gentile fees were kept. This was in the Cave of the Prince, the Rich Man, at the end of the esplanade, referred to in the second sentence in the Copper Scroll. Here were the fees paid by men like James Niceta, using the wheat emblem, as well as the shared property of men like John Mark. Large numbers of Gentiles were joining, and those supporting James were willing to pay fees, so he 'prospered'. The money was legally his, as Gentile money was kept separate from Jewish money, and he used it for further mission. James was officially the David under the high priest Caiaphas, and had used

Qumran up to now. Jesus, who did not tolerate the payment of fees, had moved to Caesarea, where he simply supervised John Mark's shared property.

James also instructed proselytes who became circumcised and paid fees like Jewish members, and this money could be claimed by Agrippa. So James turned to Himself, a way of designating Simon Magus. Simon still controlled the anti-Herodian centre that had been set up in Damascus. It was not in Judean territory, but under the control of Aretas, King of Arabia, an enemy of the Herods.[18] James, fearing the capricious Agrippa, agreed with Simon that proselyte mission should be taken out of his control. Qumran ceased to be the storage place for any money accessible to Agrippa; the 'barns were pulled down'. The storage of proselyte money was transferred to Damascus. This part of the history was taken up in the Damascus Document of the Dead Sea Scrolls.

James' 'soul' was required of him when Caiaphas was dismissed at the end of AD 36. Jonathan Annas, who used the title 'God', was appointed to succeed him. The treasure, the mission property, should not be laid up to Himself, Simon Magus, but to 'God', Jonathan Annas, who would use it for a peaceful form of mission.

## AD 37: Lazarus and the Rich Man (Luke 16:19–31)

A rich man clothed in purple and fine linen dined daily in splendour, while a poor man named Lazarus lay at his gate, covered with sores, waiting for the

233

pieces of food falling from the rich man's table. The dogs came and licked his sores. Then the poor man died and was carried into the bosom of Abraham. The rich man died also, and was buried. In Hades he lifted up his eyes, being in torment, and saw Abraham from afar, and Lazarus. The rich man called for mercy, asking Abraham to send Lazarus to dip the tip of his finger in water and touch his tongue, 'for I am in anguish in this flame'. Abraham replied that their situations were now reversed, and that between them there was a great chasm (*chasma*) fixed. Abraham, urged to help the rich man's five brothers, replied that they had Moses and the prophets. The rich man answered that if someone came back from the dead they would repent, but Abraham replied that if they did not hear Moses and the prophets they would not be persuaded if someone rose from the dead.

James the brother of Jesus was again the Rich Man of the story. In January, AD 37, the Gentiles he taught had opposing political loyalties. James Niceta could support the Herodian monarchy in the west, but proselytes in Damascus were opposed to it. While with James Niceta, under the high priest elect Jonathan Annas, Brother James acknowledged that he was merely the David crown prince. Accepted in this role by the new regime, he dressed in the purple of a bishop and presided at the meal table of this kind of Gentile. Here, Simon Magus, or Lazarus the leper, was relegated to the equivalent of the dais step, being anti-Herodian, and only received the 'crumbs' of the charity loaf. A gate, which would become the chancel gate in a church, divided the step and all below it from the room to its north.

Since the leaders had left Qumran it was used for different purposes, one of them as a school for proselytes of the type who paid fees to Thomas Herod. Thomas was accused of sodomy, and the name 'dogs' was used for his order. Simon Magus, being part of a mission to proselytes in the east, associated with him, so 'the dogs licked his sores'.

By September, AD 37, a messenger had returned from Rome confirming Agrippa's appointment, and bringing news of his strong pro-Roman stance now that his friend Caligula was emperor. Any leader who had sympathy with the anti-Roman east was firmly put down. Jonathan Annas himself, a moderate who was lukewarm in his support of Agrippa, had been appointed high priest in March 37, but held his office for only six months, then was replaced by his younger brother Theophilus who was more western in his views and who led the people in an oath of loyalty to Rome.[19] So Jonathan, who as Pope used the traditional title 'Abraham', was excommunicated and sent to Cave 4 at Qumran, the burial and excommunication cave of the Popes.

Just before Jonathan's overthrow, Simon Magus had formed a zealot alliance against him, believing that he could bring in an eastern power.[20] But when Theophilus was appointed, Simon was seen to be an even worse enemy of the state and excommunicated likewise, placed in Cave 4 as he had been in the time of Jesus. Here, he was 'in the bosom of Abraham', the two together seen as enemies of Agrippa.

James, the Rich Man, had links with both these leaders, and that meant that he too was seen as too eastern. He was similarly excommunicated in the

235

purge that was now taking place, and, since his burial cave was the cave of the Davids, Cave 8, he was placed there. It was a 'Hades', corresponding to the valley of Hinnom, or 'Gehenna', in Jerusalem. Between his cave and Cave 4 there was a chasm, the space between the two cliff projections up which ran the path from the plain below. His cave, the western one of the two, had a window looking across the chasm, through which he could call out to 'Abraham'. It is through the details in this parable that Luke gives the information about the position of the 'resurrection cave'.

The conversation between the incarcerated men concerned the Pharisee and Sadducee doctrine of resurrection. The Pharisee view was urged, upheld by zealots, that death by martyrdom would be followed by a physical resurrection. But 'Abraham', the Sadducee Jonathan, argued that such a belief was not useful. His party denied it not only on theoretical grounds but because such a belief was a motivating force behind anti-Roman militancy.

## AD 40: The Importunate Widow (Luke 18:2–8)

A judge in a certain city did not fear God and did not respect a man. A widow in that city came to him, asking to be vindicated ('made righteous') from her adversary. She was at first refused, but when she persisted the decision was changed. Because of the 'toil' the widow brought, it was agreed that she should be vindicated, lest at the end (*telos*) she should cause trouble, literally 'strike under the eye'. The narrative goes on: 'The lord said, Hear

what the judge of unrighteousness says. Will not
God vindicate his elect ones who cry to him day and
night? . . . I say to you that he will vindicate them
shortly. Nevertheless, will the Son of Man when he
comes find faith upon the earth?'

With this parable Luke's history coincides with the
history of eastern proselytization given in Josephus,
who records at considerable length that Jewish
merchants came to the eastern kingdom of Adiabene
and converted to the Jewish faith both its queen,
Helena, and her son born of incest with her brother,
Izates.[21] One missionary, Eleazar of Galilee,
required that Izates should be circumcised, but
another missionary, Ananias, said that it was not
necessary. Queen Helena subsequently gave
generous rights to the Jewish state, maintained a residence in Jerusalem, and helped them in time of
famine.

According to Acts, a certain Ananias was in
Damascus, and Paul was sent to him at the time of
his conversion. Ananias appears also with Sapphira,
holding back money and being excommunicated by
Peter. Ananias was one of the many pseudonyms of
Simon Magus, and Sapphira (meaning 'blue', the
colour that should be worn by women ministers
rather than scarlet and purple) was his mistress
Helena. He and Eleazar of Galilee, the successor of
Judas Iscariot, were co-leaders of the ascetic order
of Manasseh, Simon of its western, Magian side,
Eleazar of its eastern. From Damascus they
conducted mission in the east, holding different
views on the necessity of circumcision. Their
mission always aimed at monarchs, knowing that the

237

religion would become established in the state if the ruler adopted it.

Queen Helena was converted in June AD 40. She asked to be made a presbyter, as a Widow could be, but was refused by Eleazar at first and made to undergo three years of instruction in ascetic discipline, 'toil', as all Judean initiates were required to do. In June, AD 43, she was given her promotion, and at a council in September 43 she became part of a political plot led by Herod of Chalcis, who was the 'judge' of the story. He 'did not fear God' because his sympathies were Pharisee, not Sadducee, and he did not respect the party of his brother Agrippa, whose murder was planned at this council. Because of Agrippa's outrageous behaviour, and the dismissal of Matthew Annas, the majority of leaders banded together against him.

Matthew Annas formed a temporary alliance with Simon Magus, who was the 'lord' presiding at the council (the phrase 'the lord said' is part of the parable). He was able to report that at that season he had gained influence over the sixteen-year-old Agrippa II, who, in his view, should succeed his father. The younger Agrippa, who was to remain unmarried, represented 'the Elect Ones', Herodian celibates.

The younger Agrippa's twin sister Bernice, already widowed at sixteen, had just been married for the second time to her uncle Herod of Chalcis, and was involved in the scheme.[22] Queen Helena became the Chief Widow in the mission, a position that would later be filled by Bernice. An active missionary worked in the name of a leader, and Helena, mistress of Simon Magus, was the actual teacher and worker in the east, having instructed the queen, baptizing Gentiles as the Chief Woman had always done.

Matthew's party, however, with the younger Agrippa as nominal head, was western, and while the two sides were allied they met in Antioch, the north being the meeting place of east and west. Here, in late December, AD 43, the Christians began to use their distinctive name, approved by Matthew. The 'Son of Man', Jesus, came there, as Acts shows in its corresponding narrative, and he found there 'Faith upon the Earth', a way of saying that he found Paul, working as an active missionary for the younger Agrippa.

East and west were to remain together only for the purpose of dealing with the dangerous influence of the king. During the following year the final schism would take place and the Christians begin their independent mission.


## AD 43: The Pharisee and the Tax-Collector (Luke 18:9–14)

In this parable, immediately following that of the Widow, two men went up to the temple to pray, one a Pharisee and the other a tax-collector. The Pharisee stood and prayed 'towards himself', saying 'O God, I thank thee that I am not like the rest of men, extortioners, unrighteous, adulterers, or like this tax-collector. I fast twice on the sabbath, I tithe all I get'. But the tax-collector stood afar, and would not lift up his eyes to heaven. He prayed, 'God be merciful to me a sinner'. The tax-collector was sent away to his house justified. The concluding words are: 'Everyone who exalts himself will be humbled, and he who humbles himself will be exalted'.

In late AD 43 the conspirators against Agrippa met at Qumran, taking it over as a headquarters for their plot. But even as they met in council for their common purpose, the differences between them were expressed, preparing for the schism of the following year. On one side was Simon Magus, with whom the elderly Theudas was still associated. Theudas could hold either Pharisee or Sadducee doctrine, according to his changing attitudes to Rome, and at present he was a Pharisee.[23] On the other side was Matthew Annas. As the Annas priests all were, he was called both 'God' and the 'tax-collector', for the tribute to Rome was paid through the Sadducee priests.

At a time when prayers were offered, Theudas stood just south of Simon, so prayed 'towards Himself', since 'Himself' was Simon. At this point Matthew Annas was still the public high priest, so he stood on the platform, while Simon and Theudas were on the ground floor below. Theudas directed his prayer up towards Matthew, calling him 'God'. Theudas' prayer concerned the differences between his views and those of other parties in the eastern mission.

But then Matthew Annas was dismissed.[24] The tax-collector was sent down to the exclusion row, 'standing afar'. He would not, and could not, 'lift up his eyes to Heaven' – that is, he no longer stood on the platform, holding his 'eyes', his lamp, and he would not co-operate with Agrippa, who claimed the title of 'Heaven' as the supreme priest.

By the rule of the last referent (p. 262), it was 'Heaven', Agrippa, who said, 'God be merciful to me a sinner'. He had become aware of the plot against him, and was still hoping to retain the Sadducees on his side. But Matthew took part in the plot and was subsequently exiled to Antioch, where he founded the new Christian party: 'he went to his house justified'. The schism between the Christians and the Magians then took place, so that the one who exalted Himself (a supporter of Simon Magus) was humbled, and the one who humbled Himself (an opponent of Simon) was exalted.

## AD 43–44: The Fig-Tree in the Vineyard (Luke 13:6–9)

> In the last parable when the chronology is followed consecutively, it is said that a certain man had a fig-tree planted in his vineyard. He came seeking fruit, and when he did not find it said to the vineyard-keeper: 'Behold three years I come seeking fruit on this fig-tree . . . cut it down'. The vineyard-keeper answered, 'Lord, leave it this year, until I dig around it and throw dung. It may bear fruit into the time about to come, and if not, cut it down.'

The 'Fig-tree' was the mission on the Tiber Island in Rome that had once co-operated with the royal Herods' 'Vineyard' mission, but from the time of the split between the house of Antipas and the royal Herods it worked in rivalry to it. Simon Magus was the leading figure of the Fig-tree party. In year 3 of the emperor Claudius, AD 44, the younger Agrippa found himself head of the royal Herods following the assassination of his father. Not yet appointed king, he sought to repair the breach, suggesting that the 'fruit' of the 'Fig-tree', its income from the mission, should be merged with that of the royal house.

In September of AD 44 the younger Agrippa (aged just seventeen) had a meeting on the island of Cyprus with the leaders of the mission. One adviser was Matthew Annas, stationed at that time in Antioch. As head of the Herodian Sadducee mission, he was the 'Vineyard-keeper'. Matthew told him that he needed another year until AD 45, when Peter would come to Rome and the decision would be made about a final breach. Meanwhile Matthew was attempting to restore strict monastic rule, including the rules of uncleanness, to the Magian branch of the mission. However, the arrival in Rome in AD 45 of both Peter and, later, Jesus, gave such an independent identity to the Christians in the royal Herodian house that the two missions decisively separated, with the consequence that a few years later the Jewish Tiber Island group brought about the expulsion of Christians.

Thus through twelve parables Luke recounted 'to him who had ears to hear' all the key events in the mission, from its founding up to the separation of the Christian party, the true climax. The gospel period had seen Jesus move into the position of central figure to Gentiles, but the real history was that of the organization of which he was merely a part. Its motivating events were not in the person of

Jesus but in the spiritual and intellectual needs of the Greco-Roman world which was opening its doors to this new religion. But in Jesus the complex organization found its soul, and in his name it would grow while the culture that had now been born survived in history.

# More about the Pesher

# Outline of the History

The history of the period within which the Christian Church arose has previously been known only from a few writers of that time. Since the discovery of the Dead Sea Scrolls, it has been obvious that they are sources for far more knowledge on the subject, but there is still intense controversy about how they should be used. In the following brief outline, the well-known and established facts from the external historians will first be set out, followed by the history which, as may be argued, is found in the Scrolls and derived from the new approach to the New Testament.

## The History as Given by External Writers

In the first centuries BC and AD, the little country of Judea was as much of a 'political football' as it is now. One of the reasons was that the Mediterranean coastland, where it lay, formed a highway between east and west. The Jewish nation had always had too little territory to become a political power in its own right, but it had a long history of independence in religious thought, especially opposing any kind of polytheism or the making of images. While economically poor, Jews were conscious of intellectual superiority.

Since at least the sixth century BC very many Jews had lived in the Diaspora (the 'Dispersion'), in Babylon in the east, in Alexandria in Egypt, and in Asia Minor. They usually became prosperous, taking part in the intellectual and civic life of the cities where they lived. The homeland was regarded as their religious centre, and they supported its temple generously with financial donations, but they expressed their Jewish identity primarily through their distinctive practices and attendance at local synagogues. In the Hellenistic period (from c. 300 BC), their numbers came to exceed by far those of Jews in the homeland. Josephus speaks of 'myriads of our race' in the Diaspora.

For a brief period in the second century BC the Jews had gained independence and full control of Judea, after the heroic Maccabees had fought off an attempt by their pagan overlord Antiochus Epiphanes to set up a statue of Zeus in the Holy of Holies in the Jerusalem temple. The Hasmonean dynasty stemming from the Maccabees gradually declined in prestige, until in 63 BC the rising power of Rome, under Pompey, again made Judea a subject nation. From that time the Jews had to pay taxes to Rome, and their local rulers were appointed by the Romans.

There was an influx of talent when the Herod family succeeded in gaining rule. They were not even Jewish in origin, coming from Idumea in the south. But Herod the Great was granted the kingship, reigning from 37 to 4 BC. His personal stature, his grandiose building projects, his shrewd judgement about which side of Roman politics to back, gave the nation a surge of confidence, so that they felt independent, even though they were technically subject. Herod's numerous family, from his nine wives, remained at the centre of Jewish politics throughout the first century AD.

After Herod's death in 4 BC his son Archelaus was made by Rome an ethnarch, not a king. Archelaus was almost the sole heir left after the king in his manic last years had ordered the execution of other sons. When his own countrymen complained to Rome about him, Archelaus was removed from office, and the kingship was abolished in 6 AD. That year, 6 AD, became a turning point. The country was placed under the direct rule of Roman governors, and the feeling of independence was lost. At once a militant opposition was formed, led by Judas the Galilean. Later called zealots, they were prepared to lay down their lives to preserve their country's identity and religion.

Although there was no longer a Herod on the throne, another of Herod's sons, Antipas tetrarch of Galilee, continued to look after Herodian interests in the country. He gained the favour of the emperor Tiberias (AD 14–37) and named the newly built city of Tiberias on Lake Galilee after him. This was the tetrarch Herod who appears in the surface story of the gospels.

But in Rome the young man Agrippa Herod, a grandson of Herod the Great, began to climb the social ladder, using the family wealth that was paying for his education. Noted for his generous but unstable nature, he gave lavish banquets, and became a particular favourite of Antonia, the most influential woman in Rome. Having overspent his fortune, he was declared bankrupt and, in the twenties AD, expelled from Rome on the orders of Tiberius. He came back to Judea, where he attempted suicide, but was rescued by his wife, and helped financially by the tetrarch, who was married to Agrippa's sister Herodias. There was still tension, however, between the two parts of the family, as Herodias wanted her husband to try to regain the kingship, whereas Agrippa wanted it for himself.

Agrippa got his opportunity when the emperor Tiberius died and Gaius Caligula ('Little Boots') took his place, reigning AD 37–41. Agrippa had by now borrowed enough money to return to Rome, and after an initial setback during Tiberius' last days, his friendship to Gaius was rewarded when he was given rule over most of Judea. Gaius' insanity soon led to his assassination, but Agrippa, back in his country, had kept enough distance to survive, and his kingdom was enlarged by Claudius (AD 41–54).

However, Agrippa had been influenced by Gaius' claims to godship, and in AD 44, in a grand staged ceremony in Caesarea (on the coast of Samaria) he acted out a messianic role, dressed in a glittering silver garment. Josephus records his death five days later from agonizing stomach pains, and there can be little doubt, even without the testimony of the pesher of Acts (see below) that he was poisoned.

His son Agrippa was only sixteen at the time of his father's death, and did not receive rule until some years later. He remained at the head of his countrymen for the rest of the century, but only because of his passive nature. His twin sister Bernice was far more dominant, and at one point had hopes of becoming empress of Rome, as the mistress of Titus, a future emperor.

From the mid-century the real rule of Judea was exercised by the Roman governors, who came and went in fairly rapid succession, having to deal with the waves of attacks by militants, who were following the tradition of AD 6. An associated problem was the appearance of would-be 'Joshuas', who summoned crowds after them, promising that at their behest the waters of the Jordan would part or the walls of Jerusalem fall down, to give them 'victory over the Promised Land' – that is, the liberation of their own country.

The governor Felix (AD 53–60) became more closely involved than the others, for he married Drusilla, the younger sister of Agrippa II and Bernice. Felix adopted the Jewish religion in order to marry her. His rule was responsible for continuing conflict between different factions in the country, and he committed a particularly arbitrary act in ordering the assassination of Jonathan Annas, one of the five Annas brothers who had held the high priesthood, simply on the grounds that Jonathan kept interfering in affairs of state. Felix was arrested in AD 60 by Festus, who was sent out from Rome to replace him. He was taken to Rome, where he counted on help from his brother Pallas, one of the richest men in Rome and a current favourite of Nero (emperor AD 54–68). But Nero turned against Pallas and Felix lost his case.

The sixties AD were a time of continuing tension in Judea. It was obvious to all that Jerusalem would be attacked by the Romans, who were increasingly provoked by the guerrilla raids of the zealots. War

251

broke out in the late sixties, and Agrippa II and Bernice with their court fled the country. In August–September AD 70 Jerusalem fell to the Romans in a conflagration described in unforgettable detail by Josephus. This was, in effect, the end of the history of ancient Judaism in Palestine, although there was another failed attempt to oust Rome in AD 132. Jerusalem was declared a pagan possession with the name Aelia Capitolina.

Diaspora Judaism continued, but anti-Semitic feeling rose in the Roman empire, the Jews losing acceptance in proportion as the Christians gained it during the first three centuries AD.

During the first century AD, the references to the Christian history in external writers are:

a. John the Baptist's death, on the orders of the tetrarch Antipas, is recorded by Josephus. The reason given is that he was thought to be stirring up sedition by his popular oratory. There is no mention of the reason given in the New Testament, that John had objected to Antipas' illegal marriage with his half-brother's wife. But great popular support for the Baptist is shown, in that certain subsequent political events were said to be due to Antipas' treatment of the Baptist (*Ant.* 18: 116–19).

b. The 'Testimonium Flavianum' of Josephus (quoted on p. 163) speaks of Jesus as an extraordinary man who had been crucified by Pilate but was seen alive by his friends on the third day. 'The tribe of the Christians, so called after him, has still to this day not disappeared.' There is no textual reason for doubting this passage, although the matter has been hotly disputed (*Ant.* 18:63–4).

c. The death by stoning of James, 'the brother of Jesus who was called the Christ', is recorded by Josephus. It took place in AD 62, at the hands of the high priest Ananus, the youngest of the five Annas brothers. Ananus was removed from his office in consequence. No clear reason is given why he took this action (*Ant.* 18:200).

d. Suetonius records that in the reign of Claudius Jews were expelled from Rome 'for making disturbances at the instigation of Chrestus' (*Life of Claudius* 25:4).

e. Tacitus and Suetonius mention the punishment of Christians by Nero, who blamed them for the great fire of Rome that he had started himself. Tacitus describes the Christians as 'a class hated for their abominations' (*Annales* 15:44), and Suetonius as 'a set of men adhering to a novel and mischievous superstition' (*Life of Nero*, 16).


## The History as may be Found from the Dead Sea Scrolls and the Pesher of the New Testament

A certain group of the Dead Sea Scrolls describes conflicts between the Teacher of Righteousness and a rival teacher. At first, these were thought by scholars to be figures who had lived in the second century BC, the Teacher being a person who was not previously known. This conclusion was difficult to sustain on textual and palaeographical grounds, and has now been made even more unlikely by recent radiocarbon datings (see Note 1, p. 417). There is very good evidence that the Teacher of Righteousness was John the Baptist. However, there is still, at the time of writing, no new consensus among Scrolls scholars about the further consequences of this observation.

The pesher technique, learned from the Dead Sea Scrolls, is described and applied in this book and in *Jesus the Man* and *Jesus of the Apocalypse*. A history that converges with the public history given above is derived from it. In outline, it is as follows:

Herod the Great's magnificent reign (37–4 BC) had inspired a mission among Diaspora Jews, with the purpose of bringing Jews and Gentile proselytes into a new, hellenized form of Judaism called the New Covenant. This was at the same time a money-making venture, for initiates paid a half-shekel membership fee at the time they were baptized, and the money, stored at Qumran and listed in the Copper Scroll, was the means of financing Herod's building projects.

So great was the success of the New Covenant among Diaspora Jews that ideas of political supremacy for the Jews began to grow. The period was at the outset of the Roman empire, and there was thought to be a reasonable hope of fulfilment of a long cherished hope that the Jewish religion would predominate in the known world.

The collapse of the Herodian kingship in AD 6 was a severe blow to these hopes. Qumran, which had been evacuated in 31 BC because of an earthquake, was reoccupied by a coalition led by Judas the Galilean. It included Sadducees and Pharisees who had taken up an ascetic way of life taught to them by

254

Essenes. Some Essenes, who had been the previous occupants of Qumran, found it necessary to turn to political action and joined with the new coalition. Others, who retained the traditional discipline and name, stayed in Jerusalem; these were the peace-loving Essenes described by Josephus.

From the Sadducee element in the coalition came a less militaristic counsel, that it was better to co-operate with the occupying Romans and pay the taxes. With the backing of this element the high priest Ananus was appointed by the Romans after the uprising of AD 6 had been put down. His five sons all had the same political views.

Jesus had been born into this movement. His grandfather Heli, a descendant of a younger son of King David, had allied with Herod the Great and been appointed the 'patriarch Jacob' of the mission, the subordinate of its 'new Abraham' and 'new Isaac'. Joseph, Heli's son, was Jesus' actual father, and Jesus should have inherited the mission duties of the heir of David, but he had been conceived before his parents' wedding, and so was denied legitimacy by the Pharisees in the coalition, who upheld his younger brother James as the true heir. The Sadducees, however, accepted Jesus as legitimate, and Jesus' political views agreed with theirs.

By the time Jesus came to a position of leadership in the twenties AD, Gentiles were joining the mission in very large numbers. For many in the Greco-Roman world, this liberalized form of Judaism was an attractive option, more satisfying, intellectually and ethically, than paganism. It was part of the duty of the heir of David to minister to the Gentile membership.

With increasing numbers, the question had become pressing whether it was necessary for Gentiles to adopt Jewish identity, becoming circumcised, following the dietary laws, and attending synagogues; or whether they could simply espouse the spiritual and theoretical aspects while retaining their own ethnic identity. Jesus upheld the latter point of view, and his whole life was devoted to breaking down the barrier between Jew and Gentile (with a consequent flow-on to the breaking down of other kinds of social barriers). His brother James, however, held the former point of view, as the New Testament openly shows (Gal 2, Acts 15).

In addition to Pharisees, Sadducees and nationalist Essenes, the mission leadership included a group of Samaritans called Magians. Their leader, contemporary with Jesus, was Simon Magus. Appearing briefly in Acts 8, his history is recorded in external sources, particularly the Pseudo-Clementine books, which have been thought to be spurious but in fact are a major and early source. Simon was a man of extraordinary talent and learning, but at the same time unscrupulous in his manipulation of the fears and superstitions of ordinary people. For him, the mission continued as a money-making venture, but with a different purpose from the original one. Simon was the chief enemy of the Agrippas, opposing their attempts to regain the kingship, and the mission money coming to him was intended to support his Samaritan gnostic version of Judaism.

When Gentiles joined the mission, Simon did not require them to become circumcised, disagreeing on this point with the Pharisees. On this question he gained an ally in Jesus, and their friendship was intensified by a common opposition to Agrippa, who, as Josephus shows, was present in Judea in the twenties and thirties AD (although this fact is not openly stated in the gospels). But on the question of armed resistance to the Romans, Jesus was in complete disagreement with Simon, whose espousal of militarism gave him the title 'Simon the Zealot'. Nevertheless, Jesus was drawn into co-operation with Simon, when Pilate's tactless administration aroused all parties against him, and Jesus' help for Simon afforded sufficient evidence of complicity with zealots.

This evidence was used against him by those whom Jesus had offended on other questions: by Pharisees, under the high priest Caiaphas, because Jesus opposed the circumcision requirement; and by Sadducees, under Jonathan Annas, because Jesus claimed that ordinary laymen could exercise the privileges of priests. When the opportunity arose (as described in Chapters 4 and 5), they combined together to ensure that Jesus was crucified as the third man.

Jesus survived the crucifixion, as is shown in Chapter 6. Josephus' account of his appearance on the third day simply records a remarkable event, not a miracle, stressing the personality and influence of Jesus. The 'visions' of Jesus in the Acts of the Apostles were a way of saying, as transparently as possible, that Jesus was still alive and leading his party of Gentiles who had abandoned Jewish identity and adopted the name 'Christian'.

The assassination of Agrippa I in AD 44 was a decisive event for the Christian history. It was brought about by Simon Magus, who was the 'angel of the

257

Lord' who caused him to be 'eaten by worms' (given snake poison). All the conspirators fled to Antioch, where the final schism occurred between Simon Magus with the eastern party, and Christians with the western party. By now, Paul had joined the Christians, and he and his ascetic community were loyal supporters of the Agrippa family, especially the youthful Agrippa II. The name 'Christian' was given to the leaders of the mission to Gentiles who supported the Herodian monarchy, who taught a liberalized doctrine that did not require Jewish identity, and who held that Jesus was the true heir of David and the chief minister to Gentiles. Some, such as Peter, still believed that Sadducee priests should be involved; others such as Paul, a former Pharisee, would have no Sadducee priests, and held that laymen, with Jesus at their head, could act in all priestly roles.

Felix, the governor who had become a member of the royal Herod family by marriage, was instructed by Paul, and allowed the old enmity between Pharisees and Sadducees to break out when he ordered the assassination of Jonathan Annas. A few years later Ananus the Younger, although a Sadducee, acted in support of Paul's views on circumcision when he ordered the death of James the brother of Jesus. Felix was brought to Rome in AD 60–61, and when he lost his influence at court was punished, and Paul with him. Peter had been part of recurring demonstrations in Rome arising from the belief that heaven would intervene in the significant year 4000 to sweep the mission into power, and he too lost his life when Nero saw his opportunity to fasten blame on what was seen as a subversive movement.

On the surface, the New Testament presents the Christians as peaceful and innocent, complete strangers to the Jewish leaders before whom they were brought, and to the Roman authorities. The hostility of the authorities to them is depicted as unreasonable malevolence. But in fact the Christians, before they took the name, were part of the Jewish leadership, which was internally divided on issues concerning the mission. All were part of a concerted effort to recommend Judaism to the Greco-Roman world, and for some the goal was the supremacy of their religion, to be gained by force of arms if necessary.

Such a goal exacerbated the issue of identity, the question of which kind of Judaism should succeed. When a kind of teaching that hardly appeared Jewish at all, and was more sympathetic to Gentiles than to Jews, began to gain the greatest influence, the question became a matter of life and death. In the end, the Christian form, the one that had shifted furthest from the original, was the winner. The price it paid was such total separation from its origins that it found it necessary to deny them, and to conceal the long and intense political process that eventually gave it success.

# Notes for the Pesharist

In *Jesus the Man* and *Jesus of the Apocalypse* the theory of pesher (the second level of historical meaning) was set out, together with information needed to give the exact, technical meanings of terms on which it depends.

Further information is given here, including rules of procedure and a Lexicon relevant to the parts of the gospels dealt with in this book. An example of the pesher is given, in the section of John's gospel describing the trials before Pilate.

It is the case, unfortunately, that the pesher must be done on the Greek text. The English reader will, however, be able to make a sufficient test for consistency – on which the proof of the case depends – by studying the special meanings of terms in the Lexicon, and seeing if all occurrences of terms are accounted for as having the same special meaning.

A study of the rules of pesher will also show how exact, and exacting, the procedures are, allowing no subjective interpretation. All persons who worked on the Greek text, following the rules and with knowledge of the special meanings, would arrive at the same result.

The Greek text used is that of Codex Vaticanus, which is regarded by textual critics as a highly reliable copy. The major variant texts show an understanding of the pesher and an intention to alter it for their own institutional reasons.

## Rules of Pesher

The basic principle was one of *exactitude*. The word *akribōs*, meaning 'accurately', is the Greek word referring to the pesher technique. The principle meant that words with an apparently vague or broad meaning had, in fact, a special and technical meaning, which did not cancel out the more general meaning, but showed a specific example of it, thereby recording an event. As has been seen, 'Love your enemies' had both an ethical and a historical meaning. Another example is: 'The Spirit is willing, but the flesh is weak'. It remains a true comment on human frailty, but it also means, 'Of the two kinds of bishop, one a celibate, the other a married man, the celibate may work among married members, but a married man cannot rise in celibate ranks'. Its particular meaning concerns an actual institution. It was because of this meaning of 'Spirit', a celibate bishop, that the pesharist knew that when Jesus 'gave up the Spirit' at the crucifixion he had simply become defiled, through his illness and the permanent injury to his hands, making him physically imperfect, a disqualification for holy celibates according to the writers of the Scrolls.

Exactitude was needed also in dealing with the connections in the text. The primary example of this is the rule of the last referent, which in the gospels is used to such an extent that it can alter the surface meaning quite drastically. It treated the text in a mechanical way, contrary to normal usage, and so was a means of concealment, for the outsider would read the words differently. The rule was:

*The referent of an unstated personal subject of a verb, or of a pronoun, is the last noun, of the required person, number and gender, that has appeared.*

For example, 'Jesus saw Peter, and he said . . .' The outsider assumes that the 'he' who 'said' is Jesus. But it is Peter, because 'Peter' is the last noun that has appeared.

The word order consequently becomes important, and is often adjusted because of this rule. For example, if the writer wanted to say that it was Jesus who 'said', he would use the facility of Greek to put the subject after the verb, and write, 'Saw Peter (accusative case, indicated by the ending of the word) Jesus (nominative case), and he said . . .'

This leads to some striking changes of sense. When John 18:33 says, 'Pilate . . . called Jesus and he said to him, "Are you the king of the Jews?"', the pesharist reads that Jesus said these words to Pilate, not Pilate to Jesus. He must then enquire why Jesus would have said such a thing to Pilate (knowing also that what appears to be a question, 'Are you the king of the Jews?' is a statement, 'You are the king of the Jews'). He then uncovers an important fact, that 'king of the Jews' was a name for a graduate in Antipas' school, and that Pilate had just become an honorary graduate in order to receive a bribe. Soon after, Pilate 'washed his hands', confirming his status as a minister.

Or in another case in John 18:10, 'Peter having a sword struck the slave, and he cut off his right ear', it was the 'slave' who cut off Peter's 'ear', not the reverse ('ear' having a special meaning, not the literal ear, as is the case for all names of parts of the body).

The last referent may be in preceding quoted speech, for example in John 20:29, where the previously quoted speech names 'God' (the Sadducee priest) in its final phrase, so that the next sentence, 'Jesus said to him' means 'Jesus said to "God"'.

If an apparent last referent is in the vocative case (a form used in addressing a person), it cannot be used as the subject of a third person verb, for it is a second person. Moreover, a noun or pronoun in the genitive case ('of') cannot normally be used. In the expressions 'the Son of Man', or 'the king of the Jews', 'Son' and 'king' can be a referent, but not 'of Man' or 'of the Jews', for a genitive acts as a further description of a person, not as a separate person. It is found that this applies to all genitives, including those governed by a preposition. An exception to this is when the name of an object is followed by a person in the genitive, for the person is not simply an attribute of the object. For example, 'the hands of sinners' is found in Matt 26:45; and a later 'they' in verse 48 does refer back to 'sinners'. Similarly in the phrase 'the body of Jesus', a later 'he' refers back to Jesus (Mark 15:43 and 44).

At times the pesharist has to draw on his knowledge to go past a last referent to the previous one, for example in Mark 14:63, 'the Chief Priest tore the tunics (*chitōnes*) of him'. A priest did not wear a *chitōn*, only a layman, so 'him' means Jesus, the previous last referent. These exceptions are only found when the subject is made certain by the following context.

Some words meaning objects ('Heaven', 'Lightning', 'Earthquake') refer to persons, so that the rule of the last personal subject applies to them. These words are indicated by capital letters.

The student of the Greek text must first note all terms affected by this rule, not assuming that referents are as they appear on the surface. The rule often makes a great difference to the apparent meaning.

The converse of this rule is that some words that would normally be taken to refer back do not do so. 'This one' (*houtos*) and 'that one' (*ekeinos*) do not refer back, but act as new nouns. The pronoun for 'he' is *autos* (not normally needed as subject of the verb, which is indicated simply by an ending). When it is in cases other than the nominative it refers back. But when it is in the nominative it means a new person, a 'He', who is a person of some authority in the context, and the same applies to its plural, 'They'. Similarly the word 'himself', which is used, as may still be the case today, to refer to a particular authority. 'Let him deny himself' means 'let him deny Himself' – that is, one person is to deny another person who is called 'Himself' for political reasons (Simon Magus). Further, although a relative pronoun 'who' naturally refers back, this is only the case for other than nominatives. When in the nominative, 'who' means a new person, someone in authority.

A definite article in the nominative may be used as the subject of the verb, usually with the particle *de*. '*Ho de eipen*' means 'the person addressed said', not the immediate last referent.

A participle without article, in the nominative form, refers back to the subject of a previous verb, not to any other case. If the participle is accompanied by a noun subject, it does not refer back. A participle with article acts as a new noun.

The word 'and', *kai* in Greek, used very frequently, acts as verbal punctuation. For the pesharist, it marks the units of sense, and is best conveyed by a full stop.

Two nouns or nominal phrases side by side, both with article, are to be taken as separate, not in apposition, for the word 'and' that would be expected to indicate two persons has the special function noted above. So 'Jesus the Nazorean, the king of the Jews' in John 19:19 means two people, Jesus and Simon Magus, who was the main 'king of the Jews'.

Another rule that makes a great difference is that all events are consecutive. Every event in narrative follows another event, even if it would naturally be assumed that it was a repeated statement about a previous happening. In John 19:41, after Jesus was put in the tomb, the narrative reads, 'and in the place where he was crucified there was a garden'. This is to be read as meaning that he was *now* 'crucified', after being put in the tomb or 'garden'. Although the noun *stauros* means an actual cross, the verb 'crucify' itself has a special sense, to subject to a cursing ceremony using a rod in the shape of a cross, and the curse was now repeated. In quoted speech, however, the speaker may refer back to past events or to future events.

The reader of the Greek text notices a strange inconsistency in the use of tenses, when a narrative normally using a past tense suddenly breaks into the present, for no apparent reason. In the gospel of John this happens very frequently, and it is noteworthy that the subjects of verbs in the present tense are usually Pilate, or a woman, or Peter, or Jesus in some capacities. Gentiles, women and married men such as Peter were in the lowest class, and could act and speak as private persons, not representing the office. When acting in an office a person is said to act in the past tense, but when in a private capacity, 'off the record', acts in the present tense. Pilate when representing Rome used the past tense, but when he was asking for a bribe, present tenses are used.

Greek grammar uses double negatives, which are still negative: 'I do not not eat (*ou mē phagō*, both *ou* and *mē* meaning "not")' still means 'I do not eat'. But the pesharist applies the rules of logic, that two negatives make a positive, and reads this as 'I do not not-eat' – that is, 'I do not fast, but I do eat' (Luke 22:16).

In Greek, there is no way of indicating a question by the form of the verb, as there is in English usage, which reverses subject and verb. Only the punctuation shows that a question is intended. But punctuation is a subjective matter, not part of the word structure. The pesharist therefore takes all such questions as statements. The words 'are you the king of the Jews?' are exactly the same as 'you are the king of the Jews', and are to be taken as a statement of fact. Similarly when the interrogative pronoun 'Who?' (*tis*) begins a question, it is a statement, not a question, for *tis* also means 'A certain person' and must always be used consistently in this sense. So, when the women at the tomb appear to ask 'Who will roll away the stone?' it is a statement,

'A Certain Person (*tis*, a known individual called by this term) will roll away the stone' (Mark 16:3). When an actual question is intended, the word *ei*, meaning 'if', signals it.

A plural noun means a singular person, one who reproduces the position of another. A 'Scribe' was one person, and 'Scribes' was another person, representing the 'Scribe' in his position. 'Disciples' means one person. All plural nouns are to be read as referring to a single person. In some cases the same person is described by both the singular and the plural, for he could act in his substantive position at the main council, and at times in an outside position where he was usually represented by another.

A noun referring to a person may be used with or without article, and the difference indicates that the person is acting at a different grade. The article is used for a priest or celibate when at his highest grade, but no article when the person is 'in the body'. He could come down to be at the level of his servant, acting three grades lower (see the explanation of grades on pp. 282–7). For priests, called by such terms as 'God' and 'Spirit', the word without article may mean a different person representing the priest.

A genitive phrase also gives information about grades. 'X of Y' means that X is one grade below Y.

The particle *de* and the word *oun* ('therefore') are used very frequently in John, and *oun* is not rendered in modern translations. As shown in the Lexicon, their special meanings arise from plays on letters.

Educated Jews in the Hellenistic world were very much aware of the niceties of Greek grammar and form, and of the difference that they made to the meaning of their Old Testament when it was translated into Greek. Philo, the hellenized Jew of Alexandria, in his essay *On Dreams* (1:101), built a whole case for a secondary meaning of an Old Testament text on a distinction familiar to rhetoricians about the different forms of statements, whether explanatory, or exhortatory. He introduced his point with the comment: 'And indeed the peculiarities of the wording might well lead even the slowest-witted reader to perceive the presence of something other than the literal meaning of the passage'. It becomes apparent that the Christian pesharist, part of a scholarly community that valued Hellenistic learning, was intended to have such a degree of knowledge, and to observe every fine distinction in the gospel text.

While the use of the devices may be suspected in particular passages, the case is only proven when it is found that these rules are always applied, in every instance, and that the concealed history emerging is consistent with itself, with the overall history, and with what is known explicitly from other sources. Consistency is the essential criterion for testing.

# Example of the Pesher of John's Gospel: The Trial before Pilate

**(John 18:28–19:16)**

An example may be offered of a passage that illustrates many of the foregoing rules of pesher: the account of Jesus' trial before Pilate in John.

The passage is set out verse by verse, with a translation of the Greek text in italics, followed by the detailed history emerging when the special sense of terms is taken into account. In the Lexicon which follows the special senses of terms are explained.

A very literal translation of the Greek is necessarily given, to convey the Greek as accurately as possible. This frequently leads to unnatural English. It may be compared with a more natural translation, preferably the Revised Standard Version. Some points of Greek are not conveyed when they do not affect the pesher, for example, articles with names, and the recurring word 'therefore'. Subjects supplied by the rule of the last referent are given in brackets.

A slightly strained translation is used to distinguish words that are normally translated by the same word, for example, the different verbs 'to see', for which 'see', 'observe', 'view', etc. are used; or the different verbs 'to say', for which 'say', 'speak', 'utter', etc. are used. In the case of other words needing to be distinguished, something is added, for example, 'when' for *hotan*, but 'when now' for *hote*. A verb with prefix is rendered literally, for example, 'beside-give' for *paradidōmi*, as the literal meaning is the special one.

The historical point is sometimes drawn out by adding phrases that do not correspond to words in the text.

This section refers to detail of the area outside the vestry where the two pillar bases stood, described in Chapter 2.

## JOHN 18

28. *They (These Ones vv. 21, 25) lead Jesus from Caiaphas to the praetorium. It became morning. And They did not come into the praetorium, in order that they (They) might not be defiled, but they might eat the Passover.*

28. James the brother of Jesus brought him from the north of the vestry, where Caiaphas had tried him, to the south base outside where the Roman tribute was paid. It was 6 am. Antipas did not go to the south base, for it would render him unclean, this being the hour for unleavened bread by his calendar.

29. *Came out Pilate towards them (They v. 28). And he uttered, 'What accusation do you bring, down of This Man (gen.)?'*

29. Pilate stood on the north base, with Antipas on its north side as adviser. Pilate said formally, 'You bring a charge under Roman law against Jesus'.

30. *They answered. And they said to him (Pilate, as 'This Man' is genitive), 'If not became This One Making Evil, not to you we beside-gave him (This One Making Evil)'.*

30. Antipas spoke as a teacher. He said to Pilate, 'There is also Simon Magus to be tried; I am not his opponent'.

31. *Said to them Pilate, 'You (plu.) receive him (This One Making Evil). And according to your law judge him.' Said to him (This One Making Evil) the Jews, 'To us it is not out to kill No One'.*

31. Pilate said to Antipas, 'Examine Simon yourself. Let him be further tried for murder under Mosaic law.' Antipas said to Simon, 'I cannot say under my rules that James is legitimate, thus making him the third man and Jesus the second man, as Agrippa wants'.

32. *In order that the Word of Jesus might be fulfilled which he (Word) said, signing by which Death he (Word) was about to die.*

32. Jesus spoke to Simon in Hebrew, saying that he would be excommunicated with him in three hours' time.

33. *Came in again into the praetorium Pilate. And he (Pilate) called Jesus. And he (Jesus) said to him (Pilate), 'Are you the king of the Jews?'*

33. Pilate came to the south base to represent Caesar. He stood on the base, placing Jesus near him. Jesus said to Pilate, 'You are now a paid graduate of Antipas' school'.

34. *Answered Jesus, 'From yourself do you say this, or have others said to you around me?'*

34. Jesus spoke as a teacher, 'You may now speak as a member, or my Gentile deputy will instruct you'.

35. *Answered Pilate, 'Am I a Jew, surely not? The nation the yours. And the Chief Priests have beside-given you to me. What have you made?'*

35. Pilate spoke as a teacher, saying, 'I am a member of Antipas' mission, not using the sign of the cross. The Gentile John Mark is in your following in the same party. Jonathan Annas your opponent has handed you over to me. But you use the sign of the cross, as he does.'

36. *Answered Jesus, 'My kingdom does not become out of this world. If out of this world became my kingdom, my servants were agonizing, in order that I might not be beside-given to the Jews. Now my kingdom does not become hence.'*

36. Jesus spoke, 'My teaching mission to Gentiles is not centred in the eastern Diaspora. But do some accept my teaching in the east? James head of my eastern branch keeps ascetic rules, so the mission requiring circumcision does not overcome me in the east. Nor is my mission zealot.'

37. *Said to him (Jesus) Pilate, 'Accordingly a king you are?' Answered Jesus, 'You say that a king I am. I to this was born. And to this I came to the world, in order that I might witness to the truth. All the Being One out of the truth hears of me the voice.'*

37. Pilate said to Jesus, 'You are a lay teacher'. Jesus spoke, 'You say that I am a lay teacher. I may sometimes act as a mere layman. I may be in

the married state, teaching ascetic doctrine to Diaspora pilgrims. Agrippa when with Sadducee ascetics accepts me as a member of the council.'

38a. *Says to him (All the Being One) Pilate, 'What is truth?'*

38a. Pilate said privately to Agrippa, 'Herodian Sadducee ascetics use the sign of the cross, but I do not'.

38b. *And saying this he (Pilate) came out again towards the Jews. And he (Pilate) says to them, 'I find in him (All the Being One) a No One charge.'*

38b. At 7 am Pilate resumed his position on the north base, with Antipas on its north side. Pilate said privately to Antipas, 'I have received a payment from Agrippa to declare James legitimate, so that he will be the third man and Jesus will die in Judas' place'.

39. *'Becomes a custom to you (plu., Jews) in order that a One I will release to you in the Passover. You (plu.) counsel, will I release to you the king of the Jews (gen.)?'*

39. 'But I am not under strict law in your party, so I can release and promote a lay bishop at this hour, the meal of unleavened bread by Theudas-Barabbas' calendar. Make me a paid member of your council and I will release and promote a teacher in your mission'.

40. *They (Jews v. 38) shouted again, saying, 'Not This One. But Barabbas.' Became Barabbas a thief.*

40. After the minute's silent prayer Antipas said, 'Not Jesus. Let it be Theudas-Barabbas.' Theudas-Barabbas was released and became

the Chief Zealot, the other two being under
arrest.

## JOHN 19

1. *Then Pilate received Jesus. And he (Jesus)*
   *whipped.*
1. At 8 am Pilate began Jesus' trial. Self-flagellation was imposed on him.
2. *And the Soldiers having plaited a crown out of*
   *thorns put of him (Jesus v. 1) to the head. And a*
   *purple garment they (Soldiers) threw around him*
   *(Jesus).*
2. The guard, acting for Agrippa, made a rope
   circlet with an attached thorn, worn by illegitimates who were permanent residents in a
   Sadducee abbey, and put it over Jesus' headband. He made Jesus wear the purple vestment
   of a levite, to whom a permanent monastic was
   equal.
3. *And they (Soldiers) came towards him (Jesus).*
   *And they said, 'Rejoice, the king of the Jews (gen.)'.*
   *And they (Soldiers) gave him (Jesus) blows.*
3. The guard stood south of Jesus, who was made
   to stand on the south base as a rival to Caesar.
   The guard said, 'You claim to be legitimate
   and a teacher in Antipas' mission'. The guard
   punished him with blows for his error.
4. *And came out outside again Pilate. And he says to*
   *them (Soldiers), 'Lo, I lead him (Jesus) out to you*
   *(plu.), in order that you may have knowledge that*

*a No One charge I find in him (Jesus)'.*

4.  Pilate returned to the north base. He said privately to the guard, 'I will make Jesus stand again on the south base, to show Agrippa that I will accept his bribe to treat James as legitimate, and Jesus as a monastic illegitimate who can replace Judas'.

5.  *Jesus came out outside, bearing the thorny crown. And the purple garment. And he (Jesus) says to them (Soldiers), 'Behold the Man'.*

5.  Jesus stood on the south base, carrying the illegitimate's headdress in his hand instead of wearing it. He still wore the purple vestment, which was also that of a king. He said to the guard, 'I stand here as the New Adam, the legitimate David'.

6.  *When now saw him (the Man) the Chief Priests. And the servants shouted saying, 'Crucify, crucify'. Says to them (servants) Pilate, 'Receive him (the Man), you (plu.). And you crucify. For I do not find in him (the Man) a charge.'*

6.  At 8.30 Jonathan Annas saw Jesus, agreeing that he was the legitimate David. James, who would die if Jesus was proven illegitimate, said after the silent prayer, 'Curse both Jesus and Judas'. Pilate said privately to James, 'You should accept being crown prince, acting as servant of Annas by taking Jesus in charge. You should perform the cursings on behalf of Annas. But I have not yet received a further bribe from Antipas to release you and make Jesus the third man, with Judas as the second man.'

7.  *Answered him (the Man) the Jews, 'We have a*

*law. And according to the law he (the Man) owes to die, because a Son of a God Himself he (the Man) made.'*

7. Antipas said to Jesus, 'I am applying the law of Moses. It says that a teacher should be excommunicated if he treated the zealot Simon Magus as a fellow-priest.'

8. *When now the Pilate heard This Word, rather he (This Word) was afraid.*

8. Pilate then officially questioned James, the alternate David by Agrippa's rules.

9. *And he (This Word) came into the praetorium again. And he (This Word) says to Jesus, 'Whence are you?' Jesus did not give an answer to him (This Word).*

9. James was brought to the south base. He said privately to Jesus, 'You are the David, superior of Gentiles'. Jesus was saying a silent prayer and did not answer him.

10. *Says to him (This Word) Pilate, 'You do not speak to me? Do you not know that I have authority to release you? And I have authority to crucify you?'*

10. Pilate said privately to James, 'You are now saying a silent prayer. You do not recognize me as a member of the ministry, able to release and promote you. But I can curse you as the third man.'

11. *Answered him (Pilate) Jesus, 'You do not have No One authority down of me, if not it became given to you above. On account of this the One Beside-giving me to you has a greater sin.'*

11. Then Jesus spoke to Pilate, 'Having now received a further bribe from Antipas, you have turned against Agrippa, who says James is legit-

278

imate; and the priest Jonathan Annas supports Antipas in giving the bribe. James my rival is in Agrippa's party.'

12. *Out of This One (gen.) Pilate sought to release him (One Beside-giving me). The Jews shouted saying, 'If now you release This One, you are not a friend of Caesar. An All One making Himself a king, against-says to Caesar.'*

12. Pilate found legal reason to release James, as only the crown prince. Antipas after his silent prayer said, 'When you release James, whom Agrippa wants to be the third man, it will show that you are not allied with Agrippa, who aims to become a Caesar. There is an alternate Herodian party, of which Simon Magus is a member, opposing Agrippa's ambition to be a Caesar.'

13. *Pilate having heard These Words (gen.) led out Jesus. And he (Jesus) sat upon of a judgement-seat to a place said to be Stone-paved, in Hebrew Gabbatha.*

13. Pilate, having pronounced James to be free, brought Jesus to the south base. Then Jesus sat, as one of the three condemned men, on the west side of the south base, where Simon Magus now stood as a rival Caesar, called in Aramaic 'the Mountain Rome'.

14. *It became a preparation of the Passover, an hour became as sixth. And he (Jesus) says to the Jews, 'Lo the king of you (plu.)'*

14. It was five minutes to nine, which by the uncorrected time was five minutes to noon, when the Friday noon service and meal of unleavened bread for monastic Gentiles began. Jesus said to

Antipas, 'There stands Simon, a teacher in your mission'.

15. *Those Ones shouted, 'Lift up, lift up, crucify him (the king of you)'. Says to them (Those Ones) Pilate, 'The king of you (plu.) will I crucify?' The Chief Priests answered, 'We do not have a king, if not Caesar'.*

15. Antipas said after the silent prayer, 'Prepare crosses for Judas and Jesus, and curse Simon prior to crucifixion'. Pilate said to Antipas, 'I will curse Simon'. Jonathan Annas spoke, 'I am opposed to Simon, and to Agrippa, who aims to be a Caesar'.

16. *Then he (Caesar) beside-gave him (king) to them (Chief Priests), in order that he (king) might be crucified.*

16. At 9 am/noon Agrippa handed over Simon to Jonathan Annas for the cursing ceremony.

# The Sacred Loaves
# and the Holy Table

A pesharist who was working with an insider's knowledge was familiar with the seating order at the holy table in the vestry. It arose from a centuries' old custom, of eating the twelve sacred loaves of the Presence that had been dedicated to God. A single scheme accounted for the numbers of the loaves, the grades and seats of ministers, and the times for prayers. This scheme, as may be seen, lay behind the seating at the Last Supper and the present orders of Christian ministry.

The attention of all readers was drawn to the existence of a scheme of loaves by the Riddle of the Loaves in Mark 8:14–21. Jesus was quoted as speaking to his disciples, using the same words about 'having ears to hear' that were used when he said that there was a 'mystery of the Kingdom of God' which was given only to insiders. Then he went on: 'When I broke the five loaves for the five thousand, how many baskets full of broken pieces did you take up?' They said to him, 'Twelve'. He continued, 'And the seven for the four thousand, how many baskets full of broken pieces did you take up?' They said to him,

'Seven'. Then he said to them, 'Do you not yet understand?'

Twelve loaves of the Presence, one for each tribe, had long been set out in the sanctuary before God, as a sign of the gratitude of the Israelite people for the harvest that gave them food (Levit 24:5–9). For the exiled priests at Qumran, they became their daily food, but their sacredness was not forgotten. The priests ate them on behalf of God, and those laymen who were admitted to the meal were given a form of holiness by partaking of them. The meal, called 'the Purity', was used as a means of discipline for the laymen who had to obey the priests. If they had committed any breach of the strict monastic discipline they were excluded from the meal for varying lengths of time. The rules for exclusion are set out in the Scrolls (1QS 7; 4Q266 frag. 10; 4Q270 frag. 7).

## Loaves and Grades

Twelve loaves gave rise to twelve grades in the educational system, which was also the system through which men rose to the ministry of the table.

The school system gave education between the ages of 18 and 30, each year being called by a Hebrew letter, with the last letter, Taw, used for the highest grade at age 30. In the gospels numbers are used for the grades, the lowest (given at age 18 or to a person of equal low status) being grade 12, the next year up grade 11, the next grade 10, and so on, up to 1 for the second highest and 0 for the highest, when the Taw was given.

Initiation, grade 7, was given at the age of 23. Prior to that a person was a novice or pre-initiate (grade 8) or merely baptized (grade 9). After initiation there were four years of undergraduate study, then graduation at grade 3. A postgraduate year was spent outside the sanctuary, then a minister of the sanctuary entered it at grade 2, advancing through 1 to 0.

There were many ways of speaking of the system, one of them being to play on the Hebrew letters. One such play gave the famous number 666 (see *JA*).

These grades were not only educational but social and moral, given for advancement in religion. There was an annual promotion ceremony, given on proof of spiritual merit (1QS 5: 23–5).

The positions for saying prayers were on the centre of each successive row in the vestry, each row a cubit wide (see Figure 1, p. 37). A grade 1 or his substitute stood on row 1, grade 2 on row 2, and so on down to row 12 at the edge of the dais. A man at grade 6 said the noon prayer in the centre of row 6, but he was only an acolyte, and above him on the platform stood the highest priest at the grade called 0. When the Julian calendar was adopted noon and midnight were treated as zero hours.

There was a system of servants and masters, laymen being servants of the priests. A servant must stand at arm's length from his master, that is 2 cubits away, for a cubit was the length of the forearm. Hence there were three grades between them, for a man at grade 1 stood on row 1, two intermediate persons stood on rows 2 and 3, and the servant, 2 cubits away, was on row 4.

# The Tables, Holy and Common (Figure 7(i))

Twelve men, the leaders of each of the grades, sat each day at a table placed across the 6 cubit width of the central panel of the vestry. Six sat on either side, close together on a bench. At noon the table was placed between rows 7 and 9, with the bench for leaders on row 7, which was the row containing the 'eyes' in the anatomical imagery, giving rise to the saying about the 'beam in the eye' (Luke 6:41) (see Figure 7).

Two meals a day were taken, one at noon and one in the evening. The noon meal was considered the most sacred one, as Josephus shows (*War* 2:129–33, 'The Essenes . . . come into their refectory as into a sacred shrine'). The table placed between rows 7 and 9 was treated as holy. The evening meal was considered the common one, when outsiders such as guests could be present, as Josephus also shows. The common table was placed further down the room, between rows 10 and 12. Thus row 10, which contained the 'bosom' in the anatomical imagery, was on the low side of the holy table but the high side of the common table. Christians, who rose from the lesser ranks, were at first classed with those using the common table. It became a holy table, but different views in Christianity still lead to different placements, some putting the table near the front of the chancel close to the congregation, others further back.

The twelve loaves were divided into two sets of six (Levit 24:6). Six loaves were eaten at each of the two daily meals, each loaf being shared between two

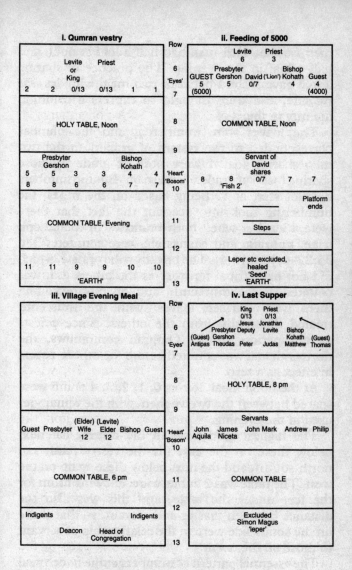

**FIGURE 7  Tables And Loaves**

men, so that each man had half a loaf at noon and half a loaf in the evening. The practice of sharing a loaf gave a bond between two men, who sat side by side, and were thought to express a common identity in this way.

The loaves were numbered, and the number corresponded to the system of grades, so the two men sharing loaf 4 were both at grade 4, those sharing loaf 5 at grade 5, and so on. But the numbers did not start at 1. Being based on the tribes, the numbering took into account the fact that there were 13 tribes when both branches of the Joseph tribe, Ephraim and Manasseh, were counted (Gen 35:22–6; Josh 16:4). The priestly tribe of Levi, which did not have tribal territory as the others did, was counted as the thirteenth, and on this reckoning there were thirteen loaves, with the thirteenth treated differently from the others. Since priests were superiors in the Qumran community, the thirteenth loaf was counted before the others, acting in effect as a zero.

At the noon meal, loaves 0, 1, 2, 3, 4 and 5 were shared between the twelve men, with the remainder used in the evening.

The highest grades sat in the centre, the next below these on the east (as the vestry room ran north-south), and the next below these again on the west. The table was 2 cubits wide, allowing room for the feet under the table, and this was also the distance between master and servant, so that those on the south side were in the relationship of servant to those on the north.

The essential pattern of numbers at the noon meal at the holy table was, then:

|   | 2 | 2 | 0/13 | 0/13 | 1 | 1 |   |
|---|---|---|------|------|---|---|---|
| W |   |   |      |      |   |   | E |
|   | 5 | 5 | 3    | 3    | 4 | 4 |   |

Loaf 0/13 was shared between the priest sitting on the east side and the levite on the west side of centre. These two men were responsible for prayers at the major hours of the sun, 6 am and noon. Under the original system, 6 am, counted as sunrise, was the greater hour, when the superior priest prayed, while noon was secondary, being the hour for the levite.

In the evenings the same twelve came down to the common table to eat the remaining six loaves, in the pattern:

|   | 8  | 8  | 6 | 6 | 7  | 7  |   |
|---|----|----|---|---|----|----|---|
| W |    |    |   |   |    |    | E |
|   | 11 | 11 | 9 | 9 | 10 | 10 |   |

On loaf 12, see below. The numbering system had developed in the Essene monastery, where the descendants of the ancient priestly and royal families lived, hoping to be restored to the positions in the temple that they had once held. They used titles, found in the Scrolls, drawn either from the names of archangels or from the Old Testament levitical families. These sources give their hierarchical order. Michael was the supreme priest, the 0/13, followed by Gabriel, 1 and Sariel, 2. Phanuel (whose position became that of cardinal) was the 3, then Kohath (a bishop) was the 4, and Gershon (a presbyter or judge) the 5. The man called Raphael was the levite who included in his duties the acolyte's work of number 6. (See further on the development of these offices in *JM* and *JA*.)

## The Village Table at Noon; the Feedings of the Multitude (Figure 7(ii))

While those who belonged to the highest grades in the monastery were normally confined to it, the men who sat on the south side of the holy table were permitted to go outside to perform duties of ministry. Phanuel at grade 3, Kohath at grade 4, and Gershon at grade 5, as well as the levite-acolyte at grade 6, all travelled to villages where they ministered to Essenes and other ascetics who had joined them. Men of the same grade travelled to the wider world of the Diaspora, ministering to Diaspora Jews and their associated Gentiles. Their positions became those of the Christian ministry.

The building that stood for all these outside places was Ain Feshkha, two miles down the coast from Qumran. It was here, at the noon meal table, that the 'feeding of the Five Thousand' and the 'feeding of the Four Thousand' took place.

The ministers who sat on the low side of the holy table at Qumran, which was at the same time the high side of the common table, now sat on the high side of a table at Ain Feshkha, one that had the status of a common table (see Figure 7 (ii)). It was placed on a raised platform at Ain Feshkha, with steps leading up to it inside the room. The same principle of pairing was used, with the bishop Kohath sharing his loaf 4 with a guest beside him, and similarly presbyter Gershon, sharing his loaf 5 on the western side.

As has been seen in Chapter 4, John Aquila, the 'Five Thousand', was ordained a presbyter by coming up to the guest's seat to share loaf 5 with Theudas, who was the Gershon in the system. At the same time (as Mark's account makes clearer), James Niceta was made a bishop by sharing loaf 4 with the man in the position of Kohath.

An additional minister exercised leadership in villages, being more important there than in the monastery. He was the heir of David under his image of the 'Lion' (one of the four 'Living Creatures' of the Old Testament and the Book of Revelation). At a period in the past, described in 1 Sam 21:1–6 and referred to in Mark 2:25–6, he had been given a loaf, one that entitled him to minister on a Saturday, the zero and seventh day, like the supreme priest, but in the villages. His loaf 0/7 had the same function as the zero loaf of the priest. When in the monastery he could sit with the priest, because of his exalted birth, in the position usually taken by the levite. When outside he sat at the centre of the table, alone. This position was at the same time that of the 'Glory', the podium. Jesus was in this position when John Mark 'beheld his Glory'.

The 'Lion' shared his loaf 0/7 with his servant sitting opposite him on the south side of the table, thus entitling him to represent him in other villages. At the 'feeding of the Five Thousand' the servant was John Mark. At the 'feeding of Four Thousand', recorded by Mark's gospel for later in the year, James Niceta took the place of servant and was given a share of 'loaf 7'. Thus in the two episodes, loaf 5 and loaf 7 were used. They were, in fact, simply part of the five loaves used in outside ministry (3, 4, 5, 6

289

and 7), but the numbers were emphasized to bring out the origin of the whole system in the twelve loaves of the Presence.

The other men who sat on the low side of this table did not share in the loaves. During the meal they ate the common food, cooked fish (the man who was the leader of these being called 'Fish 2'). At the end of the meal they were given leftover fragments in baskets. Those servants sitting on the west side represented members who would meet only monthly, so their fragments were in 'basket 12', while those on the east side, of higher status, would meet and say prayers daily, so they were fed from 'basket 7'. The baskets designated what became a presbyteral and episcopal ministry.

In the monastery vestry there were strict rules of exclusion. According to the Temple Scroll neither a leper nor a blind man was to be permitted into sacred precincts (11QT 45). Such men, and others who were defined as equal to them because of wrong-doing, were sent right outside the monastic vestry, the nearest they could come being the pillar bases. But in the village and Diaspora communities represented at Ain Feshkha, their treatment was less harsh. They were sent down only to the dais step, to row 13. When the time came for their healing or re-admission, the levite and the 'Lion' came down to the step to stand with them. Here they performed priestly duties, for it was the work of a priest to heal literal lepers, and the rule was extended to metaphorical ones. These priestly healers held another version of the levitical thirteenth loaf, one intended for the use of priests in the Diaspora. Associated with the place of the 'seed', it was said to give spiritual fertility, and the crumbs from it were put in a container called 'the body', to be carried to other parts of the world.

## The Village Table in the Evening; the Last Supper (Figure 7 (iii) and (iv))

In the monastery vestry, loaf 12 had been set aside, and was not eaten at either table. It represented the lowest grade, which included married men.

Each loaf was associated with an hour for prayer, the priest's 0/13 with 6 am, the levite's loaf 6 with noon, and this loaf 12 with 6 pm. It was thus the evening loaf, used by ordinary villagers who had meals only in the morning and in the evening. A chief villager called an elder handled this loaf, sharing it with another, who might be his wife. One of her titles was 'the Beloved'.

In a village meal chamber patterned on the vestry, the elder and his wife sat at a common table on the equivalent of row 10, that of the 'bosom', the man on the east side and the wife on the west (see Figure 7 (iii)). If the occasion was one when unleavened bread was to be eaten, it was eaten instead of loaf 12, at 6 pm, the twelfth hour.

The Last Supper was patterned on such a village evening meal, with a more sacred meal later in the evening. The 6 pm part of it is described fully only by Luke, with John dealing with the 'foot-washing' ceremony (see Chapter 5). At 6 pm Jesus played the part of the Elder at the common table, sitting beside John Mark, the Beloved, in the place of the wife, both on row 10. Jesus was quoted by

Luke as saying 'with desire I have desired to eat this Passover (unleavened bread) with you'. The word 'desire' meant that he had not yet left the married state.

John Mark began as 'number 12' in the structure of the apostles. It is he who is always indicated by this term, just as 'the 7', 'the 5' and so on refer to other individuals, the leaders of their grades. He is called 'the elder' in his epistles. The reason was that he could act in the male role as well as the female one, being a male-female 'eunuch'. He could sit on the husband's side at the village low table, as he did later at the Last Supper. His very low grade, the lowest of the twelve, made him an 'apostle', one sent out from the monastery vestry. But in the course of the history, as the servant of Jesus, he rose to be head of Christian celibates.

At 8 pm came the sacred part of the Last Supper, when the priestly loaf 0/13, in its Diaspora version, was to be shared between the two priestly leaders. Jesus at this hour returned to the celibate state, and so was entitled to sit beside the priest, Jonathan Annas, in a pair of seats that extended back from row 6. In front of them, in the usual place of the Lion in row 7, sat their deputies, Peter in front of Jesus and Judas as levite in front of Jonathan Annas (see Figure 7 (iv)):

| | | King | Priest | | |
|---|---|---|---|---|---|
| Guest | Gershon | Deputy | Deputy | Kohath | Guest |
| W | | | | | E |
| Servant | Servant | Lion's servant | | Servant | Servant |

The occupants of the positions were:

292

|       |         | Jesus   | Jonathan Annas |         |        |
|-------|---------|---------|----------------|---------|--------|
| Antipas | Theudas | Peter | Judas Iscariot | Matthew | Thomas |

W                                                 E

| John   | James  | John Mark |  | Andrew | Philip |
|--------|--------|-----------|--|--------|--------|
| Aquila | Niceta |           |  |        |        |

John Mark, the Beloved Disciple, reclined on both sides of the 'bosom', as is shown in John 13:23, 25. Peter's position is indicated when it is shown that Peter could not see what was going on behind him, and had to beckon to John Mark, who was facing north and could see. Thus Peter was sitting in front of Jesus as his deputy, and Judas Iscariot, the true levite, was sitting in front of Jonathan Annas as the levite who 'gave beside' (the verb *paradidōmi*, used of Judas, meant both 'betray' and 'give beside').

The two guests at the meal were Antipas and Thomas Herod, the former taking the place of Simon Magus, a member of his party, who had been excluded to the dais step and was limited to 'washing feet'. Guests normally sat as the outer partner in the pairs, but this was not possible in the Qumran vestry, where the holy table was on the ground floor. When the platform had been constructed after the earthquake, its supports, the remains of which are still to be seen, rested in the guests' cubits, and, since Antipas and Thomas were very distinguished guests, they went back to sit (or recline) beside the priest and king-levite. Thus Jesus was sitting beside Antipas, as several details show. When he gave the bread and wine to 'All' (*pantes*), he was giving it to Antipas, called 'All' as a Herod, but standing for the common man.

In the seat of Gershon was Theudas, and Matthew

Annas was the Kohath, the levitical bishop, the one who would become 'tax-collector' in succession to his brother Jonathan (Matt 10:3, see below on Jonathan). On the lower side of the table James Niceta and John Aquila were the pair on the west side, as is seen by the reference in John 13:22 to James Niceta under one of his pseudonyms (*allēloi*, see 'One Another' in the Lexicon). Andrew and Philip, frequently paired together in John (John 1:44, 6:7–8, 12:22) were the pair on the east.

After Judas left at 9 pm, Peter came down to share the seat of John Mark, so that he now could see Jesus and speak to him (John 13:36). Jesus and Jonathan Annas moved forward into row 7, which was that of the 'Glory', so Jesus said, 'Now the Son of Man is glorified, and God is glorified in him' (John 13:31). In these seats they were closer to those whom they were teaching during the remainder of the session. Questions were asked of them by Thomas and Philip on the east side (John 14:5, 8), and by Theudas (another levite, now called 'Judas, not Iscariot' since Judas had left) on the west side (John 14:22).

In the final stage of development of the Christian ministry, there was only one man at the centre, Jesus having combined the roles of King and Priest. The surface form of the Last Supper narrative gives the impression that it was already in operation. The identity of Jonathan Annas is concealed in the list of twelve apostles by one of his titles, 'Jacob of Alphaeus', and 'Levi of Alphaeus' (Mark 3:18, 2:14), the meaning of which may be understood through the letters for classes. (He was 'of an Aleph/Alpha', the Hebrew and Greek for the class of priests, who were in grade 1. The genitive relationship meant that he was a grade 2, the Sariel, the third of the three leading priests when the zero was counted. This placed him at the west centre of the table, making him the priestly counterpart of the 'Jacob', the patriarch of the west. An allusion to him as a Jacob, having the dream of the ladder, is given in John 1:51, where he appears as 'Nathanael', a word with the same meaning as 'Jonathan'. The name 'Levi of Alphaeus' identifies him as a priest. He was a 'tax-collector' in Mark 2:14 because the Roman tribute was paid through the high priest, a position to which Jonathan aspired.)

Intricate as the 'riddle of the loaves' is, it goes back to a single unified scheme covering most aspects of the organization. The construction of such a scheme from the more natural history of Israelite priesthood was the work of hellenized Jews deeply influenced by Pythagorean systematization, as Diaspora Jews and especially the Essenes are known to have been. Artificial as it was, it did give the means of setting up a puzzle, a 'mystery', which when solved gave a full account of the history, a history with enduring significance.

# Chronological Points Relevant to the Crucifixion

A full treatment of the chronology, basic to the whole history, is given in *JM* and *JA*. The discovery of information about the solar calendar from the Dead Sea Scrolls has proved the key to the chronology of the gospels, as has been argued in these books. A brief summary of points relevant to the date of the crucifixion may be given here.

## Intercalation

The calendar measured a year of 364 days, intercalating 420 hours (17½ days, 2½ weeks) every fourteen years. The year was divided into four quarters, each with three months of thirty days each, with an extra day at the end of each quarter, called the 31st, but treated as a zero day before the 1st of the next month. It was the day on which great events were expected. The 31sts were placed at the equinoxes and solstices, but because of the difference between the 364 day year and the true solar year, they fell back gradually over fourteen years, so that just before the quartodecimal intercalation the 31st of the March season would fall early in March instead of at the equinox, 20 or 21 March.

Because of the symmetry of the calendar, containing exactly fifty-two weeks, a date always fell on the same day each year. The 1st of the first month was on a Wednesday, and so were the 1sts of the fourth, seventh and tenth months. Thus the 31sts fell on the previous day, a Tuesday. This was the normative arrangement of the calendar.

However, the necessary intercalation of 2½ weeks resulted in a change of the days of the week. When the intercalation was needed, it began on Tuesday 31st and inserted the extra days, the 31st now falling again 2½ weeks later. This meant that it fell on Friday evening, and from now on, for the next fourteen years, the dates followed from this. This position of the calendar, the Night position, was the one in operation during the gospel period. Good Friday was a day when the 31st would begin at 6 pm, so it was a Great Day, as John 19:31 says.

The gospel period was one when the quarto-decimal intercalation was due, properly in September AD 29. But the intense politics of the previous two centuries, shown in the Book of Daniel, had resulted in the insertion of 3½ years in the year dates, the later year being numbered the same as the earlier one. Issues concerning loyalty to the Jerusalem temple hung on the two versions, and two parties were formed, which may be called 'North Solar', intercalating in September AD 29, and South Solar, in March AD 33, the season of the crucifixion. At both these seasons there was intense expectation of

298

a fulfilment of prophecy, for the year was that of the end of the Last Jubilee (see below).

The effect of having two parties was that from AD 29 the North Solarists (who included Jesus) held their 31sts on the Friday at the equinoxes and solstices, but the South Solarists, the pro-temple party, who would not intercalate until AD 33, had their 31sts earlier in the month, the date to which they had fallen back. For example, their Day position 31st might be on Tuesday, 3 March, while the Night position 31st was at the equinox, Friday, 20 March. This meant that the Passover for the Day position, the 14th of the first month, fell on Tuesday, 17 March, a few days before the 31st of the Night position. It was this set of dates that was in operation in the week of the crucifixion, for there was a South Solar party that had not yet intercalated.

| Tuesday, 3 March | Tuesday, 17 March | Friday, 20 March (6 pm) |
| Day position 31st at I | Day position 14/I | Night position 31st at I |

In summary form, the Julian dates relevant to the gospel period were:

| Year | 31st Day | 31st Night |
| --- | --- | --- |
| AD 30 | Tuesday 7 March | Friday 24 March |
| AD 31 | Tuesday 6 March | Friday 23 March |
| AD 32 | Tuesday 4 March | Friday 21 March |
| AD 33 | Tuesday 3 March | Friday 20 March |

This is indeed complicated, showing that only

calendar experts were in a position to announce the dates and deal with the different occasions for intercalation. Its complexity would account for the ready acceptance of the Julian calendar when it was introduced, needing only a one day intercalation every four years.

## The Method of Combining Feasts

It becomes apparent that a further complication of the 31sts was introduced in an attempt to reconcile the two parties, North and South, so that they could meet on the same occasion for their feasts. This process accounts for the Last Supper being called Passover.

The method arose from a different way of correcting the calendar, by intercalating 2½ days every two years. In the year the intercalation began, the 31st moved from the Tuesday at 6 am to the Thursday of the same week, at 6 pm. Consequently all dates in that month followed. Whereas in AD 33 the 14/I, the date of Passover, had been on Tuesday, 17 March, it was now on Thursday evening, 19 March. It was for this reason that the Last Supper, held on Thursday, 19 March, was called the Passover (although the actual word used means the meal of unleavened bread associated with the Passover). (See 'Passover' in the Lexicon for the reason why Good Friday is called the Passover in John's gospel.)

### 'Tomorrow's Bread Today'

There was yet another adjustment of the Great Day
to suit some parties, expressed in the phrase 'Give us
tomorrow's bread today', the literal translation of a
phrase in the Lord's Prayer (Matt 6:11). Promotions
were given on the 31st, called 'Today', and the 1st,
called 'Tomorrow', priests being promoted on the
latter day. (Simon Magus as Lazarus was 'raised
from the dead' on Day 4, Wednesday 1st in the Day
position, and was said to be a 'fourth day man', John
11:17, 39.) Once lay celibates were given the status
of priests, their promotion day, 'Today', was given
the value of 'Tomorrow'.

Consequently, the laymen promoted on the 30th,
'Yesterday', were upgraded, as if they had been
promoted on the 31st. 'Yesterday' then became a
significant day, which might be the Great Day for
fulfilment of prophecy. The Last Supper, being the
evening before the Night position 31st, was a
'Yesterday', and some hoped for a fulfilment that
night. When it did not happen, Jesus' doctrine,
which used this day to promote Gentiles, was
discredited.

### The Three Hours' Darkness and
### the Double Cockcrowing

A further point of relevance to the crucifixion story
is that an adjustment in the measurement of hours
was being made on Good Friday, the Great Day at
the March equinox. Exact hours and minutes could
be measured, using devices such as a sundial by day,

301

or at night a marked container of oil for an oil lamp, reducing as the oil was burnt at a known rate. The Roman world used an hourglass, which may also have been known to the mission leaders.[1]

It had become necessary to bring back the timing devices by three hours. The reason was that the solar year is about eleven minutes shorter than 365¼ days, and the method of intercalation disregarded this, putting in a full thirty hours for each year. Over a period of years it had got to the point where the timing devices said it was 3 pm when it was manifestly noon.

This was adjusted by the 'three hours' darkness' that took place while Jesus was hanging on the cross. It had been the custom (as is shown by several episodes including that of Paul's conversion) to remove part of the roof of the vestry room at noon each day, so as to let the sun shine down brightly into the room. The members of the congregation were then able to look up and see the priest praying on the fixed part of the roof. On this day, the custom was not observed. The part roof was left over at the true noon, because at the same time the devices registered 3 pm, and it was left over until the true 3 pm, the time when it was normally put back. Hence 'at the sixth hour there was darkness over the whole Earth (the lower part of the vestry room where the Earth circle lay) until the ninth hour'. The episode of the three hours' darkness is a very good example of a story of a miracle or marvel containing a natural, technical meaning.

The same point accounts for the fact that in John's gospel the crucifixions are said to have begun at noon, but in the Synoptics at 9 am. In keeping with their different view of the date of the feast of unleavened bread, the party of John's gospel did not adjust their timing devices on this day, and were keeping the 'fast' times. But the actual time when the crucifixions began was 9 am.

Again, this point accounts for the double cockcrowing that took place at the time of Peter's denials. The prediction of Jesus that Peter would deny him three times 'before the cock crows twice' came from a play on the different versions of the hour. There was normally a cockcrowing at 3 am, as shown in Mark 13:35. It was the hour when ascetics rose from sleep, and a loud prayer was said by the 'cock', the levitical deacon, to signal time to rise. Jesus was arrested at the true midnight, which was the 'fast' 3 am, and the first cockcrowing was heard then. The period of his trials before the priests lasted until the true 3 am, when the second cockcrowing was heard. During the hours after 3 am it was Peter's duty to celebrate sunrise (as Essenes were said by Josephus to do) by saying three prayers, one at 4 am, one at 5 am, and the final one at 6 am. Peter had not yet adjusted his timing, and said them at the 'fast' times, the true 1 am, 2 am, and 3 am. At each one he 'denied' Jesus, by refusing to follow his practices for prayer. Thus his third denial came at the true 3 am, coinciding with the second cockcrowing.

At all points the exact hours and half-hours were known to everyone in the vicinity of the Qumran vestry, for one of the main duties of monastics was to offer a prayer at significant times. This is stated in the Scrolls, which show that it was a sin to be 'early or late for all the appointed times' (1QS 1:14–15). Rising from the vestry roof, the prayers acted as a human clock. They established the custom maintained throughout Christian history of placing a clock in church buildings, its chimes giving order to the lives of everyone living nearby.

# The Lexicon

A list of terms with special meanings follows, in the form of a Lexicon. The literal meaning of the Greek word is given first, followed by the special or technical meaning that was known to the pesharist as 'insider's knowledge'.

To enable the lexicon to be followed by readers not using Greek, the entries are in English first, with the Greek in brackets. There may be varying English translations of Greek words in the different versions of the Bible, and the Revised Standard Version should be consulted first. As has been explained above, it has sometimes been necessary to use a range of terms, or to add terms, to distinguish between words that are usually translated by the same word in English.

**about** (*hōsei*). The time unit before, used especially by Luke. In Luke 3:23, 'about thirty years' means 'about year 30', AD 29, a year before AD 30, already called year 30 using the Christian millennium. In Luke 22:59, 'about one hour', means 'about hour 1', the uncorrected 6 am, an hour before 7 am. In Luke 9:28, 'about eight days' means 'about day 8', Sunday; the word order, with noun first, meaning

Saturday, 6 pm (see day), so the expression means Friday at 6 pm, Friday the Day of Atonement.

**about** (*peri*). See **around**.

**about to, be** (*mellō*). This verb is used when an action occurs in preparation for one that will occur three hours or three months later, an hour being equated with a month, as both come in sets of twelve. Luke 22:23, said in March AD 33, means that Agrippa will sail for Rome in three months' time. John 18:32, Jesus speaking at 6 am knew that by 9 am he and Simon would be finally excommunicated and crucified.

**accusation** (*katēgoria*, verb *katēgoreō*). (To bring) a charge under Roman law (John 18:29). The 'Accuser' was used as a name for the emperor (Rev 12:10).

**aeon** (*aiōn*). A long period of time in the precise sense of 'world-week', the divisions of history into sets of 490 years, as in the prophecy of Enoch (1 *Enoch* 93:3–10, 91:12–16). In the Herodian period it meant the eighth world-week, the year 3920, when the Restoration of the rightful rulers was expected, according to the prophecy. It had fallen in 21 BC, but when the expected Restoration did not come a Last Jubilee had been declared, for 3969 (AD 29 and AD 33), which would be called 3920 on the principle of a zero jubilee. Agrippa took it to refer to his own restoration, and began a new dating at this time. John 9:32 refers to his dating, and the new beginning made by the mission. Peter speaks of his regime as the 'aeon' in John 13:8, and Antipas refers to it in John 12:34, showing that an expectation for the appearance of the Christ was bound up with it, Agrippa to be the superior priest. The supporters of Agrippa are called 'the sons of the aeon' in Luke 16:8. 'The ending of the aeon' is the last phrase in Matthew (28:20), a supporter of Agrippa II. See further *JM* and *JA*.

**afar** (*makrothen*). A name for the north pillar base and its equivalents, as the place where the king stood when pilgrims came to see him. 'From afar' (*apo makrothen*), the south base as its other extreme (Mark 15:40; Luke 23:49). The corresponding positions for pilgrims who had been promoted to the north doorway of the vestry were given the same names (Mark 14:54; Matt 26:58). An excluded priest stood here (Luke 18:13).

**after** (with time expressions, *meta* + accus.). The corresponding time unit after. If with 'day', it means 24 hours after. Day 3, *treis hēmerai*, means Tuesday, and *meta treis hēmeras*, 'after three days', means Wednesday. John 20:26, 'after day 8' means Sunday at noon, because Sunday was day 8, but the word order with noun first indicates Saturday at 6 pm and Saturday noon (see **day**) so 24 hours after that, in this case Sunday noon.

**after** (*opisthen, opisō*). One of the four prepositions meaning the compass points. Also translated 'behind'. It means 'west', as in Hebrew thought the subject faced east and the west was behind him. The Hebrew equivalents, *qedem* and *achrit*, 'before' and 'behind', were used in the same sense. In Mark 8:33, 'Get behind me, Satan', means 'go to the west, to the Rome province'. In Luke 23:26 Simon was 'behind

Jesus', so Simon was at the west and Jesus at the east, each of them being cursed on both sides.

**Alexander** (*Alexandros*). A title of the Chief Therapeut when in Alexandria. In Mark 15:21 it means Theudas. 'Alexander the coppersmith' was Apollos his successor (2 Tim 4:14). In Mark 15:21 'the father of Alexander and Rufus', with the fact that Simon Magus the 'father' carried his cross, is an allusion to the Isaac story (Gen 22:6), and to Jacob and Esau the sons of Isaac (Gen 25:25–6). 'Rufus' means 'red', as does also 'Esau' (Gen 25:25). Thomas Herod was the 'Esau', the twin of the hierarchy who had lost his Herodian birthright (see *JM*), and he formed a pair with the Chief Therapeut in two related sects.

**all** (*pas*, sing., *pantes*, plu.) Used to indicate a member of the Herod family, as Herod the Great had claimed all positions in the hierarchy. An apparently vague word, used to describe leading persons in the history. 'All Ones', *pantes*, using the plural of reproduction, was a name for the tetrarch Antipas, the third Herod, in some of his functions. 'All Things' *panta*, Herodian laws. Fem. *pasai*, Matt 25:5, Bernice, the sister of Agrippa II. The word added to a term for a person who is not a Herod indicates another leader acting on their behalf. 'All the Chief Priests' meaning Caiaphas in Mark 14:53; Matt 27:1, and 'All the Ones Having Knowledge' meaning James in Luke 23:49. In John 13:11, with *ouchi*, it means Theudas (see **not**).

**already** (*ēdē*). Used with a time expression to show that the time was three hours earlier than expected, giving rise to the question 'Already?' It arose from the changes of time on a Friday, when prayers were held three hours earlier than usual, at 3 pm for 6 pm.

**amazed, be** (*ekthambeomai*). To don a minister's vestment, giving a new identity, transforming from the lay state. Jesus in Mark 14:33. Antipas in Mark 9:15. Note: in Mark 14:33 Mark draws on special knowledge about vestments to give an exception to the rule of the last referent, for Peter, James and John, preceding the verb, were all laymen and could not put on this vestment, hence the subject of 'began to be amazed' is Jesus. A similar device is used in (Mark 14:63); see **tunic.**

**amēn** (*amen*, from Hebrew 'to confirm'). Used in the Scrolls, said twice, as the words of the congregation after a liturgical action (1QS 1:20, 2:10). In the gospels, said by the bishop who leads a congregation. Its double use, 'Amen Amen' has significance, as with all repeated words. Used once, by the bishop as an outside dynast, used twice, by him in the double position at the centre of row 7 or its equivalent (John 13:16, 21).

**and** (*kai*). Used as verbal punctuation, indicating a new unit for the pesharist, sometimes disregarding the apparent sense. The student of the Greek text should first mark off all phrases beginning with *kai* as new sentences. This will not be possible in the English text.

**angel** (*angelos*). A monastic celibate. 'Gabriel' in Luke 1:11,19 was the Abiathar priest, Simon the Essene. Simon Magus had taken over his office, and the same title is used for him (Acts 12:23). Simon Magus in the tomb in John 20:12.

**answer** (*apokrinomai*). Act in the role of a teacher, who gives answers to questions. It does not necessarily mean that the previous statement was answered.

**apostle** (*apostolos*). One 'sent out'. A monastic in a state of uncleanness was sent to the exclusion cistern in the south-west part of the Qumran grounds (John 9:7, this word is used to translate 'Siloam', the name for the cistern). A Gentile monastic was defined as equal to an unclean Jewish monastic, so the word was used for him. In the plural, John Mark, unless a further identifying word is added, as in Acts 14:14.

**arise** (*egeirō*). To be promoted to the status of a Chief Initiate, one who entered the north vestry. The position was open to a celibate who was at the level of an initiate. Used of Jesus in Mark 16:6, and of Simon Magus in Matt 27:64, in both these cases used with the apparent meaning of resurrection, since to be initiated meant to receive (spiritual) life. Used of John Mark as Chief Gentile in Mark 14:42, or of an equal female in John 11:29.

**around** (*peri*). Its meaning, which indicates both a place and a time, comes from the position around the central semicircle in the vestry, in row 7 (see Chapter 2). A teacher could stand here at one of the 'eyes', as a Witness (John 1:7, 'around the Light', near the priest on row 6). The semicircle of half a cubit, 9 inches, contained the podium for the feet. Since the teacher's feet were likely to be a little bigger, three-fifths of a cubit was allowed. In the equation of time and space, a cubit also stood for five minutes, since there were twelve of them in an hour and a unit of space contained 12 cubits. Hence three-fifths was three minutes, and 'around' also indicates three minutes past the hour. The main division of the opening five minutes of each hour was at three minutes past, when a prayer was said. *Peri* has the sense of three minutes past the hour in Mark 6:48, the time needed to walk the 100 cubits of the jetty at the rate of 2000 cubits per hour, three minutes being one-twentieth of sixty, 100 one-twentieth of 2000 (see *JM*, 'Locations').

The witness standing *peri* was on the outer part of the central circle, and could move to the seat in row 7 on either side of the central 2 cubits. In John 18:19 the seats of the witnesses, on either side of the central seats of the judges, are said to be *peri* (John 18:19).

**as** (*hōs*). Used for 'and' within a sentence, as *kai* was used to mark a new sentence for the pesharist. In Luke 10:18 'Satan as Lightning' means Judas Iscariot ('Satan') and Simon Magus ('Lightning'). In John 4:6, 19:14 'it was an hour as sixth' means it was five minutes to noon (as 'hour' has no article), and on the hour it would be the sixth hour – noon – the two times being taken together.

**ask** (*erōtaō*). To direct a non-monastic to do something, or indicate that he should do it, as the priest could only 'order' a monastic bound to obey him. If a priest 'asked' a monastic, he was treating him as an excluded layman (Mark 14:60, 61).

**at once** (*eutheōs*). This term is used to indicate five minutes past the hour, when the hour's activities were said to begin. If it was a meal hour, the doors were shut at this time. (John 18:27; Matt 26:74, 27:48).

**authority** (*exousia*). The privilege given by initiation (John 1:12, 19:10; Mark 11:28, 30).


**band** (*speira*). Used to translate the Roman 'cohort'. A cohort was the tenth of a legion, which usually contained 6000 men. The mission had divided the world into ten provinces for taxation purposes, so a cohort of 600 men was the military force in the first of these provinces, containing Qumran. The men were primarily Gentile initiates of the mission, using Roman military terminology for their organization, who were prepared to take up arms in a holy war if necessary. In Acts 10:1, Luke-Cornelius was head of the 'band called Italian', the 600 of the Rome province, he himself being a 'centurion', over the first hundred. In John 18:3, 12 a name for the levitical deacon Merari (Ananus the Younger) acting as military head for Agrippa.

**Barabbas** (*Barabbas*). The title used by Theudas the Chief Therapeut in his role of servant of (*bar*, 'son' or 'servant' in Aramaic) the *Abba*. The *Abba* (Aramaic for 'Father') was the abbot of a Sadducee open monastery. Theudas, representing Alexandrian Jews, could agree with both Sadducees and Pharisees, and when more moderate in his nationalism allied with Sadducees. Consequently he was helped at the crucifixion by Jonathan Annas and by Antipas, who together were the 'Chief Priests' and the 'Crowd', who urged that Barabbas should be released (Mark 15:11).

Theudas as a Sadducee had similar nationalist views to Ananus the Younger, Merari, said to be a Sadducee in *Ant.* 18:4. He led the people in moderation at the time of the fall of Jerusalem. He and the Chief Therapeut frequently appear together, as the two guards at the tomb, and as 'the Philippian jailer' with 'Earthquake' in Acts 16:26–7.

**barley** (*krithinos*). Used with 'loaf 5', John 6:9, 13, to show that it was the loaf standing for the season of barley harvest, Passover.

**beckon** (*neuō*). To signal to another member, because not permitted to speak. Peter at the Last Supper, sitting in row 7 in front of Jesus, signalled across the table to John Mark in row 10 (John 13:24). In Acts 24:10, Felix the governor, who was an initiated member, signalled similarly to Paul.

**become** (*eimi*) (**be**). The verb 'to be' is here translated 'become', to draw out its special meaning, derived from the Hebrew verb 'to be', which is used in a dynamic sense to mean 'to become', 'come into existence'. No verb is used when a purely static sense is intended. *Ego eimi*, 'I am', contains an allusion to the divine name 'Yahweh' and indicates that the person claimed priesthood (John 18:6), so *ouk eimi*, 'I am not', said by Peter (John 18:17) means that he denied being a priest but was simply a layman, disagreeing with Jesus.

A 'Being One', using the present participle of 'to be', was a supreme priest, one able to give initiation (Rev 1:8). With 'All', it means Agrippa claiming his position (John 18:37). In the corresponding passage in Luke 23:6–12, set at the same time, Agrippa is shown to be present, named as 'Herod'.

**before** (with time, *pro* + gen.). The time unit before. If the time given is a day, 'before' means 24 hours previously. John 13:1, 'before the feast', the Thursday evening, 24 hours before Friday evening, the 'feast' in question.

**before** (with place, *emprosthen*). This is one of the four prepositions with apparently indefinite meanings, having the precise sense of the compass points. It means 'east', since in Hebrew thought a man was facing east with the east before him and the west behind (after) him. In John 1:15, 'He who comes after (*opisō*) me has become before (*emprosthen*) me' has the pesher: 'Jesus as the true David would be on the west (*opisō*) side of the priest, but he must stand on the east (*emprosthen*) because he is illegitimate and as a monastic orphan can act in the place of a levite'.

When X is 'before' (east of) Y, then Y is west. In Luke 5:19 Jonathan Annas the paralytic was let down to the step 'before Jesus', so Jesus was on the west side of the step in the place of the David, and Jonathan on the east side in the place of the levite, used also by the visiting priest. The 'east' could be not only in the east centre but further out, with two cubits between, the distance between servant and master. In the story of Peter's denials, Peter was in the outer east, which was the inner doorway at the side of the north vestry (Matt 26:70). In Matt 27:11 Jesus stood on the east side of the south base which, when Pilate stood on it, represented the west, Rome.

**before** (*enōpion*). The preposition meaning 'north', Pilate using the north base in Luke 23:14.

**before** (*apenanti*). See **opposite**.

**before** (*prin*). An hour before (John 4:49). The version of the cockcrowing saying that uses *prin* (Mark 14:30, 72; Matt 26:34, 75), refers also to the minor cockcrowing at 4 am, shown in the alternate text of Mark 14:68.

**begin** (*archō*). To act with the time value of the *archē*, the 'Beginning', the podium in row 7, within the hour after the zero hour, or at .01, the minute after the zero (John 13:5), or after the half-hour (Mark 14:19; Luke 22:23). But some treated the .03 prayer as the zero, expecting the fulfilment of prophecy at that moment, so 'began' then means .04 after the hour (Mark 14:65).

**beginning** (*archē*). The podium, the place for 'Genesis', and the beginning of time. For the Julian calendar, the beginning of the day was at midnight. See Chapter 2 (John 1:1). In John 2:11, an action on the podium at midnight.

**behind** (*opisthen, opisō*). See **after**.

**behold** (*idou*). Used to indicate a person standing on a pillar base or its equivalent, in a prominent position (John 19:5, 14; Rev 6:2).

**believe** (*pisteuō*). To believe that a person was the legitimate successor to the office and would attain it. Frequently used in the context of disputes on Jesus' legitimacy. In John 2:23, Agrippa, 'Many', accepted Jesus as legitimate when he changed to Sadducee

315

views. Hence to be 'unbelieving' is to be a Pharisee, as Thomas was (John 20:27). The Sadducee Jonathan Annas, as a Pope, was called 'the Faith' (Belief), with an additional reference to the faith of 'Abraham', the first Pope (Mark 2:5).

**belly** (*koilia*, also meaning the female womb). A part of the body of the Heavenly Man, on row 12. A man who was 'lame out of (*ek*) the mother's womb' (Acts 3:2, 14:8) was in the equivalent of the space on the east side of row 12. Mark 7:19, speaking of the unclean, says that they did not go into the 'heart', but into the *koilia*, then 'go out into the drain' – that is, they were not permitted to sit at the table in row 10 in the vestry, but must go down to row 12, then further down to row 13, the outer parts of which had the uncleanness of a latrine. In its other sense of 'womb', the part was aptly placed on the same row as the Moon (see Chapter 2), thus connected with a monthly cycle.

**beside-give** (*paradidōmi*). Used in the sense of 'betray' or 'hand over for punishment'. The exact meaning is 'to be a rival minister', a counterpart in the same position who gives the communion meal, but has been pushed aside. At the Last Supper, Judas and Jesus were both capable of acting as the levite who blessed the bread, but Judas became the one who 'beside-gave' Jesus, was passed over and so became an enemy (John 13:2, 21). In John 18:30, 35; 19:11, 16, the one who 'beside-gave' acted as a rival in the same position, and an opponent.

**Bethany** (*Bēthania*). A building used by the 'Poor' (*ani* in Hebrew), the Therapeuts. The two main sects of Therapeuts had their council centres at Mird (the 'Bethany beyond Jordan' of John 1:28, see **beyond**), and at Ain Feshkha, the 'Bethany' of John 11:18 and Luke 24:50. In Mark 11:1, 'Bethany towards the Mount of Olives' means the meeting place of Therapeuts attached to the Qumran monastery, in the outer hall.

**Bethsaida** (*Bēthsaida*). A city on the north of Lake Galilee, used as the meeting place of Gentiles of the order of individual celibates (Philip and Titus), whose missionaries were Andrew and Peter (John 1:44). Hence the word means their council centre at Ain Feshkha (Mark 8:22; Luke 9:10). A play on 'House of the Olive-Tree', as 'oil' stood for outsiders, it being contrary to the rules of Essenes to use oil on their skins (*War* 2:123).

**betray** (*paradidōmi*). See **beside-give**.

**beyond** (*peran*). Used to indicate the reproduction of one place at another. 'Beyond Jordan' (John 1:28, 10:40), means the wady at Mird (the 'Jordan river') used for baptisms, repeating the aqueduct at Qumran, called the 'Jordan' in an initiation ceremony into the abbey. 'Beyond the Sea of Galilee' (John 6:1) means the part of Ain Feshkha where married persons could also meet, as at Mazin. John 18:1, the rock podium in the outer hall, where pilgrims were given a drink of water from the aqueduct, also called 'the Kidron' in the Jerusalem scheme.

**bitter(ly)** (*pikrōs*). A word used in Revelation and the Synoptics to refer to the party of Simon Magus, with their knowledge and use of poisons (Mark 14:72; Luke 22:62; Matt 26:75; Rev 10:10).

**blaspheme** (*blasphēmeō*). Be a zealot, in the party of Simon Magus, as opposed to the peace party of Jonathan Annas. Jonathan was the 'Holy Spirit' (in the form *to pneuma to hagion*), so 'blasphemy against the Holy Spirit' meant zealotry (Mark 3:29). (Mark 15:29; Luke 22:65, 23:39.)

**blessed** (*makarios*). Monastic celibates were called 'saints' and the unmarried living in the communities of Therapeuts, not permanently committed to celibacy, were called 'Blessed Ones'. The Beatitudes of Matthew 5 refer to them. In John, they are considered as of lesser status, equal to novices who have not 'seen the light', 'not seeing' (John 20:29).

**blessing, give a** (*eulogeō*). Give a non-eucharistic blessing over the sacred bread to a member who, like John Mark, did not drink fermented wine. See thanks, give (Mark 6:41, 14:22).

**blind** (*typhlos*). One of the categories of the indigent provided for by Essenes, the 'Poor, Crippled, Lame and Blind'. The terms were used literally, and the layman responsible for giving welfare to the lame and blind was regarded as so identifying with them that he himself was called 'the Lame Man', or 'the Blind Man'. These laymen were the David princes. The 'Lame Man' was the crown prince, and the 'Blind Man' the second prince. Hence the 'Blind Man' of John 9, the subject of the sixth Sign, was Joses (Barnabas), the next brother after James (Mark 6:3).

The terms were also used metaphorically, and they then referred to ascetics who had taken up the mendicant life, being called 'lame beggars' and 'blind beggars'. The princes were the leaders of their orders.

There were two kinds of 'blind man', as shown in the saying about the 'blind leading the blind' (Luke 6:39), and in the two healings of blind men in Mark's gospel. Metaphorically, a 'blind man' was one who had not yet 'seen the light' of initiation (1QS 3:7). This could be a celibate novice, or a man in the married ranks, for there were two kinds of initiation. 'Blind Bartimaeus' of Mark 10:46–52 was the latter kind. He was found at 'Jericho', which meant that he was the current head of the order of Benjamin, whose traditional tribal territory contained the literal Jericho. He was the teacher called Gamaliel, whose successor was Paul (Acts 5:34; Phil 3:5; Acts 22:3), and Paul's 'blindness' was an expression of the same status (Acts 9:8, 18).

**blood** (*haima*). Literal blood (of Jesus in John 19:34), of which a smear was placed on the cup of fermented wine, indicating the doctrine of 1QS 8:1–4, that the monastic Suffering Servants made atonement for the sins of outsiders. As the gospels show, the sacred wine stood for the atoning blood of the Lamb (Mark 14:24). Another leader's blood could be used in the same way, in a ritual of fellowship expressing willingness for martyrdom (Luke 13:1). 'Blood' meaning fermented wine also distinguished two kinds of ascetics, the western using fermented wine, the eastern using new wine or water. In Matt 27:8 Qumran became the 'Field of Blood' because it was taken over for a Sadducee abbey, used by Jonathan Annas and visited by Peter's village Essenes; whereas in the hands of Judas and eastern Essene monastics no fermented wine had been used. The 'blood' stood for willingness for martyrdom in a spiritual form of warfare, evangelism, rather than Judas' militant zealotry.

**blow** (*hrapisma*). A blow administered for making an error, at the south base in the area where boys were taught, or its equivalent (see Chapter 2). Administered to Jesus by the levitical deacon Merari, for his 'error' in the way he addressed Annas (John 18:22) and in claiming to be legitimate (John 19:3).

**boat** (*ploion, ploiarion*). The boat used in the 'Noah's ark' drama. In the form *ploion*, the boat used in Agrippa's mission (John 6:17); in the form *ploiarion*, the boat used in Antipas' mission (John 6:22, 21:8).

**body** (*sōma*). The bread container for the small pieces left from the priestly loaf 13, to be given as symbolic of charity for the Orphan and Widow, consequently for Gentiles. Loaf 13 was the sacred priestly loaf used to give a form of priesthood to the celibate indigent, at first placed on row 13 at the level of the 'seed' and the 'body', then brought up to the highest place by a Diaspora priest.

The container was portable, given to a minister to use in conducting the Christian communion. At the Last Supper, Jesus gave one to John Mark (Mark 14:22), and to Antipas (Luke 22:19), to the latter adding words indicating a lay form of communion that was merely a commemoration.

As Mark 6:8 indicates, the container was carried attached to his waist by a travelling missionary priest (Mark 6:8 contains a list of rules for the dress of a missionary layman, such as wearing sandals, as opposed to a priest who did not wear sandals. It includes 'not bread', whereas the parallel in Matt

10:10 rules that he should not wear sandals, indicating that he was a priest, and omits 'not bread'). In John 19:31 the 'bodies' (the bread container of Simon Magus, using the plural of reproduction) were 'upon the cross', meaning attached to him on the west, his left side. The bread container and the bag for water would have been left attached to the crucified men so that they would be buried with them, as a sign of their ministry.

In the crucifixion story, the 'body' of Jesus was this container. It was attached to him while hanging on the cross, but when he was brought down, unconscious but still alive, James his brother was technically his substitute, and had to conduct the Gentile service at 4 pm which Jesus would normally have taken (John 19:38). James took the container from him, and after the service he took it back to the cave to be restored to him. Luke 23:53 and Matt 27:59 show that James on top of the cave wrapped the container in a *sindōn*, a common cloth, while John shows in 19:40 that inside the cave Merari received the container and wrapped it in the priestly garment, an *othonē*, a holy cloth. See **cloth** and **tomb.** So the 'body of Jesus' lay in the cave (John 20:12). When his 'body' was not found in the cave, it meant that he had been removed (Luke 24:3 of Jesus, Luke 24:23 of Judas).

In the singular, the word means the bread container of David or a levite; in the plural, that of a priest (John 19:31 of Simon Magus; Matt 27:52 of Agrippa, carried by James).

Note: this is a revision of *JM* on the meaning of Jesus' 'body'.

**bone** (*osteon*). The bone knife used by a layman who ate meat or fish, broken when the person died (John 19:36). In Luke 24:39 a sign that Jesus was both living and acting in his lay status.

**born, be** (*gennaō*). Be mortal, without the 'divinity' of a Sadducee priest. A man 'born blind' (John 9:32) was a layman because 'blind', a pre-initiate. Mark 14:21: ' . . . if that man was not born' asks whether a 'That Man', a celibate, was lay or a priest. In Luke 23:29 concerning the women's orders, Helena was 'not born', not mortal, because she claimed to be a priest. In John 18:37 Jesus said that when he was in the married state he was 'born', a mere layman.

**bosom** (*kolpos*). The position in the west centre of row 10, that of the 'bosom' in the diagram of the Heavenly Man. See Chapter 2. The west was the female side, where a woman could sit. John Mark was in this position at 8 pm at the Last Supper (John 13:23).

**breakfast** (verb) (*aristaō*). To take the first meal of the day, whether at 6 am (John 21:12) or noon (*War* 2: 129–31 on the Essenes, John 21:15). In Luke 11:37, at noon.

**breasts** (*mastoi*). As shown in Luke 23:29, women who were the original teachers of Gentiles, acting as 'Mothers' to 'children', were replaced by a male teacher, Jesus, who did not treat them as 'children'. The word 'breasts' indicates the substitution. It is used in the description of Jesus in Rev 1:13.

**breathe** (*emphysaō*). To act at the 'nose' of God, at the centre of row 7, the podium, giving the 'breath of God', the Spirit, to a bishop. (John 20:22).

**bridegroom** (*nymphios*). The Chief Priest, the Pope, as the superior of all women, hence of Gentiles, whose initiation ceremonies were likened to a marriage. Jonathan Annas in John 2:9.

**brother** (*adelphos*). The fellow-villager of a man who went on pilgrimage or to a Nazirite retreat, the 'brother' looking after his wife and family while he was away. He formed a pair in mission with him. He may or may not have been an actual brother (Mark 1:16, 19). A woman minister could be in such a pair (John 11:21). The plural means a literal brother (John 20:17, 21:23; Luke 8:20).

**but** (*alla*). A play on *allos*, 'other', meaning a deputy.

**buy** (*agorazō*). To pay an initiation or promotion fee, hence receive benefits from the community, such as teaching, promotion or vestments. A teacher was 'bought' by being paid teaching fees.

**Caesar** (*Kaisar*). A title used derisively for Agrippa I, who aimed to be a Caesar, at least in the east, and perhaps also in Rome. In Mark 12:14, Agrippa insisted that the tribute should be paid through him. The issue here was whether or not to support Agrippa's aim to restore the monarchy, which could lead to the result that it did in fact have, that Agrippa claimed to be a god-emperor. In John 19:12, 15 the word means Agrippa, who was present at the trial before Pilate. Antipas exploited Agrippa's ambition in order to persuade Pilate to side with him, Antipas, against Agrippa.

**call** (*phōneō*). To act as a 'voice' (*phōnē*), a person entitled to stand on one of the pillar bases, sounding the main hours, as at the cockcrowing (calling), or as an important person with a voice in a council (John 18:27, 33).

**Cana** (*Kana*). The name used in John's gospel for the part of the Ain Feshkha building where women and Gentiles were permitted (John 2:1, 4:46, 21:2).

**cave** (*spēlaion*). A place used for study by Qumran monastics, who used the caves in the area for this purpose, as shown by the Scrolls left there. In John 11:38, Cave 4. In Mark 11:17, a room in the buildings, which had become a 'cave of thieves' when zealotry was studied.

**charge** (*aitia, aition*). In the surface meaning, a legal charge; in the pesher, a payment, something 'asked for' (from *aiteō* 'to ask') by Pilate (John 18:38, 19:4, 6; Luke 23:4, 14, 22). When he said 'I do not find a charge in this man', the exact meaning was that he had not received a bribe to protect Jesus. Pilate became entitled to 'ask for' money because it was the right of a graduate teacher in Antipas' school, a 'king of the Jews'. Itinerant teachers were permitted in this branch of the mission to charge fees. The word *aitia* is also used for the writing on a band worn over the headband, showing a man's qualification to be a paid teacher (Mark 15:26; Matt 27:37).

**chest** (*stēthos*). The east centre of row 10, the male side of the 'bosom' of the Heavenly Man. See Chapter 2. John Mark moved to it at 9 pm at the Last Supper (John 13:25) and at the parallel meal (John 21:20). The position was that of an acolyte, who as a student could be beaten by a superior, so in Luke

18:13 a superior 'beat the chest' (Agrippa punished his eunuch-acolyte Blastus). In the plural form, it means James Niceta, the alternative Gentile to John Mark. In Luke 23:48 James Niceta at the Gentile service was 'beaten' by Antipas acting as a teacher.

**chief priest** (*archiereus*). The term means a chief priest but not a high priest, corresponding to a distinction found in the Scrolls (1QM 2:1). In the Qumran hierarchy the 'Michael', a Zadokite, was the potential high priest, while the 'Sariel', third in the hierarchy, of the line of Levi, was the Chief Priest. He went between monastery and village, acting also as village priest. Jonathan Annas was the 'Sariel' of the Qumran hierarchy in the gospel period. Both the singular and plural forms refer to him, as he operated in two places. Caiaphas, the public high priest, was equal to him in status, but not a member of a celibate community, and the term 'Chief Priest' refers to him when there is a qualifying word, his name added (Matt 26:57; John 18:24), or with 'All' meaning that he was in the party of Agrippa as Pharisee (Mark 14:53).

**child** (*paidion*). All Gentiles were originally treated as 'children' – that is, pre-initiates who were prevented from becoming 'men'. Two different terms were used, *teknon* and *paidion*. Of these, the latter applied to John Mark in the status of a potential monastic, the former applied to both John Mark and James Niceta. In Mark 10:14, 'Let the Children come to me', the more exact meaning is 'let Gentiles be initiated'. In John 4:49 John Mark is introduced into the story as a Gentile who had also incurred the hostility of Agrippa.

**child** (*teknon*, plu. *tekna*). 'Children', Gentiles who had become proselytes (Luke 23:28, under Helena), or John Mark whose celibate discipline gave him equal status, but under the Sadducee priest (John 1:12). Matt 27:25: Pilate as equal to John Mark, honorary status.

**Christ** (*Christos*). The term means the Messiah of Israel described in the Scrolls (1QSa 2:20), the leader of the laity, the heir of David. But while some parts of the Scrolls speak of two Messiahs, a superior one of Aaron and a subordinate one of Israel (1QSa 2:19–21, 1QS 9:11), others speak of a combined 'Messiah of Aaron and Israel', one person (CD 19:10, 20:1). In Mark 14:61–2, the rule of the last referent reverses the sense to mean that Jesus said to Jonathan Annas 'You are the Christ the son of the Blessed One'. The meaning was that once Jesus was arrested, Annas claimed the combined position. He could not call James 'the Christ', holding him to be only the crown prince. Without article, the word means either 'the David in the body', acting as a bishop (John 1:41) or 'the servant of David', since the servant used the name of the master 'in the body'. In Luke 23:2 it is said that Jesus called Simon Magus 'a Christ', his servant. This is confirmed in Acts 13:6, where Simon appears as 'Bar-Jesus', meaning 'servant of Jesus'. In Luke 23:35, in a question about the status of James, 'the Christ of the God' means James, who accepted the subordination of the David to the priest.

**church** (*ekklēsia*). The 'church', in its original sense, was a sub-sect of the mission to the Diaspora, formed by men like Peter in alliance with western

Sadducees with a strong commitment to peace with Rome, their main representative being Matthew Annas. Having begun as pilgrims to a Sadducee abbey and received some learning, they were admitted into the vestry, at the level of the dais step, where the emblem of the Lion was used. The militancy of zealots and nationalist Sadducees was transformed into a method of evangelism, using military terms in a symbolic sense, such as the 'sword of the Spirit', meaning the scriptures. Their imagery is found in Eph 6:10–17. John Aquila became their chief Gentile leader. They did not separate out until AD 43–44, when the schism of east and west took place, so the word 'church' is not found in any gospel except Matthew (16:18, 18:17). But it appears in Acts (5:11) at the time Agrippa I was about to receive the monarchy, and it was encouraged by Agrippa II who was consistently pro-Roman.

**city** (*polis*). A Gentile celibate community, imitating the New Jerusalem at Qumran. It was at first equal to the south part of the vestry used for the congregation, which was on the same line as 'Jerusalem' (plu.), the back gate. 'City of the Jews' (Luke 23:51) means a celibate community of pre-proselytes, such as James Niceta. Those Gentiles who had risen to leadership were promoted to the dais step, called the 'holy city' in Matt 27:53 and Rev 21:2.

Each of the ten provinces into which the world mission was divided contained a Gentile monastery, so when a number is used with the word it refers also to the province, for example 'city 10' (ten cities) in Luke 18:17 means the Rome province, number 10. See *JA*.

**clay** (*chamai*). The level of the Sea and the feet of the Heavenly Man in row 17, with an allusion to the 'feet of clay' of Dan 2:35. Monastic progress began at the low level of the 'clay' and moved upwards. In the Scrolls, the Teacher says 'I am a creature of clay'. (1QH 1:21–2, 3:23–4). In the imagery used in the promotion of 'Adam', the heir of David, he was said to have begun in the clay before being given 'life', and the Spirit from the breath of God in row 7. So when Brother James, having become the 'Adam' in place of Jesus, reproduced Adam's creation, he 'fell to the clay', going into the annexe to the outer hall where the dishes, fashioned from clay at the Qumran pottery, were stacked (John 18:6). Under the same imagery a 'clay', a dish to accompany his lamp, was given to Joses-Barnabas when he was appointed crown prince instead of James (John 9:6). To it was added spit, indicating that he was appointed to the Rome province (see **spit**). He took with him there the power to make other 'Adams' rise from the 'clay'.

**clay** (*pēlos*). An oil lamp made of earthenware, such as were used by Christians in the catacombs in Rome. In John 9:6 Joses-Barnabas was given such a lamp when appointed to Rome.

**Cleopas** (*Kleopas*). A name found in Hegesippus' account of Jesus' family (quoted in *Eccl. Hist.* 3:32). The ordinary name of Jesus, for whom all other names were titles (Luke 24:18). Mary of Cleopas in John 19:25 was the 'Miriam' who was betrothed to him, who would be queen if he were the legitimate David. She must have been a very young girl in AD 33, as she would not marry until AD 37 when James was 36, and it was usual to marry a virgin at the age of 17 or 18.

**cloth** (*othonē*). A priestly linen garment, as opposed to a lay one. The bread container of Jesus was wrapped in it when it was placed with him in the cave (John 19:40, using the plural of reproduction) and after his recovery the cloth was seen in the cave (John 20:6, 7), not because he was absent but because he was still present, the bread container attached to his body as was the custom of missionaries. In Acts 10:11 such a garment was let down from the third storey to Peter. It was embroidered with depictions of the 'Living Creatures'. The context shows that it could be used by travelling missionaries as a table-cloth for the holy table. As Philo shows (*Contemp. Life* 38) the Therapeuts wore such a garment in summer.

**cloth** (*sindōn*). A linen garment, worn by a layman or one reduced to the laity (Mark 14:51), and used also to enfold his bread container. In Mark 15:45–6, the rule for participles and the rule of the last referent mean that Pilate 'bought' such a garment (the word used without article), having paid his fee for promotion to the ministry, and that he told James to wear one (the word used with article) when he went to the tomb, an unclean place. 'Wrap' (*eneileō*, Mark 15:46) means to place the garment on a person. In Luke 23:53 the same rules mean that James enfolded (*entylissō*) the bread container of Jesus in the lay garment (also in Matt 27:59). But the container was also 'bound' by another person in a priestly garment (*othonē*) (John 19:40). See **cloth.**

**coals, fire of** (*anthrakia*). The cooking fire lit at 4 am in the furnace in the north part of the Qumran vestry, probably for the sacred loaves, and at Mazin (John 18:18, 21:9).

**cock** (*alektōr*). A name for Merari, the levitical deacon, whose many duties including signalling the time, and especially the 3 am and 4 am cockcrowings which aroused ascetics from sleep. Bird emblems were used by Sadducees, the 'dove' by their 'Kohath' (Luke 3:22), the raven by their 'Gershon', the Chief Therapeut as Sadducee (Luke 12:24).

**come about** (*ginomai*). An expression used at significant points of time which could be those of the fulfilment of prophecy.

**commandment** (*entolē*). One of the Ten Commandments, part of the ordinary Law (Mark 10:19; John 11:57). New (*kainē*) commandment (John 13:34), the Christian substitute (Mark 12:29–31).

**compassion, have** (*splangchnizomai*). To send down to the level of the 'entrails' (*splangchna*) at row 12 in the body of the Heavenly Man – that is, to send into the 'world', the married state (Mark 6:34, 8:2).

**converse** (*homileō*). Give a homily, a short sermon in the open air (Luke 24:14, 15).

**Corban** (*korban, korbanas*). Shown in Mark 7:11 to mean 'gift', its special meaning was the mendicants' fund of the Therapeuts, who lived in eremitical communities without holding common property. While the more westernized ones acted as teachers and received teaching fees, the eastern ones, the 'lame and blind beggars', accepted gifts as mendicants. This practice was disapproved by village Essenes led by the Sadducee Jonathan Annas (Matt 27:6) and by Peter's pilgrims under his leadership. Peter is shown not giving money to the mendicant in Acts 3:6.

**court** (*aulē*). The 2 uncovered cubits in the north of the vestry were treated as the court, an area outer to the sanctuary where matters such as judgement could be dealt with (Rev 11:1; John 18:15; Mark 14:54).

**cross** (*stauros*). A wooden structure in a T shape, usually used to hold up the tents of visiting pilgrims who camped on the esplanade at Qumran, but suitable in shape for the cross for crucifixion. See Chapter 11 on Joseph the carpenter making the cross. As detail of the pesher indicates, the upright was 7 cubits (10½ feet). Three were used, the central one being that of Simon, the eastern that of Judas, the western that of Jesus. 'The cross', used alone, means the central one, that of Simon (John 19:19, 31). In Mark 8:34, 'let him lift up his cross and follow me' means 'let him be a pilgrim visiting the monastery, erecting the stand for his tent, but adopting my version of the doctrine'. The T shape of the stand happened to be the same as the letter T used by Greek-speaking missionaries to substitute for the Hebrew Taw, a 't' but the last letter in the alphabet, indicating the highest possible grade. After the crucifixion, further significance was given to the T shape, making it a powerful emblem of the new Christian party.

**crowd** (*ochlos*). Antipas, as a married man living in the world, represented the 'crowd', ordinary people not living in a celibate community. In Mark 15:11, 'the Chief Priests stirred up the Crowd' means that Jonathan Annas advised Antipas to pay the bribe for the release of Theudas-Barabbas. 'Much Crowd', *polys ochlos*, means Agrippa as a married man (John 6:2, 5).

**crown** (*stephanos*). A metal headband worn by the Sadducee, giving him the name 'Stephen' (Acts 6:8), or worn by the David, with a star attached (Rev 12:1). An illegitimate in a Sadducee abbey wore a 'crown of thorns', and as it had to be plaited it must have been a rope circlet with a thorn attached, the emblem of Sadducee ascetics (John 19:2).

**crucify** (*stauroō*). The verb is found to mean a preliminary to excommunication, a cursing ceremony beforehand, or afterwards (John 19:41, following the rule that all events are consecutive). See **cross.**

**cup** (*potērion*). A cup holding fermented wine, not new wine, the latter being called 'the mouth' as belonging in the body of the Heavenly Man. The cup of fermented wine was used as the common drink in the early part of the Last Supper (Luke 22:17), and used again for the sacred fermented wine (Luke 22:20). Rev 16:19 shows that shortly before the fall of Jerusalem the cup used in the Herodian Christian service was taken to Rome, in order to transfer the holy table to Rome. It became the origin of the Holy Grail legend. See *JA.*

**curse** (*anathematizō*). To put a person under an anathema, forbidding him to be a fellow-worker in the mission. Peter applied it to James (Mark 14:71; Gal 1:8; 1 Cor 12:3).

**curtain** (*katapetasma*). A priest's garment reproducing the curtain of the sanctuary (Heb 9:3), which was in colours, scarlet, purple and blue (Exod 26:1). The colours were now only worn outside the sanctuary (1QM 7:10–11), by a priest such as Simon Magus. His garment was torn in half when he lost power at 3 pm at the crucifixion, and the action was seen as symbolizing a schism between east and west (Mark 15:38).

**custom** (*synētheia*). A custom rather than a law (John 18:39).

**Cyrene** (*Kyrēnē*). The country north-west of Africa, treated as the south-western point of the world in the plan of mission, and hence the place of exile. Simon Magus became a 'Cyrenian' when about to be crucified (Mark 15:21). In the list of provinces in Acts 2:10 its name is used instead of Rome, as it was the lowest point of the Rome province.


**daily** (*kath hēmeran*). Holding daily prayers and services as celibates in community did, rather than monthly ones, as the visiting village pilgrims did. In Luke 16:19 and Acts 3:2 a 'poor leper' and a 'lame beggar' were laid daily at a gate, waiting for crumbs or gifts. They were actually celibates (Simon Magus and James, the brother of Jesus, respectively), heads of the ascetic classes of the Poor, who took part in daily services, when at the end of the sacred meal fragments were given out, following the practice of Essene support for the indigent. In Luke's version of the Lord's prayer, 'give us our . . . bread daily (*kath hēmeran*)' has the special meaning 'allow us to hold daily eucharistic services in a Christian celibate community'.

**darkness** (*skotia*). Midnight (John 6:17, 20:1). In John 1:5, the person who was the opposite of the 'Light', keeping the Julian calendar beginning the day at midnight, and pro-Roman, as the Romans were the 'Sons of Darkness' in the Scrolls.

**day** (*hēmera*). A feast day, a day with special significance. With a number, a day of the week. 'Two days' means 'Day 2', Monday; 'three days' means 'Day 3', Tuesday, and so on. The word order is significant. If the numeral is placed first, it means the morning start of the day in question, but if the noun is placed first, it means the evening before, as a day began the evening before in normal Jewish practice. Hence *treis hēmerai* means 'Tuesday morning', *hēmerai treis* 'Monday evening'. A further variation arose from different views on when the day started. For villagers it began at 3 am, hence *tesseras . . . hēmeras* in John 11:17 means Wednesday at 3 am. Correspondingly, the previous evening would begin at 3 pm. In the usage of John's gospel, the start of a day was at the Julian midnight, hence the earlier version was at noon the previous day. In John 20:26 *hēmeras oktō* means Saturday at noon, as 'day 8', Sunday, began at midnight Saturday. But with *meta* the phrase means Sunday at noon; see **after**.

**Death** (*thanatos*). A person, the Chief Monk, who was able to give excommunication on his own authority. In Rev 6:8, 'the rider on the green horse whose name is Death' was the then Chief Monk in the Herodian system, Atomus the Magus. In the gospels, Simon Magus (John 11:13, 12:33, 18:32, 21:19; Mark 14:64; Luke 23:22). Meaning a person, the word can be the last referent. See **die** (*apothnēskō*).

**deny** (*arneomai*). To deny that a person was a priest, the opposite of confessing him (confess a high priest, Heb 3:1). Peter did not deny knowing Jesus, only that he could act in the place of a Jewish priest (John 18:25, 27).

**depart** (*hypagō*, lit. 'lead under'). To be at a place for a celibate minister, not a married minister (John 13:33).

**devil** (*diabolos*). A name for the 'Satan', or Chief Examiner in the monastic system, and the military leader of zealots. See **Satan**. Judas Iscariot in the gospel period (John 6:70–1, 13:2; Luke 4:2, 8:12).

**die** (*thnēskō*). This shorter form of the verb 'to die' is used in John 19:33 to say that Jesus had died on the cross. It is found elsewhere: in Acts 14:19, Paul was 'thought to have died', but had not; John 11:44 for Lazarus; Luke 7:12 for the 'son of the Widow of Nain'; Luke 8:49 for Jairus' daughter. These stories of others being raised from the dead may be seen consistently as the lifting of excommunication bans. The use of the verb is, then, an indication that Jesus had not died, but had suffered only a spiritual death

335

like excommunication, had lost his functioning, both physical and in terms of ministry.

**die** (*apothnēskō*). To be reduced to grade 12, that of excommunication, having lost the spiritual 'life' given at initiation (John 11:14). In John 21:23, the statement that a person (John Mark) 'would not die' means that he was not capable of excommunication because he did not have a comparable form of initiation to Jewish monastics, a doctrine found in the gospel of Philip: 'a Gentile cannot die, for he has never lived that he might die' (52:15–16). This was the attitude of Brother James, which Jesus corrected.

**disciple** (*mathētēs*). A Gentile celibate student of a Jewish teacher, sitting in row 10, the 'bosom', when the teacher was in row 7, so in the relation of servant to master (as 2 cubits, an arm's length, had to separate master and servant). It usually means John Mark, in both the singular and plural. In John 13:23 he was in the 'bosom' at the Last Supper. When James Niceta came to be equal to John Mark, the term was used for him, with a qualifying word, as in Luke 9:54, 'the disciples James', or Matt 26:35, 'All the disciples'. The term is also used for James the brother of Jesus when he became teacher and representative of Gentiles after the arrest of Jesus (John 18:25, 19:38).

**doorkeeper** (*thyrōros*, fem.). As shown in the pesher of Rev 22:16–17, a man and his wife in a village house formally opened the door to a visiting priest. They represented the David and the David queen, called 'the Morning Star' and 'the Bride'. At the

Qumran vestry the ceremony was performed for pilgrims each morning at the northern door near the fire, when the David and his queen acted as door-keepers. At the trial of Jesus, Peter as the Chief Pilgrim substituted for Jesus, and Mary Mother, now the Chief Woman since the unmarried James had become the acting David, substituted for Mary Magdalene (John 18:16, 17; Mark 14:66).

**doubt** (*distazō*). The attitude of Peter, who could not make up his mind on the question of circumcision (Gal 2: 11–13). (Matt 14:31, 28:17).

**dream** (*onar*). An appearance of a supreme priest to a layperson (Matt 1:20, 2:12, 13, 19, 22, 27:19).

**dry** (*xēros*). A place where Essene baths were not used was 'dry'. Therapeuts did not use such baths in their village communities, so it was said that an 'unclean spirit', a married Therapeut, went to 'waterless places' (Luke 11:24). The Chief Therapeut was called 'Not Wet' (Rev 11:6). The Rome province was 'dry' (Luke 23:31), giving rise to the meaning of 'spit', sending to Rome. See **spit**. In John 5:3 the four kinds of sick persons at the pool included 'dry'. This reflects a Jordan drama, illustrated in John 5, in which initiates went through 'Jordan', the smaller exclusion pool, and came to the steps beside it, where there was no water, interpreted as the 'dry land' appearing in Jordan when the waters parted (Josh 3:17). It was an intermediate stage, at which initiates could still marry, and had not yet entered the vestry. See also **porch**.

**during** (*dia* + gen). In the middle of. In Acts 1:3, 'through forty days' means day 20 of the forty days' fasting in the quartodecimal year (see *JM*, 'Chronology').


**ear** (*ous, ōtion, ōtarion*). A person who sat at the 'ear' of the Heavenly Man was an adviser to the priest or king, sitting in the place of a bishop on the east or a presbyter on the west. His nameband, worn over his headband, carried a term indicating his office. To 'cut off the ear' was to remove a person's right to the office. When the 'right ear' or the *ōtarion* of Peter was cut off, James was denying him the right to be a bishop in his eastern mission (John 18:10; Mark 14:47), but when the *ōtion* of James was cut off by Peter, without the word 'right', Peter was denying James the right to be a presbyter in his western mission (John 18:26; Matt 26:51).

**Earth** (*gē*). Row 13 in the vestry, where the 'seed' was found. It was the point to which members could be sent down from 'Heaven', the platform for the leaders. See Chapter 2. The 'whole Earth' (*holē gē*) was in the next cubit up, row 12. In Mark 15:33, 'darkness came upon the whole Earth' means that the cover was left over the lower half of the vestry, down to row 12. 'Upon of the Earth' means the west side of the centre of row 13 (Mark 8:6) or its equivalent (Mark 6:47). Since this was also the position where the king stood as first layman, the word could be used as a name for him.

**earthquake** (*seismos*). A name for the Chief Therapeut when he made a change of doctrine, reflecting the political tensions of Alexandrian Jews. See **Pharisees**. The term reflects the earthquake at

Qumran of 31 BC, which led to its use by the Therapeuts in the second stage of occupation. It means Theudas in Matt 27:54, 28:2, his successor Apollos in Acts 16:26.

**eat** (*esthiō*). To eat sacred loaves or unleavened bread, not ordinary food.

**elect one** (*eklektos*). An ordinary celibate. Jesus after he had ceased to be the David in Luke 23:35.

**end** (*telos*). The end of the Last Jubilee. In its South Solar version, on the 31st in March, AD 33 (Matt 26:58; John 13:1). In Luke 18:5, September AD 43, after the two extensions of AD 29, the North Solar version, called 'Woes' in Revelation. See *JA*.

**enemy** (*echthros*). A Roman governor, standing for all Romans. To 'love one's enemies' (Matt 5:43–4) had the special meaning 'admit the leading Roman to the Agape meal, thus showing friendship to Rome'.

**eternity** (*aiōn*). See **aeon**.

**evening** (*opsia*). A fellowship meeting of the Therapeuts, usually at 6 pm (Mark 14:17; John 6:16), but for those who fasted on Friday evenings, the meeting was at noon on Friday (Matt 14:15). The 'evening' was the beginning of the meeting, and food was taken later, so the term is also used for the beginning of the Gentile service on Friday afternoons, at 4 pm (Mark 15:42; Matt 26:20, 27:57).

**evil** (*kakos*). Refers to the doctrine of Simon Magus, the opponent of Agrippa, whose doctrine was called *kalos*, 'good' or 'beautiful'. The noun is used of

339

Simon in Acts 8:22 (John 18:23, 30; Luke 16:25, 23:22; Mark 15:14).

**eyes** (*ophthalmoi*). As with all parts of the body, an object used at the part. A lamp, brought up to the level of the eyes to aid in reading. Used at the podium in row 7, which was that of the eyes of the Heavenly Man. The lamp used on the east was called the 'eye', and that on the west the 'eyes', on the same principle as 'hands' and 'feet'. Since the David was the chief layman he stood on the western side, holding a lamp at the 'eyes', so when he carried the lamp he 'lifted up the eyes' (John 6:5). Similarly a village levite (Luke 18:13). The crown prince could also stand here, and when the shutter of the lamp was opened it was said that 'his eyes were opened'. In John 9 the point of the sixth Sign was that the position was given by Jesus to the second prince, putting him in the place of the crown prince James.


**father** (*patēr*). The name used for the priest in a monastery or abbey who became the adoptive father of an orphan or illegitimate, or who was the authority over a dynastic celibate living inside. Simon the Essene, the 'Gabriel' over Essene monasteries, in Luke 15:11. For the Sadducee version, with a lighter discipline, the Sadducee priest, Jonathan Annas in the gospel period, was the Father. The word for 'father' in Aramaic, *Abba*, gave 'abbot' and 'abbey'. At the foundation of the mission Jews in the Diaspora were given the opportunity to be initiated as 'sons of Abraham', and he (the first head of the mission) and his successors were called the 'Father' of all members, a word that became 'Pope'. Prayers to 'Our Father' were directed to the Sadducee Pope, who was believed to be an incarnation of God.

**father-in-law** (*pentheros*). Annas as the head of a Sadducee abbey, which included women of the Therapeuts in its system. These included the wives of priests, including the wife of Caiaphas, making Annas the spiritual father of his wife and his spiritual father-in-law (John 18:13).

**fear** (*phobeō*, verb, *phobos*, noun). To 'fear' was to keep the Essene celibate rule, obeying the priests. The royal Herod was the supreme head of the monastic system, so was the one feared (John 19:8; Mark 16:8). 'Do not fear' meant to relax the rule, as when leaving for marriage (Luke 1:13), or cease to use the strict rule (Matt 28:5). Brother James, who typified this rule, was called 'the Fear' (John 19:38, 20:19), and the next brother below him 'the Trembling' (Mark 16:8), each illustrating an aspect of the rule, of which Paul frequently spoke in his letters (1 Cor 2:3). 'The Fear of the Jews' means James when he had allied with Antipas at the crucifixion (John 19:38, 20:19). The noun is used as the name of a person, so can be the last referent.

**feast** (*heortē*). Fast, not eating a meal, since the greatest feasts were observed by fasting. It was used for: a) the Day of Atonement (John 7:10, 14); and b) the 31st, the extra day at the end of each season (John 2:23, 5:1, 6:4, 7:2, 13:1), *pro* 24 hours before, the Thursday, 18:28, Mark 15:6. Or the 30th treated as the Great Day (John 12:12, 20; Mark 14:2). The term is used at the time for a meal of the party concerned. In John 5:1 the word used alone indicates the primary 31st at the September equinox; in John 6:4 the addition of 'Passover' shows that it is March.

**feet** (*podes*). An object placed at the feet, the bowl in which the earnings of an Essene village worker were placed, to be shared with the indigent. Used also for the coins given to the indigent, the leader of the 'Poor' who, as a monastic, washed them to remove the pollution of the world before taking them into the holy precincts (John 13:5). A layman in the world carried such a bowl, together with his bread paten for the charity loaf, his 'hands', so had two objects called 'hands' and 'feet' (John 11:44; Luke 24:39).

When Jesus after the crucifixion said, 'Behold my hands and feet' (Luke 24:39) he was simply showing the bread paten and the bowl for money. His feet had not been nailed. In John 20:25 there is no mention of the feet.

**finger** (*daktylos*). A ring. In John 20:25, 27 the 'finger', that is the circular shape of a ring, was to be thrown on the 'type of the nails', the X sign, a circle added to it for use in Thomas' eastern communities.

**fish** (*opsaria*). Cooked fish, brought from Lake Galilee to the Dead Sea, as no fish could be caught in the Dead Sea. Titus was 'Fish 2', as the second in rank of the individual celibate Gentiles in the 'Noah' form of mission. At the common table at Ain Feshkha he sat in the position for sharing loaf 8, and since the numbers also gave grades and prayer times, it meant that he had reached grade 8, and that he prayed at 2 pm, the eighth hour, one hour after Philip who prayed at 1 pm.

**flesh** (*sarx*). A dynast who had left the monastery for marriage came down to the 'flesh', at the level of row 13 (John 1:14). An initiate on the west side of row 13 was 'weak', not strong, only a village initiate, not confirmed and climbed the monastic ladder. In Mark 14:38 'the flesh is weak' means that a married man while he stays in this state may only minister in the outside world, in a different category from a celibate bishop or Aaronite priest, the 'Spirit' who may visit villagers but not live among them.

**follow** (*akoloutheō*). Be a minister for, under the imagery of the 'sheep', the village pilgrims who followed the David from the outer hall into the monastic grounds where they received a higher education (John 10:4).

**for** (*gar*). Like many of the minor grammatical units, the conjunction 'for' is used for a play on letters, Hebrew Gimel-Resh (G-R), meaning a class C celibate (Gimel is the third letter of the Hebrew alphabet), and a man of grade 2, Resh, equal to a Sariel priest. (See *JA* on the Hebrew letters for classes and grades.) A celibate dining in the vestry was in this status. In Mark 16:8, the original version of the gospel ends with this word, against all the rules of grammar, showing that it meant a person, the subject or object of the preceding verb.

**friend** (*philos*). In contrast to the house of Antipas, whose communal meals were like those of the Therapeuts and called Agape feasts, from *agapaō* 'to love', the house of Agrippa held meals for villagers

343

like Peter who were simply called 'Friends'. In John 21:15–17 Peter could only accept the verb 'befriend', not the verb 'love'. To be a 'friend' of Agrippa as Caesar was to be a member of his monarchist party, so Pilate was warned not to be a 'friend of Caesar' in John 19:12. In Luke 23:12 'and' divides the two parts of the sentence, which means that Agrippa affirmed the title of 'friend', in the plural of reproduction, and Pilate did not. But Simon Magus had some Essene villagers on his side, most notably Jesus when in the married state, and Simon 'befriended' Jesus in John 11:3 (rule of the last referent).

**from** (*apo*). A point that is 'from' another, at its opposite extreme, a reproduction of a point in another place. The place 'from' may be some distance from the original. While 'Galilee' meant Ain Feshkha, 'from Galilee' meant the dais step in the Qumran vestry, of the same status (Matt 27:55). 'From (the) God' meant the dais step, row 13, the furthest limit for a priest in the vestry (John 13:3). In John 21:2 'from Cana of Galilee' meant Mazin as the limit and reproduction of 'Cana of Galilee', which was at Ain Feshkha.

**Gabbatha** (*Gabbatha*). Aramaic, a form of the word for 'mountain', *gabhut*, CD 1:15. Used to speak in Hebrew about Rome, and the plan for the zealot Simon Magus to become ruler of Rome, so it means the south base, the 'praetorium', where Simon stood, condemned for planning to overthrow Caesar (John 19:13).

**Galilee** (*Galilaia*). The northern part of the country, where Essene villagers lived. A dynast on leaving the monastery temporarily for marriage lived in Galilee, acting as a bishop to villagers in surrounding centres. Their councils at Qumran were held at Ain Feshkha, which became 'Galilee' when the bishop of Galilee came there for councils. This building was consequently the first place to which the dynast came when he left the monastery (John 1:43, Mark 1:14, John 4:3; in the latter case Jesus arrived at 'Galilee' before he arrived at 'Samaria', contrary to the geography of the literal places). More exactly, 'Galilee' was on the dais step at Ain Feshkha, from which entry was made into the higher parts of the room, so it acted as a porch. It is of interest that the word 'Galilee' was retained in Christian usage to mean the porch of a church.

**garden** (*kēpos*). The name for an 'Eden', the school for pilgrims when extended to include Gentiles such as John Mark, taught by David as 'Adam'. There was a 'garden' wherever Gentiles could say prayers: in the outer hall (John 18:1); at the south base (John 18:26, with article as the primary location); in the western cave, a place for 'uncleanness', including Gentiles (John 19:41). The latter place and its equivalents were called 'Paradise', using the pagan term (Luke 23:43; Rev 2:7).

**garment** (*himation*). The white linen vestment worn by a dynastic celibate, in a circular shape, divided by the X, so that the two side segments formed sleeves. It was the origin of the Christian surplice. It was used by missionaries to represent the map of the world (see Chapter 2). The plural of reproduction means the same garment. At the defrocking ceremony the garment was taken away and divided into its four segments, standing for the four parts of the world (John 19:23).

**glory** (*doxa*). The position at the centre of row 7, on which the 'Sun', the supreme priest, shone down, and from which teaching took place, to give enlightenment. See Chapter 2. Found on both the upper platform (John 1:14) at Ain Feshkha and the ground floor at Qumran (John 13:31). The verb means 'to cause to sit in row 7, as a teacher'. Both the Priest and the King may sit here (John 13:31).

**'God'** (*theos*). A Sadducee priest, leader of the ascetic Sadducee faction in the mission. In Acts 7:2, Ananel. In Acts 7:7, Matthias. In Acts 7:32, Ananus the Elder. In the gospel period, Jonathan Annas. In Acts 7:56, Theophilus Annas. In Luke 18:11, 13; Acts 12:23, Matthew Annas. Without article, the word may mean another person, a servant of the priest, who acts himself as a priest (John 1:1, 19:7).

**good** (*kalos*). The word means both 'beautiful' and 'good', but in the pesher is always used in the same sense. It refers to the priestly colours, scarlet and purple, worn in the outside world. (Ezek 44:19, priests change into street clothes; 1QM 7:10–11, the three colours scarlet, purple and blue, are used in the battlefield, not the sanctuary.) Jesus as the 'Lamb' wore scarlet, as did Phanuel when outside. Mark 14:21 the David wore colours when representing Herod, but white when acting as a priest in his own right.

**great** (*megas*), **greater** (*meizōn*). The Great One was the King, the third of the leading triarchy, a name used for him in Sentence 2 of the Copper Scroll ('the Great One the third'). In the original organization he was 'Jacob', the patriarch of Ephesus. Hence his son 'Joseph' was the Little One, *mikros* (Mark 15:40, James as the crown prince, also called Joseph of Arimathea). The 'Greater One' was a grade above 'the Great One', so was the 'Isaac', patriarch of the east. This title was used of himself by Agrippa (Luke 22:24; John 19:11).

**ground** (*chamai*). See **clay**.


**hand** (*cheir*). An object held in the hand. The word is used for the bread paten held in the hand, to receive the two halves of the charity loaf 13. The hands of the Heavenly Man came to row 13, where the charity loaf was placed. The eastern half given by the levite was placed in the 'hand', using the singular form, while the western half given by the Son of Man was placed in the 'hands', using the plural of reproduction. Jesus' bread paten was consequently called the 'hands'. This word was used in the surface meaning, apparently to refer to his damaged hands after the crucifixion, but actually to the bread paten which he could no longer hold (Luke 24:39). A missionary carried a paten with him, to use to give the charity loaf to outsiders, including Gentiles (John 11:44). When Pilate was admitted to the vestry as a minister (see **opposite**, *apenanti*) he was given a bread paten which he purified with water as a minister did, so 'washed his hands' (Matt

347

27:24). If the actual right hand was meant, the word *dexia* was used (Rev 1:17). Thomas, using the eastern X sign, had the X marked on the paten he used in the west, and this was forbidden by Jesus in the pesher of John 20:25. The rule used by Theudas put the 'hand', the levitical bread paten, on the west side of the high table, *epi tēs trapezēs*, with the drink on the east side, because hands could be crossed at the shoulders (Luke 22:21).

**he** (*autos*). In other cases than the nominative, this pronoun refers back to the previous referent, but in the nominative it is a new subject, meaning a member of the hierarchy.

**head** (*kephalē*). A married man at grade 12 wore a headband only over his hair, not over a cloth as celibates did (Mark 14:3; John 13:9). It was a basic sign of membership, given at the age of eighteen, and always worn, other head circlets or coverings being put over it. An excommunicant sent down to grade 12 wore the headband as a sign of his disgrace. It was John the Baptist's headband that was brought on the plate in Mark 6:27. Jesus on the cross did not wear the 'crown of thorns', which had been taken from him, but only his headband, which was lowered when his head sank down (John 19:30). As Mark 15:29 shows in the phrase 'move the head(s)', its height could be adjusted, a Jewish nationalist wearing it on the forehead in order to carry his phylactery, which had to be worn between the eyebrows. The height was used to mark the length of the hair. When during his marriage or before it a man had been under a Nazirite vow and let his hair grow long, he 'shaved the head' at the resumption of the

348

marriage, bringing his hair up to the line of the head-band (Acts 21:24).

**headcloth** (*soudarion*). The headcloth of a Magian monastic, which he wore when in the village or in the Diaspora, still in membership, but substituting this 'unclean' cloth for his priestly head covering (John 11:44). It could consequently be used for 'unclean' purposes, such as wrapping money (Luke 19:20; John 20:7).

**heart** (*kardia*). The position on the west centre of row 10, the 'heart' in the diagram of the Heavenly Man. See Chapter 2. In John 13:2 Judas Iscariot came there briefly as the elder-levite inaugurating the meal at the common table. In the same place the Chief Woman, the Beloved, sat at the common meal, so it was her 'heart' (Luke 2:19).

**heaven** (*ouranos*). A person, Agrippa as supreme head of the mission, occupying the place of 'God', the priest, on the platform, but not using the title 'God'. Agrippa in Mark 6:41; Luke 10:18, 18:13. Since Merari acted with the authority of Agrippa he used his titles. 'Heaven' means Merari in Matt 28:2; John 17:1. In the plural of reproduction, 'Heavens' means the Sadducee priest acting in an equal position to Agrippa (Luke 10:20; Matt 3:1).

**heavy, be** (*bareomai*). The 'eyes', an oil lamp with markings to show the time, became 'heavy' every two hours, when new oil was put in, 9 pm, 11 pm, 1 am. Hence it gives a time. 11 pm in Mark 14:40. 1 am in Luke 9:32.

**hence** (*enteuthen*). The north pillar base, when a zealot teacher used it (John 18:36). In John 14:31,

349

those who had been in the vestry went outside, first reaching the pillar bases. In Rev 22:3, the north base is called *enteuthen* and the south base *ekeithen*. Hence in John 19:18, *enteuthen kai enteuthen*, Simon and Judas as levitical occupied two of the crosses, centre and east, at the level of the north base on a zero row, while Jesus in the *mesos* was at the level of the row below a zero, called 'middle', so was the lowest in rank, put on the layman's cross on the west.

**Herod** (*Hērōdēs*). Agrippa, the potential Herod who would restore the monarchy, who was in Judea during the gospel period (Luke 23:7, 8). In Mark 6:14–22 'Herod' is not the tetrarch Antipas, as appears on the surface, but Agrippa, who changed his policy in September AD 31 and turned against the Baptist. In this passage Antipas is 'the king', meaning simply a graduate of the schools (Mark 6:22, 25, 26, 27). In Luke 3:1 Antipas is called 'the tetrarch Herod', the added word showing the difference.

**high priest** (*archiereus*). See **chief priest**.

**hill** (*buonos*). Like 'Mountain', this word and its plural of reproduction means the head of an institution and the place where he stands. The context of Luke 23:30–31, which is a 'prophecy' of events in AD 50 when the Rome province separated, shows that it means the Gentile monastery in Corinth, where Jesus was 'hidden' during the years AD 50–58. There may be an allusion to the striking hill rising from the plain beside the city of Corinth. The superior at that time was Titus (Acts 18:7). He had succeeded to the position of John Mark, who did not have a monastery in the Rome province. John Mark becomes the 'Hills' as referent of the verb in v. 32.

**himself** (*heautos*). Simon Magus, called 'Himself' as claiming to be an independent superior of monasteries rivalling Herod. In Mark 8:34, 'let him deny Himself' means to deny Simon Magus and his party. John 13:4: 'he (Jesus) girded Himself', Jesus put the sash around Simon's waist. John 21:1: 'Jesus revealed himself', brought Simon Magus to Mazin. Luke 18:11, 14 refer to Simon Magus as Himself at the time of the schism of AD 43–44.

**hope** (*elpizō*). To expect a successor to a royal line. In Luke 23:8, Jesus is the subject by the rule of the last referent, and he tells Agrippa that Mary Magdalene is pregnant. In Luke 24:21 it refers to the hope that Agrippa will become the successor to the Herodian monarchy.

**hour** (*hōra*). The hour for fulfilment of the prophecy, at the time held by the different parties. With article, on the hour (Mark 14:41), without article, at five minutes to the hour (John 4:6, 19:14) or five minutes past (Mark 15:25).

**hundred and fifty-three** (*hekaton pentēkonta treis*). The numbers of 'fish caught' in John 21:11 have great significance, as do all numbers. They indicate the structure of a Gentile monastery, based on the Essene system. Christian monasteries up to medieval times had 150 members. As the letters for grades show (see *JM* and *JA*), an Essene monastery held six classes of 25 each, two of novices, giving 50 (the Hebrew letter Nun for the higher novice grade was used for the number 50), and four of undergraduates, giving 100 (reaching the letter Qof, meaning 'eye of a needle', with the numerical value of 100). A graduate was a superior, and could be a grade 3, a Phanuel.

**I** (*egō*). When used in narrative, on the same principle as 'we' and 'you', this means Luke, before he became the eunuch 'we'. John 21:25, Acts 1:1, 4: accounting for the ungrammatical introduction of a 2nd person (James Niceta) and a 1st person (Luke) into a 3rd person narrative.

**if** (*ei*). This word is used to indicate a question, as punctuation cannot be used.

**if not** (*ei mē*). Translated literally, but normally meaning 'unless', 'except'. Its special meaning is 'and also', from the sense 'A if not B', meaning 'A and also B'.

**immediately** (*euthys*). The actual beginning of the hour or half-hour's session, at five minutes past after the preparations. Used in John 13:30 to mean 9.05 pm, and in John 19:34 for 3.35 pm, when a test for death a few minutes after Jesus lost consciousness at 3.30 showed that he was still alive.

**immediately** (*parachrēma*). Used by Luke as an equivalent of *eutheōs*, for five minutes past the hour (Luke 22:60).

**increase** (*auxanō*). Arrive at twenty, the age of sexual maturity (Luke 2:40, Jesus in AD 14; Acts 19:20, Jesus Justus in AD 57). Or have a son (Acts 6:7, 12:24 for Jesus; Acts 7:17 for Joseph at the birth of James).

**indeed** (*men*). A particle, which in the fashion of most minor grammatical units, is used as a play on the letters M and N, meaning Hebrew Mem and Nun, the letters for grades 9 and 8 in the educational system, below the grade of initiation, 7. It indicates that the subject is acting at a low grade.

**in order that** (*hina*). The word indicates consequence, not purpose as in normal use, and is used additionally as a play on 'the N' in Hebrew, referring to an action by the Therapeuts who were associated with this letter and its numerical meaning of 50, governing their pentecontad feasts.

**Israel** (*Israēl*). Used to mean the third class of members in the Qumran organization, the 'sons of Israel' (CD 14:4–5), including proselytes who were admitted to this class. Hence it refers to a teacher of proselytes. The 'king of Israel' means Judas representing Agrippa in Matt 27:42 and Mark 15:32, Agrippa in John 12:13 and Luke 24:21.


**Jerusalem** (*Ierousalēm*, sing. form, *Hierosolyma*, plu. form). In the singular form the Essene gate on the south flank of the literal Jerusalem, the place to which Essenes had at first retreated when they were expelled from the temple. The same word is used for the Mount of Olives building, counted as a one to the zero of the Essene Gate (Luke 13:34, the word used twice, indicating two places; Luke 24:13).

In the plural, Qumran, to which Essenes had subsequently been expelled. It was conceived as a 'New Jerusalem', and the names of places in the literal Jerusalem applied to it.

More precisely, 'Jerusalem' (plu.) was in the entry gate through which outsiders to Qumran came, the back gate beside the south vestry (see Figure 4). This spot is described in John 5:2, the row which also contained the pool and 'porch 5', the small pool and the steps beside it leading to the larger exclusion pool. In John 11:55 Agrippa was there, performing a purification rite for Antipas in the 'dry' pool, the steps. See **pool** and **dry**. Agrippa also stood there in Luke 22:7, in the role of king in the gate of the city.

**Jews** (*Ioudaioi*). The special sense of 'the Jew' was one who had become a Jew, by being circumcised and living just like ordinary Jews, including in the married state. The Herods had done this, being previously Idumeans. In the plural of reproduction the term means Antipas the tetrarch, a Herod who was a married man. The term is found frequently in John's gospel, in a negative sense, less often in the Synoptics. This was because of the preference for celibacy of the Johannine books, marriage standing for 'the world' which they must not have communion with. Antipas was called 'the Jews' when he acted in outer parts as a man of the world, and by other terms when he took his place as a guest in the vestry. In Acts 18:1 'a certain Jew', without article, means John Aquila, who was not circumcised but a servant of the married Herod, so the form without article meaning a servant was used.

**John** (*Iōannēs*). The name 'John', meaning 'Grace', originally meant a person in grade 11 at the level of a Gentile who did not pay fees, so was 'free', 'saved by grace'. It was used of the Gentile leaders John Mark (although only after his rejection in AD 44,

Acts 12:12) and John Aquila. Applied to John the Baptist, it was a derogatory term, meaning that he was an outsider, a Gentile, or a boy (Luke 1:60), so is not used of him as the Teacher of Righteousness in the Scrolls. His successor Simon Magus, however (said to be a successor in *Clem. Hom.* 2:24), took the title John (II) because with Jesus he accepted uncircumcised Gentiles. 'John' means Simon Magus as Pope in John 10:40, 41; Acts 4:6.

**Joseph** (*Jōsēph*). The title of the David crown prince, as son and successor of 'Jacob', the title of David when acting as the patriarch of the west. It was used for Joseph the father of Jesus while still crown prince (Luke 1:27), and James as the crown prince to Jesus before his own son was born. James was called 'Joseph of Arimathea' (John 19:38), and 'Joseph Barsabbas Justus' (Acts 1:23). The next son was also called 'Joseph' (Joses) when he acted as deputy to his older brother (Mark 6:3), and when he was appointed crown prince by Jesus instead of James (Acts 4:36, Joseph Barnabas). This point accounts for the association of Joseph of Arimathea with British Christianity, for the far western part of the mission field, including Rome and Britain, was assigned in the original Herodian plan to the 'Joseph', the subordinate of the 'Jacob' who was the patriarch of Ephesus in the near west.

**joy** (*chara*). A name used for the wife of a dynast. The wife of John the Baptist in John 3:29. Mary Magdalene the wife of Jesus in Luke 10:17. When the David queen became a mother, she was called 'Great Joy', either at the birth (Matt 2:10; Luke 2:10) or when she was three months pregnant

355

(Matt 28:8; Luke 24:52) or later in her life (Acts 15:3).

**judgement** (*krima*). A name for a person, the one who would be leader at the Last Judgement. Simon Magus in Luke 23:40, 24:20.

**judgement seat** (*bēma*). The name for the south pillar base, used as the punishment stand for the school (see pp. 47–8) (Matt 27:19; John 19:13).

**Justus** (*Ioustos*). Latin for 'righteous'. A title of the David crown prince. Joseph is called a 'righteous man', *dikaios*, in Matt 1:19. James (publicly called James the Just) in Acts 1:23. In Col 4:11, Jesus Justus, the son of Jesus. Also in Acts 18:7, where Jesus Justus used the name of his teacher Titus, as was usual. In Eusebius' *Ecclesiastical History* (3,39, 9–12) the tradition is recorded that the daughters of Philip had spoken of a man called 'Justus surnamed Barsabbas' who 'drank poison but by the Lord's grace suffered no harm'. The story actually concerns Jesus, the true record preserved by the order of nuns whose leaders were present at the 'resurrection' (Acts 21:9, 'daughter 4' of Philip was the chief nun). 'Justus' and 'Barsabbas' were both titles of the David brothers (Acts 1:23 used for James, Acts 15:22 for Jude). But Eusebius, writing about AD 300, no longer knew the meanings of the names, and rejected the doctrine of Papias who had transmitted the tradition, condemning him for his belief that 'there will be a millennium after the resurrection of the dead, when the kingdom of Christ will be set up in material form on this earth'.

**kill** (*apokteinō*). To send down to the lowest grade 12, either into excommunication, spiritual death, leading sometimes to physical death, or to the grade of marriage, regarded as a temporary equivalent of excommunication (Mark 10:34; Luke 18:33; John 18:31).

**king** (*basileus*). A graduate of a school like those of the Therapeuts, including the school headed by Antipas. Their doctrine was non-monastic, allowing marriage. On graduation a man received a 'crown', a special headdress, and was said to be like a king. He was now qualified to teach, although he was still a layman, not admitted to the sanctuary. As a teacher he received payment, of a denarius a day (Matt 20:10), so when Pilate was made an honorary graduate it gave him the legal right to receive mission income (John 18:33 by the rule of the last referent). He wore a sign indicating his qualification to teach (possibly the Hebrew letter Qof, given at graduation) on a band worn over his headband (Matt 27:37).

Jesus and Simon Magus as members of Antipas' house and school on the Tiber Island in Rome were both called 'king of the Jews', as 'the Jews' was a title for Antipas (Jesus in Mark 15:2, 9; Simon in Luke 23:3; Mark 15:12). When the Magians applied this title to Jesus at birth (Matt 2:2) it meant that he was the legitimate David, who would become the chief layman, hence one of these teachers. But Jesus had acted independently of Simon's zealotry, espousing peace principles, and at his trials doubt was expressed as to whether the title should be used of him.

In John 19:21, a distinction is made between 'a

king of the Jews', a title that was correct for Jesus, and 'the king of the Jews', which was said not to be correct. The meaning was that Jesus in some capacities, when in the married state 'in the body' (*sōmatikō*, Luke 3:22), was only a deacon, the servant of such a teacher. Hence the word should be used without the definite article for him, as its omission indicated being 'in the body'. Pilate, whose duty was to write the name in three languages, said in response to the objection, 'The things I have written, I have written'. A repeated word means that it happened twice, but Pilate should have written three times. A piece of special knowledge about Hebrew grammar is needed: the language cannot distinguish between 'a king of the Jews' and 'the king of the Jews', as there can be no article with the first word in a construct expression. Pilate, not knowing Hebrew, was unable to convey this point. This is one of the many plays on language intended for the pesharist.

**kingdom** (*basileia*). A school, like that of the Therapeuts, bringing men to graduation. See **king**. 'The kingdom of God' was such a school under a Sadducee priest. It became an abbey, combining a monastic type of organization with the more open attitudes of the Therapeuts (Mark 14:25). The aim of the mission was to establish a chain of such schools throughout the Diaspora, to educate Jews and Gentiles in the doctrines, bringing them to both initiation and graduation. The 'Kingdom of Heaven' (sing.) was the form in which Sadducees allied with the royal Herods, Agrippa being called 'Heaven'. The 'Kingdom of the Heavens' was the same system under the Sadducee priest, representing Agrippa but acting as the superior.

**kiss** (*philēma*). The form of greeting given to Gentiles, equal to women, using the marriage imagery. In Mark 14:45 (the verb), the kiss was given by Judas to indicate that Jesus was equal to a Gentile. The Gospel of Philip (59:1–5) shows that it was used by Gentile permanent celibates, sublimating sex with marriage imagery.

**knees** (*gonata*). An object used at the knees, a portable prayer-stool for kneeling (Luke 22:41; Acts 9:40).

**know** (*eidon*). To recognize a person as a member, or to approve a practice or point of view. Used frequently to indicate political differences and alliances.

**know** (*ginōskō*, noun *gnōsis*). To have elementary knowledge, of the kind given to pilgrims visiting the monastery. 'One Having Knowledge', gnōstos. The word was used for monastic servants – for example, in their function of lighting the fire. With the article, the word means Brother James (John 18:16 (sing.); Luke 23:49 (plu.)). Without the article, John Mark his co-firelighter in John 18:15. These 'servants' developed as Christian celibates, giving the word 'gnostic'.

**lame** (*chōlos.*) See **blind**.

**law** (*nomos*). The Law of Moses, considered to be lesser knowledge by monastic celibates, but the basic law for ordinary members. It was observed by the Therapeuts, whose leader used the title 'Moses'. Those first joining the community promised to 'return to the Law of Moses' (CD 15:9–10). In John 18:31, 19:7 it refers to the ordinary Mosaic law as known to Antipas, under which the zealots should be tried for murder.

**legs** (*skelē*). An object placed at the beginning of the legs above the feet, the ankles, so an ankle-chain. All three crucified men wore ankle-chains, and when it was decided to break the legs of Simon and Judas to prevent them escaping from the dungeon, the chain was pulled together from behind, thus breaking their ankles, then snapped. As Jesus was thought to be dead, his ankle-chain was simply removed. In Acts 3:7, *sphydra*, 'ankles', means the ankle-strap of sandals, not the ankle-chain of a prisoner.

**leper** (*lepros*). A man who was reduced to row 13, given the social status of a leper. According to the Temple Scroll (11QT 45:7–18) a leper was one of those who would not be admitted into sacred precincts. Simon Magus, as the rival Pope, the leader of the anti-monarchists, was frequently reduced to the status of leper when his party was in opposition. At the Last Supper he was in disgrace after the failed uprising, and was not permitted to sit at the table. On row 13 he 'washed the feet' (as 'Himself', by the rule of the last referent for John 13:4–5), cleansing the bowls for shared property.

**levite** (*leuitēs*). Originally, a man born into a levitical tribe, doing inferior work to that of an Aaronite priest. In the Scrolls, the second class of members

(CD 14:4–5). But when Jesus claimed to be fully equal to an Aaronite priest, his crown prince accepting this doctrine, Joses-Barnabas, was called 'levite' (Acts 4:36). In Luke 10:32 Theudas was the levite who 'passed by on the other side'. He also had begun as a layman, but when as the Prodigal Son he was given the 'first stole', the robe of a priest, he became an honorary levite (Luke 15:22).

**lifeless** (*nekros*) ('dead', but may be translated 'lifeless' to distinguish from *thanatos*). A married man at grade 11 and grade 12 was spiritually 'dead', from a monastic point of view. Nekros is used for grade 11, *thanatos* for grade 12. In the singular it refers to the David crown prince, who was head of all outside orders. Normally a Nazirite at grade 8, he also represented married men 'in the body' at grade 11. The word means James in Luke 7:15. In the plural of reproduction it means Antipas and his later successors as the head of the class of married men.

**Light** (*phōs*). The supreme priest, the Pope. John the Baptist, the 'Michael', calling himself the Light in 1QH 7:24, using the Menorah as his emblem. In John 1:6–8 it is shown that when John the Baptist stepped down from his position in order to enter the married state he was replaced by his deputy Jonathan Annas, who now became the 'Light' (v. 6) and 'the true Light' (v. 9). John was no longer the Light but only a subordinate bishop (v. 8).

Jesus, claiming to be a priest to Gentiles in the Diaspora, used the title 'the Light of the world' (John 8:12, 9:5; Acts 12:7). This was a higher title than that of 'Morning Star', applied to the Davids in the role of leaders of village and Diaspora communities.

When Agrippa was in the ascendant as supreme head of the community, the title 'the Light' referred to him (Mark 14:54; Luke 22:56). The word is used as the name of a person, so may be the last referent (Luke 22:56).

**lightning** (*astrapē*). The pseudonym of Simon Magus as Pope, in the group also containing 'Thunder' (the Annas priest when with Simon), and 'Earthquake', the Chief Therapeut. In Luke 10:18 it means Simon at the time of his deposition in December AD 32; in Matt 28:3, at the time of his restoration.

**linen cloth** (*sindōn, othonē*). See **cloth**.

**lo** (*ide*). The counterpart of *idou*, 'behold', indicating a person standing on the south base (John 19:4, 14).

**look** (*emblepō*). Be in the next cubit, so look closely at (Mark 14:67; Luke 22:61).

**lord** (*kyrios*). A superior and teacher of Gentiles and of women, drawing on the marriage imagery, in which the superior was the 'husband' in an initiation ceremony. Jesus in John 11:2, 21, 20:13, 18, 20, Simon Magus in John 11:3, 13:6, 20:2, Jonathan Annas in Mark 12:29–30. The corresponding verb means 'to teach Gentiles' (Luke 22:25).

**love** (*agapaō*). Admit to the Agape meal, originally the fellowship meals of Therapeuts at which women were present. In John 11:5 'Jesus loved Martha' means that he shared his meal with her and others. It was extended to include celibate Gentiles in the place of women, who were then called Beloved (*agapētos*). The word thus came to mean a meal of

Gentile monastics such as John Mark. When the verb *phileō* was used ('befriend') it meant a village meal of the married, of the kind Peter attended, hence the distinctions in John 21:15–17, where Peter was asked whether he 'loved' Jesus, using *agapaō*, but could only reply with the verb *phileō*, meaning that he did not attend a celibate's Agape meal but only the common fellowship meal of a married man. This point is obscured in the English translation, which uses 'love' for both verbs.

**maid** (*paidiskē*). The woman who was officially the 'Virgin' in the hierarchy of women (Virgin, Widow, Sister, Wife). Mary Mother as Chief Woman occupied this position, and was at the same time a Widow, so occupied two places at the door near Peter in the story of the denials (Mark 14:66, 69).

**make** (*poieō*). The common word 'to make, to do' is used in the precise sense of 'to perform a ceremony, to officiate as a minister at a service'.

**Malchus** (*Malchos*). The Latin (Malchus) form of Hebrew *melek*, 'king', a name for James as the acting David once Jesus was under arrest (John 18:10).

**malefactor** (*kakourgos*). A person in the party of Simon Magus, whose doctrine was called *kakos*, 'evil'. Judas in Luke 23:33. 'Malefactors Two', Theudas in Luke 23:32.

**Man** (*anthrōpos*). An 'Adam' (meaning 'man'), one who was appointed to teach Gentiles in their 'Eden', at the pillar bases and corresponding places. This was a position to which the heir of David had been appointed at the outset of the mission. When Jesus stood on the base and said 'Behold the Man!' he was claiming that he was the legitimate David (he said the words himself, by the rule of the last referent). 'This Man' means Jesus as lay only, unable to act as priest to Gentiles (John 18:27, 29). The title was also used for a man teaching Gentiles on David's behalf (Mark 3:5; John 4:50, 9:24). In John 1:9 Jesus was for a brief time 'Every (all, *pas*) Man coming into the world', since Agrippa when with Sadducees accepted him as the David, but the relationship was soon broken. In the plural of representation, 'the Men' means Agrippa claiming to be an alternative New Adam to Gentiles.

**many** (*polloi*). A name for Agrippa as the head of the Many, the governing body of celibates in the Scrolls (1QS 6:8). Agrippa in John 2:23. The members of the Many were celibate graduates, of levitical rather than lay status, equal to a Phanuel, who was number 3 in the hierarchy. Hence 'Many Days' (*polloi hēmerai*) means Tuesday, Day 3, and it indicates the Day position of the calendar when the 31st fell on Tuesday. In John 2:12, 'not Many Days' means 'not Tuesday, but Friday the 31st'. In Acts 1:4 'not after Many Days' means not Wednesday the 1st, the day after Tuesday, but Saturday the 1st, the day after Friday, the date when Pentecost began according to this calendar. In Acts 16:18, 'upon Many Days' means 'on Tuesday'.

A man at the level of levitical graduate could also act as a levite servant of Michael on the holy day Saturday, the zero day, and the term in Matt 14:24 means a zero. See **stadion**. In Matt 27:52

with 'bodies', it refers to James as a servant of Agrippa.

**Mary** (*Maria*). The Greek equivalent of 'Miriam', the name of the sister of Moses (Exod 15:20). As Philo shows (*Contemp. Life* 87), the chief woman of the Therapeuts played the part of Miriam in an Exodus liturgy enacting the crossing of the Red Sea, a choir of men led by a 'Moses' singing the Song of Moses, and a choir of women singing the Song of Miriam (Exod 15). The position of Miriam was that of the David queen mother or queen. This meant that because of the doubt about Jesus' legitimacy there were three Marys in his time: his mother Mary, who was queen mother and acting queen with the crown prince; Mary Magdalene his wife; and Mary the betrothed of James, called Mary of Cleopas (John 19:25). In Mark 15:40 Mary of Cleopas is called 'Mary of James the Little One', and Mary Mother the 'mother of Joses' (allied with Joses-Barnabas as crown prince). In Mark 16:1 Mary Mother is called 'Mary of James' (not 'the Little One') as James was now crown prince only.

**meet** (*hypantaō*). Be at the meeting place for pilgrims, either the pillar bases (John 11:20) or their equivalent at the queen's house (Matt 28:9; John 12:13, the noun).

**midst** (*mesos*). Middle, the intermediate row 7, or 13, where a deputy stood. Jesus as the lay leader stood in this position, below a priest (Luke 22:27; Rev 1:13), so this word was used in John 19:18, in the description of the crosses, to mean that Jesus was the layman to Simon and Judas, both *enteuthen* – that is, belonging at the north pillar base on a zero row. Hence Jesus as the layman was on the third cross. Its apparent meaning was that he was on the central cross.

**mock** (*empaizō*). To reduce to the status of a 'child' (*pais*), a pre-initiate. In the area of the pillar bases, to send to the punishment stand, to which a schoolboy was sent (Mark 15:20; Luke 23:11).

**morning** (*prōi*). 6 am (Mark 15:1; John 18:28). *Lian prōi* 'exceedingly morning', 3 am, the time when villagers rose for the day's work (Mark 16:2). *prōi skotias*, 'morning of darkness', John 20:1, midnight, as the Julian start of day.

**morsel** (*psōmion*). The coin symbolizing the property of Jesus, handed over when he re-entered coenobitic life. It had to be cleansed in water, as it came from the unclean outside world. Jesus handed it to Judas, who was monastic treasurer (John 13:26).

**Moses** (*Mōüsēs*). The pseudonym of an Essene priest who predicted the future as the Prophet (Acts 7:20, Simon the Essene) or of the Chief Therapeut in the same role, and acting as 'Moses' in the Exodus liturgy (Mark 9:4; Luke 24:27, 44).

**mother-in-law** (*penthera*). The Chief Widow, a female minister, who was Mother Superior of all women in the ascetic orders, including the wives of married missionaries. Mary the mother of Jesus was the Chief Widow, and so was the 'mother-in-law' of Peter, a married man (Mark 1:30).

**mountain** (*oros*). The 'Mountain' was a name for the Sadducee priest when he was acting in an outside building reproducing Ain Feshkha, under the discipline of the Therapeuts, where the high table for meals was on the platform. The place where he stood was a 'Mount Sinai', from which the Law was given (John 6:3, 15). In the plural of reproduction it was used of the Sadducee who was head of hermitages in the Rome province, specifically Matthew Annas from AD 50. This is its meaning in Luke 23:30, which contains a 'prophecy' of the events of AD 50, recorded in Acts 16–18, when the Roman province separated (Acts 18:8; 1 Cor 1:14).

**mouth** (*stoma*). An object used at the mouth. The cup for new wine, brought to the mouth, covered, so it can be 'opened'. The cup for fermented wine was called 'the cup'. For some ascetics, a cup of new wine could be placed at the common table in row 11 and, since the 'heart' was on the west side of row 10, the row below it was the 'overflow of the heart' (where the leftover fragments of bread were placed) and the cup/'mouth' was 'out of' it, giving rise to the saying, 'Out of an overflow of a heart the mouth speaks' (Luke 6:45). At the crucifixion, the poisoned wine was brought to 'the mouth' of Jesus, meaning that it was put in the cup (John 19:29; Mark 15:36), then the cup was attached to a 2-cubit reed and brought to the literal mouth of Jesus.

**name** (*onoma*). The David, who gave the new name at baptism (Matt 28:19). Used for Jesus in Mark 14:32.

**nation** (*ethnos*). The word for 'Gentile', since in Hebrew *goiim* means both 'nations' and 'Gentiles'.

In the singular, John Mark (John 11:48, 52, 18:35; Luke 23:2). In the plural, Agrippa as 'Noah' the father of all nations/Gentiles (Luke 18:32; Mark 10:33; Luke 22:25; Acts 10:45).

**Nazirite** (*Nazōraios, Nazarēnos*). Both terms refer to the discipline of a man who was married but spent periods of a season away from his family for the purpose of spiritual retreat. A dynast outside the monastery, as Jesus was in the gospel period, was under this discipline, his meetings with his wife being limited to short periods only. The centre for the order was in Nazareth of Galilee, and at the times between councils Jesus would have come to this place. But their main council centre was in the Wilderness of Judea. The form *Nazōraios* ('Nazorean') was used for men attached to a monastery or abbey, but living outside it, while the form *Nazarēnos* ('Nazirite') was used for a man attached to a community of Therapeuts. In the latter case he used retreat caves along the route from Mar Saba to Mird where the Therapeuts lived as hermits. See *JM*, 'Locations'. The detail shows that their retreats were counted in periods of days, normally 90 days for the season, but 100 for the season from the June solstice to Atonement (on the 10th of the 7th month), consequently 80 from Atonement to the December solstice, and they were called by these numbers, so that 'sheep 100' was the chief Nazirite, and a '90' (with a man at grade 9) was in the 'wilderness', at Mird (Luke 15:4).

**near** (*engys*). Two times that were side by side in two different calendars, falling on the same date, were said to be 'near' (John 6:4, 11:55). Consequently two places having the same status were 'near' – the pillar bases at Qumran and Ain Feshkha (John 11:18).

**neither** (*oude*). A play on 'not (*ou*) D', the letter for the fourth class of members, the married. A 'Not-D' was a 'C', a member of the third class, celibates. The four classes were: A, priests; B, levites; C (Gimel in Hebrew, a 'g') celibates; D, the married. 'Neither' alone is not a negative but a positive (Mark 14:59).

**new** (*kainos*). Used for the Christian version of the New Covenant (Mark 14:25).

**next day** (*epaurion*). The beginning of a quarto-decimal intercalation, on the 31st, in its different versions, and in different years according to different parties. See *JM*, 'Chronology'. In Matt 27:62, Friday, 20 March, AD 33, the Night position 31st, using the alternative method of intercalation that gave a post-position. It was placed at 9 pm, the uncorrected midnight.

**Nicodemus** (*Nikodēmos*). A name for Theudas in his Pharisee zealot role, in John 3:1, 19:39. The name Barabbas expressed his Sadducee role.

**night** (*nyx, nyktos*). 'Night' alone is used at 9.05 pm (John 13:30), the beginning of the six hours' sleep period for villagers who did not keep vigils. 'Of night' is used for six hours before it, at 3 pm, (Rev 4:8), or six hours after it, at 3 am (Matt 28:13), but the fast time still used by John Mark, so actually midnight. In John 19:39 the addition of *to prōton*, 'first' to *nyktos* makes it 4 pm, the first hour after it.

**no** (*oudeis* as adjective). Used to mean the same as

the pronoun, on the principle of consistency. See **No One**. In John 18:38; 19:4, 11, 'no charge', literally 'No One charge', means a bribe (see **charge**) to make a decision about James, who was called 'No One' or 'Nemo'.

**no longer** (*ouketi*). An expression indicating the end of the 'wilderness wandering' in the Exodus imagery, when the Israelites said 'No Longer!' Used at its 'year 38' (John 6:66, March AD 32), and its year 40 (Rev 10:6; Mark 14:25) in their different versions.

**No One** (*oudeis*). 'Nemo'. A name for the acolyte saying the prayer at noon, but below the platform as he was not important, so the prayer was said by an invisible 'No One' (illustrated in Acts 9:7). The David crown prince was the Chief Acolyte, and in the gospels the term usually refers to James (John 18:31, 38, 19:41). But John Mark was called an acolyte when on the east side of row 10, as he was at the Last Supper (John 13:28, 21:12). Joses, when appointed crown prince instead of James, was called by this name in John 9:4.

**nor** (*oute*). A play on 'not-*te*', the word used for the initiation sign used by the Sadducee in the east, the Hebrew letter Taw, not the X but the later form (Mark 14:68).

**not** (in the form *ouchi* or *mēti*). Both words are used as a play on letters. Both *ou* and *mē* mean 'not', and *ti* is always used as a play on 'T', the T sign of the cross used by Greek-speaking missionaries as an initiation symbol, in place of the Hebrew Taw, with its X shape. *Chi*, a Greek letter in an X shape, is used as a play on the X sign. A person who was *ouchi*,

'Not-X' did not use the X sign (John 13:10), and a person who was *mēti*, 'Not-T', did not use the T sign. *Mēti* was normally used in a question expecting a negative answer, to mean 'surely not', so was used when Pilate said 'Am I a Jew?' in John 18:35. It gave an indication to the pesharist that he had joined Antipas' party, which although western did not use the T sign that was used by the royal Herods' house. John Mark, also a member of Antipas' party, although of its celibate wing, was a 'Not-T' (Mark 14:19).

**not yet** (*oupō*). Not a negative, but an event happening at a 'Not Yet', when an unexpected prophecy had not been fulfilled (John 2:4, 6:17, 20:17). *De* is added, giving *oudepō*, as a play on 'Not Yet for Grade D' (John 19:41, 20:9).

**nothing** (*ouden*). The time for a prayer, treated as a zero point, a beginning, in the first five minutes after the hour or the half-hour, or at five minutes before the hour at the end of the session.

**now** (*nyn*). A significant time, the 'Now' of prophecy.

**officer** (*hypēretēs*). See **servant**.

**ointment** (*myros*). The anointing oil used by a woman in marriage (Mark 14:8), so also in a Gentile service using the wedding imagery, the chrism. The Gospel of Philip lays great emphasis on the chrism. 'It is because of the chrism that "the Christ" has his name' (74:15). In Luke 23:56 Mary Magdalene kept the chrism.

**one** (numeral, *eis*, masc.). Used without a noun to indicate a position in the hierarchy. Masculine form, a man who was either a One in the hierarchy, or a 13, since counting began again after 12. Judas as the 13 (Mark 14:10). Since the 13, the levite, could sit in row 10 to supervise the common meal, John Mark in the same position is called a One (John 13:23).

**one another** (*allēloi*). A plural of reproduction, referring to one person. Used to refer to James Niceta as an alternative Chief Gentile to John Mark (John 4:33, 6:52, 11:56, 13:14, 22, 34, 16:17, 19:24; Mark 9:34, 15:31; Luke 24:14; Matt 24:10, 25:32).

**opposite** (*apenanti*). The precise meaning of this word is 'south-west', and it is an important indicator of place. Its meaning comes from the fact that *enanti* has the special sense of 'south', and the whole word means 'from the south', at one of its limits. *Katenanti* means 'south-east'. The NE, SE, NW and SW points of the world map were on rows 12 and 13 in the vestry, as shown in Chapter 2. When Pilate 'washed his hands before (*apenanti*) the crowd' in Matt 27:24, the meaning was that he was admitted to row 13 in the vestry, the position of south-west in the world map. On the west side of the step, he was in the place of the left hand of the Heavenly Man, called 'the hands', and he received a bread paten (the special meaning of 'hands'), which he purified with water as a minister did. Having been admitted inside the vestry, he was attending the service there on the afternoon of Good Friday, so did not see what was being done in Jesus' tomb, where the antidotes were placed.

In Matt 27:61 the women waited 'before (*apenanti*) the burial place' – that is, at the queen's house, whose two parts were south-west and south-east of the end of the esplanade. The word *katenanti* is used of the building in Mark 11:2.

Just as the expression 'X was east of (*emprosthen*) Y' means that Y was west, so 'X was south-west (*apenanti*) of Y' means that Y was north-west. Pilate was south-west of the 'Crowd' (Antipas) in Matt 27:24, and in Mark 12:41 (Vaticanus text) Jesus was south-west of the 'treasury'. Both 'the Crowd' and the 'treasury' were on the west centre of row 12, the north-west in the world map. See **treasury**.

**opposite** (*katenanti*). See the entry above. This term is used for the point 'south-east' in the world map. In Mark 13:3 'south-east of the temple' means the east side of centre of row 13, the 'temple' being north-east, at the east side of centre of row 12 (see **temple**). In Mark 11:2 the term refers to the queen's house, south-east of the end of the esplanade.

**opposite** (*enanti*). One of the four prepositions meaning the compass points. South (Mark 15:39; Luke 1:8).

**or** (*ē*). An equal alternative in the same function.

**other** (*allos*). A deputy, one who can be the substitute in the position. 'Others . . . around Jesus' (John 18:34) means a reproduction of a deputy who was 'around' Jesus, treating him as a priest, so a Gentile.

**out, be** (*exestin*). Meaning 'it is lawful', literally 'it is out'. More exactly, 'it is done outside', as the rule for the village class.

**out of** (*ek, ex*). One place to the east. Always indicating a place on the east, this preposition is used to disguise the fact that Jesus was on the western cross. Mark 15:27, 'One out of the right, One out of the left', draws on the position of Priest, called 'right' and that of King, called 'left', while the Levite to the Priest was an extra on the east of the Priest. Thus Judas was 'out of the right', and Simon, east of Jesus, was 'out of the left'.

**outside** (*exō*). Outside a sanctified place. The pillar bases in the area outside the vestry (John 18:29, 38, 19:4, 5).

**own** (*idios*). A married villager with his own property, typified by Peter. In John 1:41 Peter is 'the Own Brother' (John 1:11). In John 13:1, 'Own Ones' means Peter representing the class. Village Essenes worked for a living as tradesmen, and shared their income with the indigent.

**parents** (*goneis*). Plural of reproduction for 'the (first) Parent', Adam, one of the parts played by the David teaching Gentiles in the Eden imagery. Joseph the father of Jesus in Luke 2:27, James in John 9:18.

**Passover** (*pascha*). The meal of unleavened bread associated with the Passover, not the meal for eating the paschal lamb. Two rules for its date given in the Old Testament (Exod 12:18 the 14th; Levit 23:6 the 15th of Nisan) led to different practices by different parties, John's gospel using the 15th, the Synoptics the 14th. It was held both at the regular occurrence

374

of the date (Mark 14:1 the 14th, Tuesday in the Day position; John 2:13 the 15th, Wednesday) and at the +2½ version coinciding with the 31st (Mark 14:16 for the 14th; John 13:1, 19:14 for the 15th), or the 30th as the Great Day (Mark 14:12). See Chronological Points (pp. 298–300). The term is used at the meal hour at which this food, regarded as common, was eaten, and this again varied with different parties. In John 18:28 the 6 am meal, the first of the day for villagers. In John 18:39 an hour later, according to the practice of the Therapeuts of using the first hour rather than the zero. Others holding different views would be fasting at the same time (John 2:23, 6:4, 18:39; Mark 15:6).

In the Qumran vestry the unleavened bread was eaten during the first two hours of the evening session at the low table between rows 10 and 12, defined as a common table. See **table**. Only Luke shows this part of the meal, in 22:14–18. At 8 pm participants moved up to the high table for the sacred bread. Since Ain Feshkha was a non-sacred building, its table, although between rows 7 and 9 on the platform, was defined as a low table, and at the March seasonal meeting the unleavened bread was taken there at noon, followed by some of the loaves of the Presence at 1 pm (John 6:4; 10–11).

**pause** (*anapauō*). Observe a cessation of work at 3 pm, as village workers did (Rev 4:8), consequently hold a ceremony at its counterpart, 3 am (Mark 6:31, 14:41).

**peace** (*eirēnē*). The teaching of Sadducees advocating peace with Rome, such as Ananus the Elder, appointed high priest by the Romans in AD 6. Their policy was summed up in the word 'peace' (Luke 2:14). At the services of this party, the opening formula was 'Peace to you' (John 20:19, 21, 26). The word is used as a name for Matthew Annas when high priest (Acts 9:31). The dove emblem was used by this party, by Jonathan Annas in Mark 1:10, Luke 3:22.

**people** (*laos*). The 'laity', used in the special sense of Gentiles. The person who was the head of Gentiles was called by this name. For the Pharisees and the eastern party, this was the David crown prince as head of married Gentiles (Acts 7:17, Joseph; Luke 22:66, James). The Sadducees and the western party allowed a Gentile to act in the position, and it became temporarily that of Pilate when he received initiation (Luke 23:13, 14; Matt 27:25, where 'All' is added to show that he was in the house of Antipas). This minister stood on the dais step at the 4 pm service for Gentiles. The base is called 'the presbyterate of the People' in Luke 22:66. At the crosses John Mark, as a deputy to Jesus, acted as the chief Gentile celibate (Luke 23:35).

**Pharisees** (*Pharisaios*). In the plural of reproduction, this word means Caiaphas the high priest, holding eastern Pharisee views on the necessity of circumcision of proselytes. The 'Scribes and Pharisees' were Judas Iscariot and Caiaphas, the current leaders of the circumcision party, successors of Judas the Galilean and Joazar (Boethus), the Pharisee high priest of AD 6.

At that time, according to Josephus, 'Saddok the Pharisee' had joined in the uprising (*Ant.* 18:3).

Pharisees believed in life after death, and ascetic Pharisees who joined the zealots saw this as a reason for giving their lives for their country. 'The Pharisee' is a name for the same Saddok, also called Theudas, in his militant mode, and is used for him, by now an old man, in Luke 7:37, 39 and 18:11. But he was also the 'Prodigal Son' who repented, turning back to Sadducee views. His changes of opinion reflected the problems of Alexandrian Jews at this period of crisis when Judea fell under the power of Rome. Another of his titles, 'Earthquake', also reflects the changes of political attitude.

**place** (*topos*). A place defined by monastics as unclean, with an allusion to a defiled temple. A temple was called a 'place' (Heb. *maqom*) in Deut 12:14, and 2 Kings 10:27 shows that a defiled temple was reduced to a latrine. One such 'place' was the area containing the latrines, the 'place of the Skull' (John 19:17; Mark 15:22). It was the 'place of the city' from which the inscriptions on the crosses were read (John 19:20). Another was the outer hall for the married (John 18:2), another was the western burial cave (John 19:41).

**pool** (*kolymbēthra*). One of the two parts of the exclusion cistern at Qumran (see Figure 4). In John 5:2, the smaller pool inside the wall, which was likened to the 'Jordan' crossed by initiates, with the 'dry land' of the steps and 'porch 5' beside it. See **porch** and **dry**. In John 9:7 the larger cistern, used by monastics after episodes of uncleanness, called 'Siloam' following the Jersualem imagery. The word *kolymbēthra* may perhaps contain a play on *columba*, the Latin for 'dove', because the same pools

377

were employed for a 'Noah' drama, the steps being again the 'dry land' on which the dove, sent out by Noah, rested (Gen 8:6–12).

**porch** (*stoa*). The 'porch of Solomon' in the Qumran reproduction of Jerusalem was at the west side of row 12 in the vestry, the same cubit as the 'treasury', hence Jesus taught 'in the temple, in the porch of Solomon'. This meant the same as when he taught 'in the temple, in the treasury' (John 10:23, 8:20). The 'porch' was used by a subordinate grade, that of a presbyter preparing to become a bishop in the 'temple'. 'Porch 5' in John 5:2 was used by the same grade, but by a married man who was equal to a Gershon grade 5. Here he was on 'dry land', in the Jordan imagery. See **dry**.

**pound** (*litra*). (A pound weight, Latin *libra*, 12 oz.) One hundred pounds of aloes (John 19:39) was a very large quantity.

**power** (*dynamis*). The Phanuel of the hierarchy, who acted as priest in the village. Simon Magus claimed to be the Great Power of God (Acts 8:10). Simon in Mark 14:62.

**power** (*exousia*). See **authority**.

**praetorium** (*praitōrion*). The south pillar base (see pp. 45–50). Having associations of uncleanness because married men who were pilgrims stood on it, and because it was used for corporal punishment, it came to be the place to put the tribute money paid to Rome, so stood for the Roman power and Caesar. Pilate stood on it when representing Caesar (John 18:33), and a man accused of attempting to usurp

Caesar was placed on it to be mocked (John 18:28; Mark 15:16).

**pray** (*proseuchomai*). Bring a petition to the priest, who was 'God'. Jesus in Gethsemane, after the Last Supper when his return had commenced (Mark 14:32).

**preparation** (*paraskeuē*). The 'Preparation' was Friday in ordinary Jewish usage, and in the pesher it means 'the Friday service for Gentiles'. Jewish members did not hold a meal on Friday afternoon and evening, nor Friday noon in some cases, because of the Essene prohibition of defecation on the sabbath, but this did not apply to Gentiles, who held services on Friday afternoons for their different parties (John 19:31, 42; Mark 15:42; Luke 23:54; Matt 27:52).

**promise** (*epangelia*). The 'Promised Land' of triumph for the mission, to be reached at the end of the forty years of the New Exodus. In Acts 7:17, in AD 1, after the New Exodus of Herod the Great. In Luke 24:49, Acts 1:4, the end of the revised New Exodus begun at the re-occupation of Qumran, in September AD 33 and March AD 34.

**prophet** (*prophētēs*). In the singular, a priest in the role of a 'Moses', counted as the original Prophet (John 1:21, 23, 25). Simon the Essene was the earlier 'Moses' (Acts 7:20 refers to him in the pesher), and had a public reputation for foretelling the future (*Ant.* 17:346–7). The plural is used for a leading Essene or celibate, Brother James in Luke 24:25.

**proselyte** (*prosēlytos*). A Gentile who had become circumcised and lived in every respect as a Jew, including adopting the celibate discipline. He was permitted to rise to the level of deacon (Acts 6:5, Nicolaus). It was this treatment of Gentiles that Jesus opposed, believing they should retain their own ethnic identity. James Niceta, while not becoming circumcised, adopted aspects of Jewish identity, as a pre-proselyte.

**purple** (*porphyreos*). One of the three colours – scarlet, purple and blue – worn by priests when outside the sanctuary, according to 1QM 7:10–11. It became the colour worn by a Christian bishop because it was in the next grade below scarlet, and a levite-bishop, an office found at Qumran, was in the next grade below a priest. The woman called Lydia in Acts 16:14 was a 'seller of purple' because as a female bishop she gave the office to other women. The heir of David when acting as a levite also wore purple. In a monastery, an orphan admitted to the permanent monastic life became equal to a levite, so he wore the same colour, and was distinguished from a levite or king only by his 'crown of thorns', the headdress of an illegitimate.

**recline** (*anakeimenos*). The participle refers to a person occupying both positions in the centre of row 10. The man in the double space was able to recline across the 2 cubits. The word refers to John Mark in both the singular (John 13:23; Luke 22:27) and the plural (John 6:11, 12:2, 13:28; Mark 14:18).

**reed** (*kalamos*). The 2 cubit measuring stick of a Scribe or a teacher (Rev 11:1). Used as an instrument of punishment of boys at the place where Jesus was tried before Pilate (Mark 15:19). At the crosses, it was used to make up the distance between the raised hand of a man standing on the ground (4 cubits + his forearm of 1 cubit) to the mouth of the man standing on the cross, at 7 cubits (Mark 15:36; Matt 27:29).

**rejoice** (*chairō*). To be at the level of marriage, as there was rejoicing at a wedding. Since the married state was unclean by monastic standards, a person on the south pillar base, defined as unclean, was said to 'rejoice' (John 19:3; Mark 15:18; Luke 23:8).

**release** (*apolyō*). To release from either the state of being a prisoner, or the state of marriage, the two being equated. Used for the former in the crucifixion story. Since release from marriage meant a promotion in the celibate ranks, a released prisoner was also promoted, and the release performed at his promotion time (John 18:39).

**remember** (*mimnēskomai, anamimnēskō, hypomimnēskō*). To make a written record, as a memorandum (Matt 26:75, 27:63; Luke 23:42, 24:6, 8; Luke 22:61).

**repent** (*metanoeō*). Hold Baptist-Pharisee doctrine (Mark 1:4). 'Not repent', be a Sadducee (Luke 13:3, 5). In Luke 24:47 (the noun), the Baptist doctrine of James, taught in Jerusalem by Jewish Christians.

**rich** (*plousios*). The David was entitled to retain the initiation fees of uncircumcised Gentiles such as

James Niceta, because originally it was considered unclean money that should be kept apart from Jewish fees. Jesus abolished the charging of fees, so 'overturning the tables of the money-changers', but James when acting as the David retained them, so was called the Rich Man (Matt 27:57 as 'Joseph of Arimathea') and in the parables concerning the Rich Man. The money from the fees was stored in the dungeon section of his burial cave, as Sentence 2 of the Copper Scroll shows, hence the cave where Jesus was placed was called the cave of the 'Rich Man', 'Joseph of Arimathea' (Matt 27:57).

**right** (*dexioi*). Of the central pair at the table, the Priest sat on the right, and the King on the left. In Mark 16:5 Simon Magus was 'in the right', in the eastern cave and in the priest's position. These terms are used for the positions of the crosses (see **out of**). *Dexia* means 'right hand' (Matt 27:29; Rev 1:20), as the word for 'hand' has another meaning.

**rise up** (*anistēmi*). As 'arise' (*egeirō*) meant to be an initiate, to 'rise up' meant to graduate. Both terms are used with the apparent sense of 'resurrection' for those who were not familiar with the hierarchical terms.

**rock** (*petra*). In 1 Cor 10:4, 'the Rock' is seen to be a name for the David, who acted as guide to pilgrims in his capacity of 'shepherd', giving them a drink of water when they arrived in the outer hall at Qumran. For the Exodus imagery, this was to be the 'rock' that Moses struck to produce water in the wilderness (Exod 17:6). The tomb in which Jesus as 'the Rock' was placed then became the 'Rock' (Mark 15:46).

Peter, who would act for the David as head of pilgrims, was called by this name.

**Romans** (*Rōmaioi*). In John 11:48 the word means Agrippa as head of the party meeting in his house in Rome, to which Paul addressed his Epistle to the Romans. Paul with this party, in its later version under Agrippa II, preferred the name 'Romans', whereas Peter used 'Christians'.

**sabbath** (*sabbaton*). In the singular form, the 31st of the solar calendar, both at the Day position on a Tuesday (Luke 13:14) and the Night position on a Friday (John 19:31). The name was derived from the fact that the Night position 31st coincided with the sabbath, but was used to mean simply the 31st, at its varying occurrences. On a strict view the sabbath began at the time on Friday afternoon when walking any distance was forbidden. For those who normally walked one hour away to the building at 2000 cubits (1QM 7:7–8), it began at 3 pm; and for those of higher rank who walked half an hour to the cave at 1000 cubits (4Q491) it began at 3.30 (John 19:31). See also **week**.

**Samaria** (*Samaria*). In the gospels, the place to which the bishop of Samaria came for council meetings, Ain Feshkha (John 4:4). He shared the building with 'Galilee', the bishop of Galilee, both being visitors from the northern part of the country.

**sanctuary** (*naos*). Originally the long north–south courtyard at Qumran used as the substitute temple, then after the earthquake the building at Mird where the Atonement ceremony was held, called 'the sanctuary of the lord' (Luke 1:9).

**sanhedrin** (*synedrion*). The Jewish council in the person of Caiaphas the high priest, representing the orthodox Jewish Sanhedrin, which was only remotely involved in the events of the crucifixion. But Caiaphas attended the mission councils as a political figure needing the support and financial help of Diaspora Jews, among whom the mission flourished (Mark 14:55; Luke 22:66).

**Satan** (*Satanas*). The Tester or Adversary (Zech 3:1; Job 2:1–7) the levite who acted as Chief Examiner in the monastic system. Judas Iscariot (Mark 1:13, 8:33; Luke 22:3; John 13:27). The name also connected him with the Eden imagery.

**save** (*sōzō*). To act as a 'Noah', bringing men into the 'ark' to give them religious salvation and an afterlife at the cataclysm shortly expected (Mark 15:31). Since escape from literal death was included, 'save yourself', said to Simon Magus (Mark 15:30), meant 'escape crucifixion'. Simon was being told of a rescue plan through these words.

**scribe** (*grammateus*). The monastics at Qumran and its outposts in the east continued the strict Essene tradition described by Josephus of being permanent celibates, their main occupation being the copying of manuscripts, such as the Dead Sea Scrolls. Such Scribes were found in Babylon also at the beginning of the Essene tradition, using the X mark (archaic Taw, the last letter of the alphabet) to mark their initiates and promise them salvation (Ezek 9:2–4, a passage alluded to in CD 19:12). Their Diaspora order was that of East Manasseh, half of the 'tribe' or ascetic order of Manasseh, whose western half were the Magians. In AD 6 Judas the Galilean had been the head of the 'Scribes' at Qumran, responsible for the writing of the War Scroll, and his successor was Judas Iscariot. The plural is used of him because he was only the representative of Agrippa, the actual head of the order, which had come under Herod the Great (in Acts 19:35 the 'Scribe' is Agrippa II). Once Judas was arrested, he was immediately succeeded by another head, probably Eleazar of Galilee, named in Josephus as insisting on circumcision for proselytes (*Ant*. 20:43) (Luke 23:10; Mark 15:31).

**season** (*kairos*). A quartodecimal period of the solar calendar, at its varying occurrences in the intercalation period.

**secure** (*asphalizō*). To place on guard the jailer Merari (Matt 27:64, 66; Acts 16:23).

**send** (*pempō*). To send out a missionary, without the derogatory associations of *apostellō* (John 9:4, 13:20).

**send out** (*apostellō*). To send out as an 'apostle'. See **apostle**.

**servant** (*hypēretēs*). A servant but not a slave, the lay servant of a priest, who performed such duties as lighting the fire in the vestry, and other menial duties. In the plural of reproduction, James the brother of Jesus in this capacity (John 18:12, 18, 19:6). John Mark as a freeman performed the same duties and was given the same title (Acts 13:5), and in the story of Peter's denials it is shown by the detail that John Mark replaced James in the position of fire servant a few minutes after the hour (John 18:17). The term is used of John Mark in Acts 13:5.

**servant** (*paidion*). See **child**.

**serve** (*diakoneō*). Be a deacon, equal to an acolyte, the lowest rank of ministry. Luke 22:26, 27. The position could be taken by a woman (John 12:2).

**sheep** (*probata*). Village Essenes attached to the Qumran monastery, who visited it as pilgrims, meeting the David in his role of shepherd (John 10:1–5). Peter as the Chief Pilgrim was to act as the substitute for David, so told to 'shepherd my sheep' (John 21:16). When such a man acted as a Nazirite he let his hair grow long, but on resuming marriage his hair was cut, so 'shorn' like a sheep (Acts 18:18).

**sheepgate** (*probatikos*). A name for the back gate at Qumran (see Figure 4), used by the 'sheep', a name for the visiting village pilgrims (John 5:2).

**shepherd** (*poimēn*). The David in his role of village bishop, either outside, or in the outer parts of Qumran when meeting pilgrims. Jesus in Mark 6:34. In Mark 14:27, Jesus was about to leave this role in order to return to monastic life, so was 'smitten', sent away from tending the 'sheep'. The bishop of the 'camps' is likened to a shepherd of sheep in CD 14:9.

**shout** (*kraugazō*). To speak after the minute's silent prayer that was offered just after the hour and the half-hour, the contrast making the speech sound like a shout (John 18:40, 19:6, 12).

**sick** (*asthenēs*). The word means both 'weak' and 'sick'. A 'weak' person was one who was not yet confirmed, given monastic initiation, so did not have 'strength'. In John 4:46, Philip as initiated but not yet confirmed was 'sick'. A person on the downward route to excommunication was also 'sick' (John 11:12). On the view that marriage was 'death', a man on the way down to marriage was 'sick' (John 11:3, Jesus, by the rule of the last referent, in December AD 32).

**side** (*pleura*). A portable water container carried at the side of the body at the waist, next to the skin. In Matt 27:49 an addition to the text says that the side of Jesus was pierced 'and there came out water, and blood', reversing the order in John 19:34. The missionary's container of holy water, like the container of bread, was carried with him, and would be buried with him, so these objects were left on the crucified men. To test for death, John Mark from the west side pierced through the water container to the skin, drawing blood, which was washed away by the spilt water, the bag covering the wound. Acts 12:7–8 shows that Peter wore this bag next to his skin, even under his belt.

**sign** (*sēmeion*, noun; *sēmainō*, verb). The grades in the monastic schools were indicated by Hebrew letters and called 'signs'. In John 2:11, 4:54, an uncircumcised Gentile was given the letter indicating initiation. A 'not sign' (John 4:48) was a grade expressed in Greek, for Gentiles. The verb 'to sign' consequently meant 'to speak Hebrew', doing so in order that outsiders would not understand (John 12:33, 18:32, 21:19). These grades were bestowed

387

by a priest, and the words also indicate a priest. In John 9:16 the question was whether Jesus while a 'sinner', in the married state, could act as a priest and give promotion to a high grade.

**Siloam** (*Silōam*). The exclusion cistern in the south-western quarter of the Qumran grounds, named for the corresponding area in Jerusalem (John 9:7; Luke 13:4). See **pool**.

**sinner** (*hamartōlos*). The position of 'Adam' excluded from 'Eden' as a Sinner, consequently in the married classes. Jesus while in the married state was called a 'sinner' (John 9:16) and Peter, normally in the married state, called himself 'a man a sinner' in Luke 5:8. Agrippa, head of all categories, was called 'the Sinners', reproducing the role of chief villager. Merari, his servant, the levitical deacon who rose no higher than the north base, was called 'a Sinner' (Luke 19:7). He also acted as 'the Sinners' on behalf of Agrippa (Mark 14:41). 'Tax-collectors and Sinners' were the married classes and their priests, who collected the tithes and tribute from them (Mark 2:16).

**sister** (*adelphē*). A woman married to a man in the dynastic order of Essenes, who normally did not live with him, but was in a relationship like that of a sister (1 Cor 9:5; John 11:3, 19:25).

**sit** (*kathēmai*). To be a bishop-teacher, one who sits to teach, reproducing the 'Seat of Moses'.

**slave** (*doulos*). Literally 'slave'. A chief celibate in a Sadducee abbey, representing those who had no property so were legally like slaves (John 13:16). It was one of the positions of the David as a dynastic celibate, so fell to James when he became the David (John 18:10). The Sadducees used the imagery of the Vineyard, so a 'slave' was sent into the Vineyard to collect fees, which he could not keep for himself (Mark 12:2). Herod as representing all positions was called 'slaves' (John 4:51; Rev 1:1) and Merari, his servant representing him, was called by the same term (John 18:18, 26).

**sleep** (*katheudō*). To sleep rather than stay awake during the midnight vigils. This was permitted to women members (Matt 25:5; Mark 5:39) and to married men (Mark 14:37) so was practised also by John Mark in the role of a woman (Mark 14:37, 40), until treated as a man by Jesus and given sermons.

**sleep** (*koimaō*). To begin observance of the sabbath, the day of rest (Matt 27:52, 28:13).

**soldier** (*stratiōtēs*). In the singular, Agrippa as head of the form of mission prepared to take up arms (John 19:23). In the plural, his servant Merari representing him (Ananus the Younger). Merari's actions were counted as those of Agrippa (John 19:2; Mark 15:16; Matt 27:27, 28:12).

**Son of Man** (*ho huios tou anthrōpou*). The institutional meaning of this distinctive name for Jesus was 'the Chief Layman', since the Man was 'Adam', the layman who taught Gentiles. When Jesus went outside for marriage he went down a grade below 'the Man', so was called 'son', meaning deputy of the Man. The Man taught on row 12, but the Son of Man was outside on the dais step, row 13, the position in which he stood in the episode of Mark

2:1–12, when the 'paralytic', the visiting priest, came and stood beside him. Jesus then argued that it was still possible for him to give absolution: 'the Son of Man upon (of) the Earth (the west side of the dais step) has authority to forgive sins' (v. 10).

Jesus spoke of himself in the third person in this role, just as the visiting priest spoke of himself as 'God', for each was filling an office, and could at times be in another position.

In the Old Testament and the Similitudes of Enoch, the 'Son of Man' is the emissary of the 'Ancient of Days' to the outside world (Dan 7:13–14; 1 Enoch: 46). They formed a pair of Priest and Layman, and these offices were preserved in the later form of the same community.

**sorrowful, be** (*lypeō*). Be at one of the grades of villagers, who wore black, not the white of celibates. In Mark 14:19, John Mark wore black to act as the Widow, the female representing Gentiles. In John 21:17 Peter wore black as a married man who did not attend the Agape meal.

**soul** (*psychē*). A person who sat on the east side of row 6, at the head of the Heavenly Man. See Chapter 2. Agrippa as a priest sat here, being 'Souls 3000' of Acts 2:41. Jesus sat here when he acted as priest to Gentiles, so spoke of his 'soul' (Mark 14:34). In Luke 12:20 the priest Caiaphas was the 'soul' of James, treating him as the David. His 'soul would be required of him' – he would lose his position – when Caiaphas was dismissed. In Acts 20:10 John Mark-Eutychus was restored to act as a priest to Gentiles on behalf of Jesus, so 'his soul was in him'.

**speak** (*laleō*). To address another while standing on holy ground. But 'to be silent' was to be on unholy ground at a time for prayer, having to give a silent prayer. Zechariah, on leaving the sanctuary for marriage was 'dumb', and 'did not have power to speak' (Luke 1:22). In Acts 18:9 Jesus told Paul at marriage to 'speak and do not be silent', lifting the distinction between holy and unholy ground.

**spices** (*arōmata*). The censer of incense used in Gentile services, given a different name from that used for Jews (Luke 23:56; John 19:40; Mark 16:1).

**spirit** (*pneuma*). An Aaronite or a physically perfect celibate acting at the podium in the centre of row 7, the place of the Spirit of God in creation. See Chapter 2. When Jesus became ill and his hands were permanently damaged he lost the Spirit (John 19:30; Luke 23:46). This definition was challenged by Jesus in Luke 24:39, 'a Spirit (is) flesh'. In Revelation, the Sadducee priest, Matthew Annas at that time, was the 'Spirit' (Rev 2:7). The position was that of a third in rank below the Priest and King who both sat in row 6, giving the formula 'Father, Son and (Holy) Spirit'. 'Holy' (*hagios*) was added for the levitical bishop of Kohath, in the form *to hagion pneuma* (in Matt 28:19; Matthew is referring to himself, the Kohath of the Annas family of priests). The David prince who could sometimes substitute for Kohath was called *pneuma hagion* if he were in a celibate state (Luke 1:35), and a person appointed as a bishop of the same status received *pneuma hagion* (John 20:22).

**spit** (*ptyō*). To send to a place of exile, the Rome province, where no immersion baths were used and there was no holy water, so spit from the mouth of a Jewish teacher was used as a substitute, to give a mark on objects to be used in that province. Spit was used in the 'healing' of a 'blind man' (Joses-Barnabas in John 9:6, Mark 8:23; he preached in Rome, *Clem. Rec.* 1:7), and of a 'deaf-mute' (Simon-Silas the youngest brother of Jesus, in Mark 7:33, working with Paul in the Rome province as a substitute for Barnabas in Acts 15:39–40, 16:25). So when Jesus was 'spat on' at his trial he was reduced to the level of an exile in Rome (Mark 14:65).

**split** (*schizō*). To be in schism. In Mark 1:10 'the Heavens split', meaning that a schism broke out between the Baptist and Jonathan Annas, leading to the formation of the Twelve Apostles. In Mark 15:38, when the 'curtain of the sanctuary split', there was a schism between eastern and western celibates. In Matt 27:51 'the rocks split', for Peter's pilgrims divided between east and west. The noun *schisma* is used for a division in the council in John 7:43.

**stadion** (*stadion*). The Greek measure of distance, about 192 metres. It was counted as equal to 400 cubits, and 5 stadia to the 2000 cubits that must separate an unclean place such as a latrine from a holy place such as a monastery. See *JM*, 'Locations'. In Matt 14:24 *stadioi polloi* is used to mean a zero stadion, because of the use of the word 'Many' for the zero in the hierarchy, and it refers to the last stadion before the watergate at Mazin.

**stand** (*histēmi*). The verb without prefix is used for the action of standing for the prayer, in the first five minutes of the hour, or at the half-hour (John 18:5, 16, 18, 19:25).

**stand beside** (*paristēmi*). To be the deputy and potential replacement. James to Jesus in Mark 15:35. 'Gabriel' to 'Michael' in Luke 1:19.

**Star** (*astēr*). The David, using the Star of David emblem, one of the lesser powers under 'Sun' and 'Moon'. He led prayers at sunrise as the Morning Star (Rev 22:16). His crown prince could take his place (Matt 2:7; Rev 2:28).

**stir** (*tarassō*). Used in the context of the Exodus imagery, in which the waters of Jordan were 'stirred up' prior to the crossing (John 5:7; Acts 12:18).

**stone** (*lithos*). A word reflecting the anatomical imagery, the testicles on row 13. The burial caves, which were at this level, had stones on either side, not at the centre, to close the openings on the roof of both caves. With article, the heavy stone closing the eastern cave, the dungeon, is meant (John 20:1; Mark 16:3). Without article, the secondary stone closing the entrance to the western cave (Mark 15:46).

**strength** (*ischys*). The condition of a man who was confirmed, beginning the rise up the monastic ladder of progress, given to a dynast at the age of 20 when he deferred marriage. In Acts 19:20 Jesus Justus the son of Jesus, born June AD 37, was confirmed in June AD 57, so 'was strengthened'. As the 'strength' he sat on the east side of row 10. See Chapter 2. See **sick** (weak).

**suffer** (*paschō*). Enter the celibate life of self-imposed suffering, that of the Suffering Servant, including the renunciation of sex (Luke 22:15, 24:26).

**sufficient** (*hikanos*). Also meaning 'worthy, equal to'. Refers to the equinoxes, as the time when day and night are equal (Luke 23:8; Acts 27:9). Also to parties using the equinoxes rather than the solstices as the seasons for promotion.

**sun** (*hēlios*). A person, the successor of Michael as the controller of the solar calendar. Simon Magus claiming his position (Luke 23:45; Mark 16:2). His subordinate or wife was called 'the Moon'.

**supper** (*deipnon*). A common meal, as held by the Therapeuts, either the common part of a monastic meal (John 13:2, 21:20), or the midnight meal at which women were present (John 12:2).

**surely not** (*mēti*). See **not**.

**sword** (*machaira*). A copy of a scroll of the Law, in its wrapping likened to a sword in a sheath, used in the outer hall under the 'Eden' image to give rulings to prevent 'Adam' from returning inside, as the cherubim with their swords did in the Eden story (Gen 3:24). Used in the outer hall (John 18:10; Luke 22:36, 38). When applied to the New Testament, it became 'the sword of the Spirit, which is the Word of God' (Eph 6:17).

**table** (*trapeza*). The table in the sanctuary used for the twelve loaves of the Presence (Heb 9:2), and so for the holy table in the Qumran vestry. The holy table, called the *trapeza*, where the sacred part of the Last Supper was held (Luke 22:21), was placed between rows 7 and 9 in the north vestry, and the common table was placed further down, between rows 10 and 12, and called the *trapezai*, using the plural of reproduction (Mark 11:15), or *trapeza* without article (Luke 19:23). The tithes and initiation fees were placed on the common table, which was set up in the late afternoon. See **temple** and **treasury**.

At Ain Feshkha, the outside building, where education for marriage took place, there could be no holy table. But a reproduction of the Qumran vestry was used, where the 'feedings of the multitude' took place. A platform stood within the room, reached by internal steps up to which the procession of leaders came, extending down to row 10 (as came to be the case in Herodian cathedrals, see *JA*), and on it a table was placed between rows 7 and 9. But it had the status of the common table at Qumran, so the numbering of seats was as at the north side of the common table. This table was used for the 'feedings of the multitude' (see Figure 7(ii)).

**taste** (*geuomai*). To sip fermented wine used as communion wine, preventing drunkenness (John 2:9). Hence used for the tasting of the poisoned fermented wine (Matt 27:34).

**teacher** (*didaskalos*). This title belonged to the supreme priest as head of monastic schools, John the Baptist, the Teacher of Righteousness (Luke 3:12).

Jesus claimed it when acting as priest to Gentiles (John 13:13, 14).

**temple** (*hieron*). This word is used in the pesher to refer to the 'temple-tax', the annual tax that was paid in Old Testament times (Exod 30:11–16). The tax is referred to in 4Q159, which shows that it formed the basis of the subsequent system of initiation fees charged by the mission, bringing in an enormous income from the Diaspora. The money was placed on an exact spot in the vestry – the same row, 12, as the monthly tithes for the 'treasury', and this spot was called the 'temple'. As the special sense of 'opposite' (*apenanti* and *katenanti*) show, the 'temple' and 'treasury' were at the NE and NW points respectively, of the world circle on rows 12 and 13 (see Chapter 2, **opposite** and **treasury**). Teaching was given from the same row, so Jesus, using both sides of the space, taught 'in the treasury, in the temple' (John 8:20). In Mark 11:15, Jesus had come to 'Jerusalem' (plural form, Qumran), 'went into the temple', and began to throw out 'those who sold and those who bought in the temple' – that is, he went to this spot where the initiation fees were paid (described in 4Q159 as a 'ransom for one's soul', giving salvation), and illustrated his objection to the principle of charging fees for salvation. He 'overturned the tables of the money-changers', because the common table was placed in the late afternoon on this row, and the money was placed upon it. See **table**.

In Luke 18:10, 'two men went up to the temple to pray', means that Simon Magus, 'Man 2', stood on the east side of row 12 in the Qumran vestry. The Pharisee, 'towards Himself', was on row 13.

**temptation** (*peirasmos*). The married state, where temptation to sex was permitted. Used for the far end of the outer hall, to which married men came, and which John Mark was told to avoid (Mark 14:38). Antipas had been with Jesus in his 'temptations', in the married state (Luke 22:28). While in this state Jesus could exercise military and political power, and when 'tempted' or 'tested' by Judas, the 'Satan' who ruled on marriage questions in the village, Jesus defined the kind of power that he wanted, not the zealotry of Judas (Luke 4:2–13).

**thanks, give** (*eucharisteō*). To give a eucharistic blessing to the elements of the communion meal for those members who, like Antipas, set out both bread and sacred fermented wine. A different kind of blessing (*eulogeō*) was given to those who, like John Mark, used bread and new wine; (Luke 22:17, 19; Mark 14:23; Matt 26:27). But when there was bread only, and no wine, as at the noon meal at Ain Feshkha, John Mark's half-loaf was given this kind of blessing, according to John 6:11, but the other kind according to Mark 6:41.

**that** (*hoti*, conj.) Also meaning 'because'. As with many conjunctions and particles, it is used as a play on letters, *ho ti*, 'the T'. The T was the peace sign, the initiation symbol used by Greek-speaking Sadducees of the mission, giving the sign of the cross. Hoti is used before direct quoted speech to indicate that what was said was in conformity with the doctrines of the party.

**that (one)** (*ekeinos*, demonstrative adj.). A new subject, not referring back. See **this** (**one**). 'That One' in each context was on the east.

**themselves** (*heautoi*). See **himself.** As Simon Magus claimed to be 'Himself', a head of the monastic system in rivalry with Agrippa, the Herod in his party, opposing the royal Herods, was called by the same term, using the plural of reproduction. It means Antipas the tetrarch in Luke 22:17 and Mark 6:36; Herod of Chalcis in Rev 10:3; another rival Herod in Rev 2:9. In the feminine, Helena (Mark 16:3).

**then** (*tote*). Indicates a new time point for a prayer or ceremony.

**therefore** (*oun*). Used to correspond to the Hebrew for 'therefore', '*al ken*', which was a play on 'upon the Kaph to Nun', the Hebrew letters for grades 10 to 8, the pre-initiate grades. An initiate at grade 7 was 'upon' these grades. The word, then, signified an initiate, and is used very frequently in John's gospel, in the way letters for qualifications are used with a name. It is not translated, except when it makes a difference to the meaning, the sense in which the Synoptics prefer to use it. In Luke 22:70, 'You therefore are the Son of God', it means that although Jesus was the true David, he was now at the level of an initiate only.

**They** (*autoi*). A new subject, not referring back. A person reproducing a 'He'. Refers to the Chief

Therapeut Theudas (Luke 22:23), or to James, the brother of Jesus (Luke 24:14, 35) or Antipas as the Herod (John 18:28; Luke 22:71). Matthew's Beatitudes (Matt 5:3–9), each one speaking of 'They', concern the class led by James, as his gospel was directed at Jewish Christians.

**thief** (*lēstēs*). A zealot, for in the zealot uprising of AD 6 the militant party used the mission funds to buy arms, being accused of theft by their opponents. Theudas-Barabbas in Mark 14:48 and John 18:40. Judas, prior to his arrest, was the Thief, the Chief Zealot (John 12:6).

**third** (*tritos*). Ordinal numbers refer to a succession, not having the fixed value of cardinal numbers. With 'day', 'third' means the third of the three council days (not 'day 3', Tuesday). It was used in either Day or Night position. There were two views on the ordering of the council days, and this variation was drawn on to give an alternative to the day of the 'resurrection', allowing Christians to celebrate it on the Sunday rather than the Saturday morning. According to one view, the three days were the 29th, 30th and 31st, making the Friday the 31st the third day, as in Matt 27:64. But for another view, they were the 30th, 31st and 1st, making the 30th the 'first day' (Mark 14:12) and the 1st the 'third day' (John 2:1). The same rules for word order apply, so that John 2:1, with the noun placed first, means the early beginning of the day, on Tuesday evening.

**this (one)** (*houtos*). A new subject, not referring back. 'This One' and 'That One' (*ekeinos*) belonged on the west and east respectively. In each context

'This One' means the western person, the lay leader. The plural means the representative of the lay leader.

In John 1:7–8, 'This One' means Jesus, as it does also in v. 2, standing as king on the west side of the centre of row 7, while the Baptist was 'That One', now reduced to levite, standing on the east side of the centre of row 7, with Jonathan Annas as the 'Light', the priest, in the centre of row 6.

**thorns** (*akanthai*). The emblem of the discipline of some parts of a Sadducee abbey, drawn from the 'thorns and thistles' that made Adam work outside Eden (Gen 3:18; Heb 6:8; 1QH 8:25). When the 'seed fell among thorns' (Mark 4:18), the Sadducee ascetic rule had gained power in the mission. Both monasteries and abbeys took in illegitimates, and a plaited 'crown of thorns' (John 19:2, 5) may be seen to be a rope headband with a thorn, worn by illegitimates in contrast with the gold crown worn by a Sadducee priest (Rev 4:4).

**thus** (*houtōs*). A play on 'Yes', as *ken* in Hebrew meant both 'yes' and 'thus'. Used to refer to a dynastic bishop in the village who is saying 'Yes' to marriage, not 'No', as a permanent celibate did. John 4:6, Jesus in this state. Luke 22:26, addressed to the married man Antipas, 'you are not Thus', 'you cannot be a dynastic bishop as you are married'. In Luke 24:24, with 'down-as' added, a lay bishop, James Niceta.

**time** (*chronos*). A forty year generation in the Exodus series. See *JM* and *JA*, 'Chronology'.

**today** (*sēmeron*). The 31st at the quarters of the solar calendar, as the Great Day, the central one of

Yesterday, Today, Tomorrow, the 30th, the 31st and the 1st. Used on the regular 31st (Luke 23:43), including its early start when it fell on Friday in the Night position (Mark 14:30; Luke 22:34). Since some treated the 30th as the Great Day, the word was used also on this day (Luke 5:26).

**tomb** (*mnēmeion*). The word was used as synonymous with Egypt, the place of pyramids, tombs. In Mark 5:5, 'in tombs and mountains' means 'in Egypt and Rome'. Since the place of the 'Lion' of the south was Egypt, and at the same time row 13 and its equivalents, the caves at the south end of the esplanade were called 'tombs', both as places for literal burials, and for other unclean purposes. The word referred to the top of the cave, not inside it. More exactly, the inner roof of the east cave was 'the tomb', and the inner roof of the west cave was called either 'tombs' (Matt 27:52), using the plural of reproduction, or 'a New tomb', meaning a cave used for the Christian version of the New Covenant, including James as a Jewish Christian (John 19:41). The word was also used for Cave 4 as a burial place and latrine (John 11:17, 12:17). When the 'tombs were opened' in Matt 27:52, it means that the western cave at the end of esplanade was opened at 4 pm on Friday for use as a sabbath latrine.

Prepositions were used to indicate exact spots. 'Out of the tomb' meant the outer eastern roof of the east cave, the segment containing the hole for the opening (John 20:1). 'To the tomb' meant the inner roof of the eastern cave, the point to which the steps came down (John 20:4). 'Into the tomb' meant inside the eastern cave (John 20:6). 'Out of the tombs' meant the inner roof of the east cave, east of the inner roof of the west cave (Matt 27:53).

**tomb** (*mnēma*). This word is used by Luke only in his account of the burial of Jesus (23:53) to mean the inside of Jesus' burial cave, as opposed to the top, for which *mnēmeion* was used (see **tomb** *mnēmeion*). Luke is thus able to show that while James stood at the top of Jesus' burial cave (John 19:41) he did not go inside it at 6 pm. Hence Luke says in the following phrase that James ('No One') was *not* laid there at the 'Not-Yet' (the time for fulfilment), while in John 19:41 James *was* laid on the *mnēmeion* at the 'Not-Yet'.

**tomorrow** (*aurion*). The third of the three council days, the 1st of the month (Luke 13:32, 33; Acts 4:5).

**towards** (*pros* with accus.). A person who was 'towards' another stood in the cubit below him in a north–south direction. This word is an important indicator of place. In John 1:1–2 Jesus was 'towards God' twice. The precise sense of the four phrases is that he was first alone in the centre, in the *archē*; then on the east side of centre below the priest who was on the east centre of row 6; then further down in the centre as a *theos*; then as a 'This One' on the west side of centre, still in the *archē*, below the priest who was on the west centre of row 6.

In John 6:5, the uses of *pros* indicate the processional order, with the initiate Philip as least important going first to prepare the place of the priest, then Jesus as king-levite coming next, then last Agrippa as the priest (*polys ochlos*). Similarly in

John 4:47–9, the priest Jonathan Annas (the 'royal one') stood south of Jesus in processional order, so 'towards' him, and both men, Jesus and Jonathan, stood south of the healed man.

**treasury** (*gazophylakion*). Both 'treasury' and 'temple' were positions on row 12 of the vestry where tithes and taxes were placed. 'Treasury' was north-west of the world circle (described in Chapter 2), and 'temple' was north-east. See **opposite** and **temple**. In the 'treasury', on the west side of centre of row 12, the monthly tithes were placed, in the same row as the Moon, which stood for monthly occasions. The system of monthly tithes is set out in CD 14:12–15. Of the thirty day month, the earnings of three days, one-tenth (the meaning of 'tithe') were to be given, and of these two days' earnings were for the indigent. Since the centre of row 12 was used for teaching, Jesus taught 'in the treasury, in the temple', using both sides of the space (John 8:20).

**tribe** (*phylē*). One of the twelve ascetic orders, named after the tribes of Israel, into which the Jewish form of the mission was organized. See *JA*. 'Tribe 12' was the order of Asher in the Temple Scroll, the lowest order, for married Gentiles (Luke 22:29).

**tribune** (*chiliarchos*, 'a thousand'). A term used in the organization of Gentiles in the mission, preferring Roman military terminology. Married Gentiles were organized in thousands (the Three, Four and Five Thousand) and their Herodian superiors were called the One Thousand (the Herod crown prince) and the Two Thousand (the third Herod, the tetrarch Antipas). The 'tribune' is the One

Thousand, either the deputy Thomas Herod (John 18:12) or Herod himself (Mark 6:21, plural of reproduction, Agrippa I; Acts 21:31, Agrippa II).

**troubled, be** (*adēmoneō*). Used as a play on *dēmos*, 'populace', a way of referring to Merari the levitical deacon, who always wore a black vestment. (Acts 12:22; Demas in 2 Tim 4:10.) 'To be amazed and be troubled' (Mark 14:33; Matt 26:37) means to put on a black levitical vestment.

**truth** (*alētheia*). The ascetic doctrine taught in Herodian Sadducee abbeys. The Hebrew word for 'truth' (*'emet*) appears frequently in the Scrolls as the doctrine of Qumran ascetics. In the gospels the Greek equivalent is used only for the Herodian Sadducee ascetic teaching, given also to village Essenes led by Peter, so the word came to mean Peter's version of Christian doctrine. In John 18:38, Pilate's apparent question 'What is Truth?' means 'The Herodian Sadducee peace party use the T-sign (the sign of the cross) as their emblem'. The 'Way, the Truth and the Life' mean the three kinds of Sadducee doctrine; the 'Way' to Gentiles, the 'Truth' to pilgrims like Peter, the 'Life' to celibates.

**tunic** (*chitōn*). The vestment worn by a celibate under his surplice, consisting of a straight strip of cloth with a hole for the head, without shoulder seams. Its sides were open, and it was bound by a girdle, being the garment referred to in 1QS 7:15–16 that must be secured sufficiently to prevent nakedness being seen (John 19:23). An Aaronite priest was better covered, not wearing a *chitōn*, and Mark 14:63

requires knowledge of this fact to overcome the rule of the last referent, in 'the Chief Priest tore the *chitōn* (plu.) of him'. He did not wear a *chitōn*, so 'of him' must refer to someone else. A similar device is used for the vigil priest's vestment; see **amazed**.

**Twelve** (*dōdeka*). Person 12 in the hierarchy, at the grade of the excommunicated, the 'dead', or the actively married. His loaf 12 was taken outside the vestry, in the village, at a common table at which an elder presided. John Mark, called an Elder in two of his Epistles, was the 'Twelve' in the original Twelve Apostles, being equal to a Jewish monastic who had been sent outside as unclean.

Being a derogatory term, 'the Twelve' is used only once in John's gospel (6:67), but more frequently in the Synoptics (Mark 3:14, 6:7, 14:17, etc.). The word is used to mean a person, and can be the last referent.

**Two** (*dyo*). A person at grade 2 – that is, one equal to a Sariel or western guest, a high position. Simon Magus held several positions, including that of western guest representing Antipas, so was 'Man 2' in Luke 18:10, and 'angel 2' in John 20:12. But 'a Two out of his disciples' (John 1:35) used the Julian times for Gentiles, and it meant a grade 8 novice praying at 2 pm.

**unless** (*ean mē*, 'if not'). John 20:25. Since '*ean*' has the special sense of 'when', then 'if not' means 'when not', altering the sense of John 20:25 to 'when I do not see the print of the nails'.

**until** (*heōs*). This word has the special meaning of 'when', an event happening at the time of speaking, not in the future.

**upon** (*epi*). This preposition is used with three different cases in Greek, and the case gives important information about position. When with the accusative, it refers to the centre; when with the dative, to the east side of centre; when with the genitive, to the west side. Hence *epi tēs trapezēs* in John 22:21, using the genitive, means that the object is on the west side of the table. *Epi tēs gēs* means on the west side of the dais step, the 'Earth' (Mark 2:10, 8:6).

**utter** (*phēmi*). To speak formally, as an authority.

**view** (*theaomai*). To see from a distance (John 1:14). In Luke 23:55, Mary Mother saw the caves on the end of the Qumran esplanade from the queen's house on the plain.

**vine** (*ampelos*). The celibate who acted as priest giving wine at the sacred meal. Jesus to Gentiles (John 15:1). 'Product of the vine' (*genēma tēs ampelou*), grapes used for new wine, not fermented wine (Mark 14:25).

**vinegar** (*oxos*). Spoiled wine, spoiled with poison (John 19:29).

**voice** (*phōnē*). The voice of a person of superior or levitical status, entitled to say prayers to mark the main hours of the day, to preach, and to have a vote in the governing council. The 'Great Voice' was that of the King, the 'Great One' the third of the leading triarchy, the 'Jacob' patriarch of Ephesus, so 'with Great Voices' in Luke 23:23 meant a person acting in 'Jacob's' position, drawing on the funds of Ephesus, which as the head of five provinces received half the income of the mission.

**walk** (*peripateō*). Act as a peripatetic teacher of Gentiles (John 10:23, 6:19).

**warm** (*thermainō*, 'to warm oneself'). To be in the inner cubit in line with the open north door of the vestry after the fire was lit, rather than in front of the fire where one was 'scorched' (Rev 8:7). Peter was here in row 1 in Mark 14:54 and John 18:18, and in the cubit below it in John 18:25.

**wash** (*niptō*). To wash an object using a bowl of purifying water (John 13:5). In John 9:7 a person was sent to the area of the exclusion pool in the south-west of the Qumran grounds ('Siloam') but was told to 'wash' only – that is, avoid full immersion and only wash his hands.

**watch** (*grēgoreō*). To keep a midnight vigil, in the manner of the Therapeuts (*Contemp. Life* 83–7; Mark 14:34).

**water** (*hydōr*). Three kinds of water were used for lower grade baptisms, still water in a cistern (grade 9), running water (grade 10) and sea water (grade 11). The three kinds are named in 1QS 3:4–5. Still water in a container used for washing persons or objects, and also for drinking at the communion meal, was also called *hydōr* (John 2:9, 13:5, 19:34).

**we** (*hymeis*, pronoun and in the verb). When in narrative, the eunuch, speaking the words of or acting for Jesus. He was double, as both 'male and female', going between husband and wife in dynastic marriages, and when speaking for the husband said 'we'. Its use, for John Mark (John 1:14, 21:24) and for Luke (Acts 16:9, 10, etc.) meant that Jesus was in the status of a husband, in the flesh.

**week** (*sabbata*). The plural of *sabbaton*, apparently 'week', is used to mean the beginning of the sabbatical year, as seven years was called a 'week' in the literature drawing on the solar calendar. AD 33 was such a year for the South Solar calendar, 3969 from creation (3920 when the Last Jubilee was intercalated). It began for some on the 1st of the solar month, at its Julian beginning on Friday at midnight (Night position), giving the opportunity of dating the 'resurrection' and making it appear to have happened on the first day of the week, Sunday, the day on which Christians commemorated it. John 20:1, midnight; Mark 16:2 and parallels, Saturday at 3 am.

**weep** (*klaiō*). To act as a 'Widow', a woman minister. Either a woman, or a Gentile of the same status, wearing black, or Jesus representing such a Gentile (Mark 14:17).

**what** (*ti*, interrogative pronoun). The pronoun is used as a play on the letter T, referring to the initiation symbol preferred in the west when the Greek language was spoken, by Sadducees liberal to Gentiles. The original Hebrew symbol of evangelists was a Taw, 't', the last letter in the alphabet, in the shape of the archaic Taw, an X-shaped cross, so a T was used in Greek, giving the shape of the Christian cross. It was used by the royal Herods when allied with Sadducees, and, being the symbol indicating a policy of peace with Rome, it became the property of Christians led by Peter, derived from this party. In John 18:35 the meaning of 'You have made What' after the reference to Jonathan Annas means that both Jesus and Jonathan used the sign of the cross, yet were opponents. Mark 14:36 shows that the sign was made by both Jonathan Annas and Jesus when they spoke Greek to prepare for initiation. The meaning does not apply to the interrogative adjective 'what', *tis* agreeing with the noun.

**wheat** (*sitos*). The emblem of married Gentiles, keeping a Nazirite rule in which bread was eaten and not wine. David led a mission to them as the Sower (see Chapter 12). In Luke 22:31, 'Wheat' is used as a name for Jesus in this role.

**when** (*hotan*). Indicates the hours 3 pm, 3 am, 9 pm, 9 am.

**when now** (*hote*, translated 'when now' to distinguish from *hotan*). Indicates the half-hour, (John 19:6, 8). The use of the word in John 19:23 and 30 shows that Jesus was put on the cross at 9.30 am, after the other two, and that he drank the poison at 3.30 pm, having been first offered it at 3 pm.

**whence** (*pothen*). A word used for the fees and property of Gentiles, being income unaccounted for in the Jewish system. The David controlled this money (Rev 2:5; John 2:9, 6:5, 19:9).

**whip** (*mastigoō*). Apparently meaning self-flagellation in John 19:1, the subject being Jesus through the rule of the last referent.

**who?** (*tis*). The same word is used in Greek for the interrogative and for 'anyone'. Its special meaning is always the latter sense, 'a Certain One'. An apparently vague word, it means the Chief Celibate, a person who had given up personal identity and was nameless. Used alone, it means Agrippa, or his servant Merari acting in his name. Agrippa in Luke 22:24 (with article). Merari in John 13:22, 25, 21:20; Mark 16:3. With qualifying words, it means another Chief Celibate, Simon Magus in Mark 15:21, Jesus in Mark 15:24. In the plural of reproduction it means Thomas Herod as Agrippa's deputy and representative (John 13:18). When with added words or phrases, Antipas who also acted as Agrippa's deputy (Luke 24:24; John 20:23).

**whole** (*holos*). From the point of view of married men, a celibate was a 'eunuch' and a married man was 'whole'. Peter's party came to be called *kat holon*, 'according to the whole', permitting marriage, giving the word 'Catholic'.

**wilderness** (*erēmos*). A place used by Therapeuts, who had an eremitical rather than a coenobitic discipline, their main place of retreat being at the Mird wady (Mark 1:4).

**will** (*thelēma*, and verb *thelō* 'to wish'). A man outside the monastery was under his own will, but inside it was under the will of the priestly superior, as set down in the Scrolls (1QS 7:1–3). In March AD 29 when Jesus had left the monastery for marriage he 'willed' to go to 'Galilee', the building outside (John 1:43) and on his return in March AD 33 he said to the Abbot Jonathan Annas 'not my will but thine be done'.

**wine** (*oinos*). Fermented wine, as opposed to new wine (*gleukos*). See 'blood'. From the Diaspora point of view, fermented wine was 'good wine', and new wine, spoiled some months after the September harvest, was 'worse wine' (John 2:10).

**with** (*meta* + gen.). Equal to another. In Mark 14:18, Judas as levite equal to Jesus as King. In Luke 1:15, Jesus and John Mark equal in the common part of the Last Supper.

**withdraw** (*anachōreō*). Be at the grade of a hermit. The word gave 'anchorite' (Mark 3:7; John 6:15).

**witness** (*martyreō*, verb). To be a bishop, a person permitted to stand at the podium, in the place of the 'eye' or 'eyes', and to act as a witness of the Atonement (John 1:7).

**witness** (*martyria*, noun). A person, a bishop. In John 19:35 John Mark and in John 21:24 James Niceta, accepted as the bishop to whom John's gospel was to be re-assigned.

**woe** (*ouai*). As used in Revelation, a cry, characteristic of the Old Testament prophets, meaning that the expected appearance of the Restoration had not come, and, with an added meaning, that there was a further seven years to wait. One 'woe' seven years, two 'woes' fourteen years, three, twenty-one years. Used of Agrippa's restoration of the monarchy. In Mark 14:21, Mark 15:29 and parallels, a prediction that Agrippa would have the monarchy in seven years from AD 33. He did, in fact, receive rule in AD 37 from Caligula, and a confirmation and extension in AD 41, from Claudius.

**woman** (*gynē*). A woman minister, corresponding to *anthrōpos*.

**womb** (*koilia*). See **belly**.

**wonder** (*thaumazō*). To become converted to the mission, undergoing a process likened to the miraculous crossing of the Red Sea, an image used by the Therapeuts in mission, derived from their Exodus liturgy. Pilate 'wondered' when he became an honorary initiate (Mark 15:5) and added 'exceedingly' when he took a further step (Matt 27:14).

**wood** (*xylon*). Means both 'wood' and 'tree', from the double meaning of the word in Hebrew. The word was used for the original south base and its equivalents, which had become the punishment stand (Acts 16:24). At the same time it was the 'tree of life' for Gentiles (Rev 22:2). The cursing rod may have been kept here, hence the association between the cross and the 'tree' (Gal 3:13). In the plural it refers to a person who had been reduced to this point, Simon Magus in Mark 14:43.

**word** (*logos*). This name was used for the heir of David when he was outside the monastery, bringing the learning of the monasteries to the villages while he lived their during his marriage. See Chapter 3. The 'Word of God' means the David, Jesus, and is used as a code name for him in Acts 6:7 and 12:24, at the time of the birth of his sons, when 'the Word of God increased'. It is used also in the coded message sent by Paul to Timothy shortly before Nero's persecution – 'the Word of God is not fettered' (2 Tim 2:9). 'The Word' also means Jesus in John 1:1, 14.

'This Word' means James acting as the substitute for Jesus (John 19:8, 21:23; Matt 28:15), also in the plural (John 7:40, 19:13).

**word** (*hrēma*). Words of lay status only, given to women or Gentiles (Luke 2:15, 19, 22:61, 2:19).

**work** (*ergazomai*). Not obey the sabbath law, which forbids working on Friday night and Saturday (John 5:17, 9:4).

**world** (*kosmos*). The Diaspora, the outside world as opposed to Judea, its centre in Antioch under the authority of the Agrippas, for non-monastic members represented by Peter. It was divided into west and east, the former called 'this world' according to the usage of 'this', and the latter 'out of this world' according to the usage of 'out of', so when Jesus said 'My kingdom is not out of this world' (John 18:36), the meaning was 'I do not have a teaching mission in the eastern Diaspora'.

Since the Diaspora was counted as unclean, men in the married state, equally unclean, were said to be 'in the world'. When Jesus came 'into the world' (John 1:9, 10) he took his first step outside the enclosed life of the monastery to begin preparation for marriage, coming down to row 12. In John 1:10–12 ('the world did not know him') it is emphasized that Peter did not accept Jesus at first, but that John Mark did, for to John Mark the 'world' was not to be 'loved', both because married and supporting the royal Herods (1 John 2:15). See **love**. But in Rev 11:15 the triumph of the 'kingdom of the world . . . and of his Christ' is proclaimed, for this book upholds the Diaspora Christian party of Peter that was formed in AD 44 in Antioch, the date and place of this passage. Jesus left 'the world' on his return from marriage to the community (John 13:1). When the gospel of John was re-assigned to the married classes, it went 'into the world' (John 21:25). The word is not used as a name for a person.

**world** (*aiōn*). See **aeon**.

**writing** (*graphē*). With the article, a text from the Septuagint, the Greek translation of the Old Testament, which at Qumran was classed with the Writings, the inferior section of the Hebrew Old Testament. Such texts were quoted and said to be 'fulfilled' (their pesher given) at times that were not part of the vestry session, in the five minutes before the hour (Mark 14:27, 49; Luke 22:37; John 19:36–37), so the word is a means of giving the time. In the alternate text Mark 15:28, such a text is quoted in the place of the crucifixion, an unhallowed place. The Septuagint was formally read in outside places at 3 pm (Rev 5:1–5) hence referred to at 3 pm at the crucifixion (John 19:28). In the plural it means a new writing, such as the apocryphal and pseudepigraphical books, classed with the third division of the Old Testament (Mark 14:49; Luke 24:32, 45; John 5:39).

**year** (*eniautos*). The Jewish year by the solar calendar, beginning on the regular 31st, not the 1st of the Julian month. Caiaphas used this method even when beginning the year in December–January, so used the December solstice (John 11:49), and Annas did so when allied with him (John 18:13, at the March equinox). The use of the December solstice combined with 1 January, observed in Antioch (Acts 11:26) gave the calendar basis for Christmas.

**year** (*etos*). The Julian year, starting on the 1st of the Julian month. With a number it means the year of the emperor. In Luke 13:7, 'year 3', AD 44, the third year of Claudius (41–54). In Acts 19:10, 'year 2', AD 56, the second year of Nero (AD 54–68).

**yesterday** (*echthes*). The first of the three council days, the 30th of the month. Monday in the Day position of the calendar, Thursday in the Night position. In John 4:52 Thursday, as the calendar was in the Night position in the gospel period.

**you** plu. (*hymeis*, pronoun, and in the verb). When used in narrative (not speech), the word refers to James Niceta, as a counterpart of John Mark who was called 'we' (John 19:35, pronoun; John 20:31, in the verbs). In Acts 1:4, both 'you' and 'I' appear in a third person narrative in an ungrammatical way. When they are taken as names for James Niceta ('you') and Luke ('I') there is no breach of grammar.

# Notes

## Preface

1 Recently announced radiocarbon datings (1996) have given strong support to the Christian dating of the Teacher of Righteousness, who is the subject of the pesharim and the Damascus Document. See *Atiqot*, vol. XXVIII, Israel Antiquities Authority, Jerusalem, 1996. The essential document given the test is 4Q171 (pPs^a), the pesher on the Psalms, of which the subject is the current danger to the Teacher from his enemies. There was only one edition of each of the pesharim; it cannot be a copy of an earlier work. Its radiocarbon dating is announced to be AD 6, ± 23 years, with a 1 sigma calibration AD 22–78, 2 sigma AD 5–111 – that is, the animal whose skin was used for the writing material was not killed until the first century AD. Consequently the Teacher, who was still alive at the time of writing, lived in the first century AD.

Another piece tested, 1QpHab, also deals with the Teacher, and is given an earlier date, the writing material having been prepared before the Christian period. But its internal contents firmly date it in the Christian period (the Romans are a terrible force, 'marching across the land', a situation that arose after AD 6, and, if the specifics of the work are taken into account, in AD 37 with the march of Vitellius near Qumran). A work composed in the Christian period could have been recorded on an older piece of writing material, but the original of a work composed in the pre-Christian period could not have been recorded on material prepared in the Christian period.

This finding for the pesher on the Psalms accords very well with the dates for the Teacher that, as may be argued, are given indirectly in the Scrolls themselves, in CD 1:5–11, where a corrected translation together with a principle of consistency gives his date of appearing as AD 26, twenty years after the 'Period of Wrath', the Roman occupation of Judea in AD 6. Further, CD 20:13–15, shown from the context to refer clearly to the destruction of Jerusalem in AD 70, says that the Teacher died forty years previously, in AD 30. These two dates give a precise period for the ministry of the Teacher of Righteousness, between AD 26 and 30.

Contrary to the consensus view, which placed the Teacher in the second century BC, I have argued, from these dates and from numerous parallels, that the Teacher of Righteousness was John the Baptist. The rival teacher with whom these documents are pre-occupied, called by many different polemical pseudonyms, was, I believe, Jesus. This identification accounts for the numerous and pervasive links between the Scrolls and the early Christian Church.

418

# CHAPTER 1: The Conception

1  *Clem. Hom.* 2, 32.

2  Philo, *On Dreams* 1, 102.

3  For example, Hab 2:15 is quoted, in the form 'Woe to him who makes his neighbour drink, pouring out his fury, and makes him drunk to gaze on their festivals'. The pesharist writes: 'Its pesher concerns the Wicked Priest, who pursued after the Teacher of Righteousness to consume him in his venomous fury, and at the period of the festival, the rest time of the Day of Atonement, he appeared to them to consume them and to cause them to stumble on the day of fasting, the sabbath of their rest' (1QpHab 11:2–8). The same document says that only a person to whom the special knowledge had been revealed was able to see the pesher, in this case the Teacher of Righteousness, 'to whom God made known all the secrets of his servants the prophets' (1QpHab 7:3–5).

4  The concept is given in 1 Cor 3:1–3, Heb 6:1–8.

5  2 Kings 6:5–7, Exod 16:1–36, Exod 14:21–31, Josh 10:12–14.

6  Plutarch, in his essay '*On Isis and Osiris*' wrote to Clea the priestess at Delphi, 'Therefore, Clea, whenever you hear the traditional tales which the Egyptians tell you about the gods . . . you must not think that any of these tales actually happened in the manner in which they are related' (355).

7  Mark 8:17–21.

8  The enemy of the Teacher of Righteousness was called by a number of opprobrious names, including 'Man of a Lie' and 'Wicked Priest'. See Note 1 to Preface.

9 S. Sambursky, *The Physical World of the Greeks* (London: Routledge & Kegan Paul, 1956), p. 32.

10 1QpHab 7:3–11, in which the Wicked Priest/Man of a Lie is said to fulfil the description of the 'Arrogant Man' of Hab 2:5–17.

11 Acts 16:10–17; Acts 27–8.

12 1 Cor 16:22.

## CHAPTER 2: How He Invented the Language

1 For detail and sources of the calendar and related questions, see the 'Chronology' sections in *JM* and *JA*.

2 John 1:39.

3 *Ant.* 15:371.

4 See J.B. Humbert and A. Chambon, *Fouilles de Khirbet Qumran et de Ain Feshkha*, (Göttingen: Vandenhoeck & Ruprecht, 1994), plates 278–91. For a fuller description of the vestry, see *JA*, Part II, Chapter 2.

5 C.D. Ginsburg, *The Essenes, The Kabbalah* (London: Routledge & Kegan Paul, reprinted 1956 from the original in 1863). D.C. Matt, *The Essential Kabbalah, The Heart of Jewish Mysticism* (San Francisco: Harper 1994). On the Therapeuts, see Philo, *Contemp. Life*. Their close involvement in the Christian history is discussed in *JM* and *JA*.

6 Humbert and Chambon, Plate 272.

7 ibid., Plates 293–301.

8 Ezek 46:1–3.

9 *Ant.* 17:149.

10 1QH 8:20, 4Q265.

11 Rev 22:1–2.

12  Rev 11:8. See *JA*. The rule that all events are success-
    ive means that this is not a reference back to the actual
    crucifixion, but took place at the time of events in the
    chapter, which the chronological information shows
    to be March AD 44.

## CHAPTER 3: 'In The Beginning Was the Word'

1  2 Tim 2:9.
2  See Chapter 8 on the birth date of Jesus.
3  11QT 57:14–15, 58:16–21.
4  See Note 1 to Preface.

## CHAPTER 4: The Seven Signs

1  Acts 2:13.
2  *Gos. Phil.* 52, 15–16.
3  *Ant.* 18:156–7. Protos was a freedman of Agrippa's
   mother and a retainer of Antonia, a leading woman in
   Rome, who had returned to Judea with Agrippa. His
   links with the Roman court would have given him
   great influence.
4  Deut 2:14.
5  *Ant.* 20:70, 73; 20:169–71. Acts 21:38.
6  *Contemp. Life* 83–7 (Moses and Miriam).
7  Josh 3:14–17.
8  See *JA*, Chapter 7.
9  Luke 17:27, in an account of the recent history under
   the guise of biblical history.
10 The boat rate was counted as one-third the walking
   rate. See *JM*.

11  *Clem. Hom.* 2, 24. Dositheus succeeded John the
    Baptist as leader of his sect, and Simon Magus seized
    the leadership from Dositheus. Dositheus is to be
    identified with Jonathan, also called Nathanael,
    all names having the same meaning 'God gave'.
    Jonathan had inherited the leadership of the
    Samaritan Dositheans, one of the ascetic orders (the
    tribe of 'Reuben') which had been founded by
    the original Dositheus before his time.

12  Acts 1:23 (Joseph was the title of the David crown
    prince when the David acted as 'Jacob' in the patri-
    archate of 'Abraham, Isaac and Jacob' of the 'New
    Israel'. James or Jacob acted also in this role when
    Jesus was filling other roles). Matthias, the alternative
    replacement in the Twelve Apostles (Acts 1:23), was
    said to be Barnabas in *Clem. Rec.* 1, 60. Mark 6:3 gives
    the list of the brothers of Jesus. Joseph Barnabas (Acts
    4:36) is shown to be the brother Joses by 'son of
    (deputy, next grade below) *paraklēsis*', a title of James
    as a lay 'paraclete' in the Herodian triarchy listed
    through pseudonyms in Acts 9:31. He accepted the
    role of 'levite' (Acts 4:36) to Jesus' 'priest'.

13  *Clem. Rec.* 1, 6–11.

14  *Ant.* 18:60–2.

15  *Ant.* 18:85–9. A Samaritan staged a demonstration on
    Mt Gerizim, provoking Pilate to attack with undue
    force, then laid a complaint against him with the
    governor of Syria, resulting in his dismissal.

16  John 10:40, in which 'John' means Simon Magus,
    using the title 'John' as a successor of the Baptist.
    Similarly in Acts 4:6. This follows from the rule that
    all events are successive (p. 266). 'Beyond Jordan',
    Mird-Hyrcania, was Agrippa's stronghold.

17  Luke 10:18.

## CHAPTER 5: Jesus' Own Account of His Sufferings

1 *Every Good Man*, 85–7.
2 1QSa 2:11–22.
3 1QH 8:16–26.
4 *Didache* 9:3–4.
5 Matt 11:19. 1QpHab 11:14 (on the Wicked Priest).
6 *Ant.* 18:172. Tiberius is said to have held that 'it was a law of nature that governors are prone to engage in extortion'. The apocryphal Pilate literature arose from the fact that Pilate became an initiate. It contains useful historical information.
7 Due to the fact that double times were in use because their measurement of time was ahead by three hours, this was 12 noon for John's gospel (John 19:14). See pp. 301– 4; 'Chronology' in *JM*.
8 Deut 23:12–13.
9 Sentence 16, concerning a grave in the north-east corner of the *m-l-h*, a word taken to mean 'esplanade'. It possibly is the Hebrew word *melach*, 'Salt', referring to this area as the 'Sea', a place of the level of uncleanness of the lowest kind of water.
10 See **king** in the Lexicon.
11 1QS 7:13–14. Its shape as a strip of cloth open at the sides, bound by a girdle, is implied by the rule.
12 1QS 7:12. *War* 2:161.
13 Josephus, *Life* 420–1. Mark 15:44.
14 See pp. 301– 4; Chronology in *JM*. This point accounts for the second cockcrowing at the time of Peter's denials, and the fact that the Synoptics put the crucifixion at 9 am while John puts it at noon.

# CHAPTER 6: Jesus' Attempt to Tell the Truth About the 'Resurrection'

1 See **die** (*thnēsko*) in the Lexicon.
2 Acts 12:23.
3 The words having an exact time sense show that although he was offered the poison at 3 pm, he did not drink it until 3.30, and the test for death, the pricking of his side, was made at 3.35. See **when now** (*hote*) and **immediately** (*euthys*) in the Lexicon.
4 See *JM*, Chapter 26, on the location of the caves.
5 See p. 236 on the 'Hades' cave.
6 Copper Scroll, Sentence 2, which may be translated: 'In the tomb of the son of the Third Great One' (the king in the hierarchy of priest, prophet and king). One hundred gold bars were said to be stored there.
7 See **body** in the Lexicon.
8 Luke 19:20.
9 Luke 14:5, where *ouk eutheōs*, 'not at once' has the special meaning 'not after five minutes past the hour'. See **at once** in the Lexicon. The rule, understood in this way, gives an exception to the rule in CD 11:13, that if a beast fell into a cistern or pit on the sabbath, it was not to be lifted out.
10 John 20:14, by the rule of the last referent.
11 *Gos. Pet* 9:36–10:39.
12 See *JA*, Chapter 8.

# CHAPTER 7: What Peter Did with Jesus' Book: Mark's Gospel

1 *Ant.* 19:332–4, on Simon of Jerusalem, a man 'with a reputation for religious scrupulousness'. All leading

figures in the history were in Agrippa's household or circle, and Simon is shown to have declared Agrippa 'unclean', but subsequently was invited to Caesarea to discuss the question with him. He became convinced that Agrippa's liberal kind of Judaism was not contrary to the law, and begged the king's pardon. This was soon after Matthew Annas was appointed high priest. The story parallels that told in Acts 10, when Peter in Joppa was instructed by Jesus in a 'vision' to declare nothing unclean, and travelled to Caesarea, where he met the centurion Cornelius. When 'the Holy Spirit' fell on Gentiles (*ethnē*) (Acts 10:45), the special meaning concerns Agrippa, who was the 'Noah' to Gentiles. His servant Cornelius-Luke was representing him.

2  *Ant.* 18:63, 20:200.

3  1QSa 2:18–21.

4  John 21:7–8.

5  Mark 8:29.

6  *Epistle of Clement to James*. In this letter (here accepted as genuine, like all the Clementine literature), Clement says that Peter in Rome in the early sixties AD, knowing that his death was approaching, entrusted to Clement his 'chair of discourse'.

7  *Eccl. Hist.* 2, 15, 1–2. Eusebius reports that Mark made a written record of the teaching that Peter gave verbally, producing the gospel of Mark. This Mark was referred to by Peter as 'my son' in 1 Pet 5:13. Eusebius also quotes from Papias, that 'Mark became Peter's interpreter and wrote accurately (*akribōs*) all that he remembered, not, indeed, in order, of the things said or done by the Lord. For he had not heard the Lord, nor had he followed him, but . . . followed Peter, who used to give

teaching as necessity demanded' (*Eccl. Hist.* 3, 39, 15). The word *akribōs* is, it may be argued, an indication that the gospel was capable of a pesher.

8 In the ancient Syriac document *The Teaching of Simon Cephas in the City of Rome* it is stated that in the third year of Claudius Caesar (AD 44), Simon Cephas departed from Antioch to go to Rome. Eusebius states that Peter came to Rome in the reign of Claudius (*Eccl. Hist.* 2, 14, 6). In Acts, he as Simeon Niger was present in Antioch at a date shown by the chronology to be June, AD 44 (Acts 13:1). After the assassination of Agrippa I in March, AD 44, Peter 'went to another place' (Acts 12:17), at first to Antioch. Peter does not appear in the history for two years, until the Council of Jerusalem in June, AD 46, for which he would have returned (Acts 15:7).

9 See *JA*, Chapter 9.

10 The Herodian leaders of the Four Thousand and the Five Thousand were called the One Thousand and the Two Thousand, following the rules for grades (pp. 282–7). The One Thousand was the *chiliarchos* (Acts 21:31). The Two Thousand was Antipas, of grade 2 in the Herodian hierarchy.

11 Origen, *De Principiis* 4, 2, 4.

12 Mark 1:21–31, 40–5; 2:1–12; 3:1–6; 5:1–43; 7:24–37; 8:22–6; 9:14–29; 10:46–52.

13 1 Pet 1:3.

## CHAPTER 8: Luke and Jesus Improve Peter's Book

1 *Ant.* 20:14.
2 See Chapter 2, Note 12.
3 See the Chronology in *JM*.
4 See Note 1 above.
5 Suetonius, *Life of Claudius*, 25, 4.
6 *Ant.* 18:63–4.


## CHAPTER 9: Matthew Adds the Finishing Touches

1 *Ant.* 19:315–16.
2 *Eccl. Hist.* 3, 24, 6–7; 3, 39, 16; 6, 25, 4–6.
3 Rev 10:1–7. See *JA* for the full pesher.
4 See *JA*, Chapter 8.
5 *Ant.* 17:78. See *JM* and *JA* on Thomas as Herod.
6 1 Tim 5:9.
7 *War* 2:123.


## CHAPTER 10: Behind the 'Visions': Jesus in the Acts of the Apostles

1 *Ant.* 18:168, 179, 183–6, with Acts 20:7–12. All leading figures in the history were part of the household or circle of Agrippa.
2 Acts 13:5, 13; 16:37–40.
3 *Eccl. Hist.* 3, 39, 6.
4 In Col 4:10 and 2 Tim 4:11 he is shown to be associated with Paul in Rome.

# CHAPTER 11: The Gospels of Thomas and Philip

1 See Elaine Pagels, *The Gnostic Gospels* (London: Weidenfeld and Nicolson, 1979).
2 Saying 19.
3 *Gos. Phil* 74:10–24.
4 *Gos. Phil* 51:29–52:24.
5 *Gos. Phil* 59:1–5.
6 *Gos. Phil* 57:29–58:10.
7 Acts 21:9.
8 *Gos. Phil* 59:6–10; 63:34–5.
9 *Gos. Phil* 55:23–30.
10 *Gos. Phil* 56:15–20.
11 *Gos. Phil* 73:8–19.
12 *Every Good Man*, 86.
13 1QH 8:4–39.

# CHAPTER 12: The Unrecognized History of the Church in Luke's Parables

1 *Ant.* 15:22, 34, 39–41, 56.
2 *Ant.* 17:19–22.
3 *Ant.* 17:151.
4 *Ant.* 18:34.
5 *War* 2:94–8.
6 See *JA*, Chapter 8.
7 See *JM*, Chapter 11.
8 *Ant.* 18:26.
9 *Ant.* 19:316, 342.
10 Acts 2:9–11. See *JA*, Part Two, Chapter 4.
11 See *JA*, Chapter 9.
12 *Ant.* 18:82–3.

13  *Ant.* 19:316.

14  *Ant.* 17:224–7, 238.

15  Suetonius, *Life of Claudius*, 25, 4.

16  *Ant.* 18:36–8.

17  John 12:35–6.

18  *Ant.* 18:109–15, 2 Cor 11:32.

19  *Ant.* 18:95, 123.

20  Acts 6:9. One of Jonathan's pseudonyms was 'Stephen', from the crown (*stephanos*) worn by Sadducee teachers. His 'death' (excommunication) is presented sympathetically because he was in favour of the promotion of Gentiles.

21  *Ant.* 20:17–53.

22  *Ant.* 19:354.

23  Theudas appears in *Ant.* 18:4 as Saddok, a Pharisee.

24  *Ant.* 19:342.

## Chronological Points

1.  The sundial found at Qumran, published in 1997, was not exact enough to give daily measurements. It gave a rough indication of the equinox and solstice days, and used seasonal hours. It was suited to the position of Babylon rather than Qumran. It may have been a relic of an earlier age, while more precise methods were used in the Roman period. See M. Albani and U. Glessmer, 'Un instrument de mesures astronomiques à Qumran', *Revue Biblique* 104/1 (1997), pp. 88–115.

# Bibliography

## Sources

### The Bible

English, *Revised Standard Version*
Greek, *The Greek New Testament*, K. Aland, M. Black,
   C. M. Martini, B. M. Metzger, A. Wikgren (eds)
   (Stuttgart: United Bible Societies, 1966)

### Dead Sea Scrolls

G. Vermes, *The Dead Sea Scrolls in English* (London:
   Penguin, 1995)
F. G. Martinez, *The Dead Sea Scrolls Translated* (Leiden:
   Brill, 1992)
E. Lohse, *Die Texte aus Qumran, Hebräisch und Deutsch*
   (Munich: Kösel-Verlag, 1971)
*Discoveries in the Judaean Desert*, vols I–XXX (and
   further to come) (Oxford: Clarendon Press,
   1955–1997).

## Other sources and ancient writers

*Collections and Series:*

Charlesworth, J. H. (ed.), *The Old Testament Pseudepigrapha*, vols I and II, (London: Darton, Longman & Todd, 1985)

Hennecke, E., *New Testament Apocrypha*, vols I and II (London: SCM, 1963, 1965)

Roberts, A., and Donaldson, J., *The Ante-Nicene Fathers*, vols I–IX (1875, re-issued by Eerdmans Publishing Company, Grand Rapids, Michigan, 1951)

Robinson, J. M. (ed.), *The Nag Hammadi Library in English* (Leiden: Brill, 1988). (*NHL*)

Stevenson, J. (ed.), *A New Eusebius* (London: SPCK, 1975)


The Loeb Classical Library (London: Heinemann)


*Acts of Pilate* in *The Gospel of Nicodemus*, in Hennecke, vol. 1

*Clementine Homilies, Recognitions, Epistle of Clement to James*, in Roberts and Donaldson, vol. VIII

*Didache* (The Teaching of the Twelve Apostles), in *Apostolic Fathers*, Loeb Library, vol. 1

*1 Enoch*, in Charlesworth, vol. 1

Eusebius, *Ecclesiastical History* (Loeb Library, 2 vols)

*Gospel of Peter*, in Hennecke, vol. 1

*Gospel of Philip*, in Robinson, *NHL*

*Gospel of Thomas*, in Robinson, *NHL*

Josephus *Antiquities* (Josephus, *Works*, Loeb Library, vols 4–9)

    *Jewish War* (*Works*, vols 2–3)

    *Life* (*Works*, vol. 1)

Philo *Contemplative Life* (Philo, *Works*, Loeb Library,
    vol. 9)
    *Every Good Man is Free* (*Works*, vol. 9)
    *On Dreams* (*Works*, vol. 5)
Plutarch *On Isis and Osiris* (Plutarch, *Moralia*, Loeb
    Library, vol. 5)
Origen *De Principiis*, extract in Stevenson
Suetonius *Life of Claudius* (*Works*, Loeb Library, vol. 1)
*Teaching of Simon Cephas in the City of Rome*, in Roberts
    and Donaldson, vol. VIII

## Modern Works Cited

*Atiqot*, vol. XXVIII, Israel Antiquities Authority,
    Jerusalem, 1996 (Journal)
Ginsburg, C. D., *The Essenes, The Kabbalah* (London:
    Routledge & Kegan Paul, reprinted 1956 from the
    original in 1863)
Humbert, J.-B. and Chambon, A., *Fouilles de Khirbet
    Qumran et de Ain Feshkha* (Göttingen, Vandenhoeck
    & Ruprecht, 1994)
Lasserre, F., *The Birth of Mathematics in the Age of Plato*
    (London: Hutchinson, 1964)
Matt, D. C., *The Essential Kabbalah, The Heart of Jewish
    Mysticism* (HarperSan Francisco, 1994)
Milik, J. T., *Ten Years of Discovery in the Wilderness of
    Judaea* (London: SCM, 1959)
Pagels, E., *The Gnostic Gospels* (London: Weidenfeld
    and Nicolson, 1979)
Sambursky, S., *The Physical World of the Greeks*
    (London: Routledge & Kegan Paul, 1956)
Schürer, E., *The History of the Jewish People in the Age of
    Jesus Christ*, revised edition, vols I–III (Edinburgh: T
    & T Clark, 1973)

Thiering, B. E., *Jesus the Man* (Sydney: Transworld, 1992) (published in the US as *Jesus and the Riddle of the Dead Sea Scrolls*, HarperCollins 1992)

—— *Jesus of the Apocalypse* (Sydney: Transworld, 1995)

# Abbreviations

## Bible

### Old Testament

| | |
|---|---|
| Gen | Genesis |
| Exod | Exodus |
| Levit | Leviticus |
| Num | Numbers |
| Deut | Deuteronomy |
| Josh | Joshua |
| 1 Sam | 1 Samuel |
| Ezek | Ezekiel |
| Dan | Daniel |
| Hab | Habakkuk |
| Zech | Zechariah |

### New Testament

| | |
|---|---|
| Matt | Matthew |
| 1 Cor | 1 Corinthians |
| 2 Cor | 2 Corinthians |
| Gal | Galatians |
| Eph | Ephesians |
| Phil | Philippians |
| Col | Colossians |

| | |
|---|---|
| 1 Tim | 1 Timothy |
| 2 Tim | 2 Timothy |
| Heb | Hebrews |
| 1 Pet | 1 Peter |
| Rev | Revelation |

## Ancient Sources

| | |
|---|---|
| *Ant.* | Josephus, *Antiquities* |
| *Clem. Hom.* | *Clementine Homilies* |
| *Clem. Rec.* | *Clementine Recognitions* |
| *Contemp. Life* | Philo, *The Contemplative Life* |
| *Eccl. Hist.* | Eusebius, *Ecclesiastical History* |
| *Every Good Man* | Philo, *Every Good Man is Free* |
| *Gos. Pet* | Gospel of Peter |
| *Gos. Phil* | Gospel of Philip |
| *Gos. Thom* | Gospel of Thomas |
| *Life* | Josephus, *Life* |
| *NHL* | Robinson, J. M. (ed.), *The Nag Hammadi Library in English* |
| *War* | Josephus, *Jewish War* |

## Dead Sea Scrolls

| | |
|---|---|
| 1QS | Manual of Discipline, Community Rule |
| 1QSa | Rule of the Congregation, Messianic Rule |
| 11QT | The Temple Scroll |
| 1QH | The Thanksgiving Hymns |
| 1QM | The War Scroll |
| CD | Damascus Document, Damascus Rule |
| 1QpHab | Pesher on Habakkuk |

| | |
|---|---|
| 4Q159 | Ordinances |
| 4Q265 | Fragment of the Damascus Document |
| 4Q266 | Fragment of the Damascus Document |
| 4Q270 | Fragment of the Damascus Document |
| 4Q171 (pPs<sup>a</sup>) | Pesher on the Psalms |
| 4Q491 | Fragment of the War Scroll |
| 3Q15 | The Copper Scroll |
| 11QMelch | Melchizedek |
| *DJD* | Discoveries in the Judaean Desert, vols I–XXX |

## Earlier books in this series

| | |
|---|---|
| *JA* | *Jesus of the Apocalypse* |
| *JM* | *Jesus the Man* (published in the US as *Jesus and the Riddle of the Dead Sea Scrolls*) |

# Index

443

## JESUS THE MAN
### by Barbara Thiering

'The impact of *Jesus the Man* . . . may be as profound as that of Darwin's *Origin of the Species* on theories of human origins'
*Focus*

*Jesus was the leader of a radical faction of Essene priests. He was not of virgin birth. He did not die on the Cross. He married Mary Magdalene, fathered a family, and later divorced. He died sometime after AD64.*

This controversial version of Christ's life is not the product of a mind which wants to debunk Christianity. Barbara Thiering is a theologian and a biblical scholar. But after over twenty years of close study of the Dead Sea Scrolls and the Gospels she has developed a revolutionary new theory, which, while upholding the fundamental faith of Christianity, challenges many of its most ingrained supernaturalist beliefs.

*Jesus the Man* will undoubtedly upset and even outrage those for whom Christianity is immutable and unchallengeable. But for many who have found the rituals of the contemporary church too steeped in medieval thinking, it will provide new insights into Christianity in the context of the 1990s.

'[The] sensational nature [of the book's assertions] may disguise the strength of the research and scholarship which Thiering has displayed in the course of her narrative'
Peter Ackroyd, *The Times Saturday Review*

'Some will see her as an anti-Christ, a mischievous scholar determined to destroy Christianity. To others she will be a source of comfort and peace enabling them to live Christian lives without having to accept as fact Jesus's divinity, his miracles, the virgin birth and resurrection'
*The Australian Magazine*

0 552 13950 5

## JESUS OF THE APOCALYPSE
### by Barbara Thiering

The Life of Jesus *after* the Crucifixion.

In her controversial bestseller *Jesus the Man*, Barbara Thiering first presented a completely new historical interpretation of the life of Jesus Christ. Now, in this work of remarkable research and scholarship, Dr Thiering sets out to unravel the mysteries that have long surrounded the elusive complexities of the Book of Revelation. *'It was not,'* she writes *'about vision and apocalypse, but about the profoundly important history of the Christian movement from AD1 to AD114.'*

In *Jesus of the Apocalypse*, Dr Thiering presents a new and significant view of the development of Christianity from the time of the Crucifixion until the second century AD. She argues that Jesus was no solitary preacher appearing suddenly on the shores of Lake Galilee: he was a central figure in a major political movement to overthrow the pagan Roman empire. Although crucified, he did not die on the cross, and he, and subsequently his sons, took an important role in the evolution of the new underground religion which was developing out of Judaism

With detective-like perserverance Dr Thiering unfolds the mystery of words, meanings and places that have been allowed to pass unchallenged, including a radical new interpretation of such mystical themes as the four horsemen of the Apocalypse, the seven seals, the Beast whose number is 666, the Great Harlot clothed in scarlet and purple. In so doing, she provides an absorbing and enlightening background to a period that has been seen more through the implications of scripture than the facts of history.

0 552 14238 7

# A SELECTION OF RELATED TITLES
# AVAILABLE FROM CORGI BOOKS

| | | | |
|---|---|---|---|
| 13878 9 | THE DEAD SEA SCROLLS DECEPTION | | |
| | | Michael Baigent & Richard Leigh | £6.99 |
| 99065 5 | THE PAST IS MYSELF | Christabel Bielenberg | £6.99 |
| 14493 2 | THE JIGSAW MAN | Paul Britton | £6.99 |
| 09828 0 | THE PROPHECIES OF NOSTRADAMUS | | |
| | | Erika Cheetham | £5.99 |
| 14582 3 | BAPTISM OF FIRE | Frank Collins | £6.99 |
| 14465 7 | CLOSE QUARTER BATTLE | Mike Curtis | £5.99 |
| 13582 8 | THE GOD SQUAD | Paddy Doyle | £6.99 |
| 14239 5 | MY FEUDAL LORD | Tehmina Durrani | £5.99 |
| 13928 9 | DAUGHTER OF PERSIA | Sattareh Farman Farmaian | £6.99 |
| 12833 3 | THE HOUSE BY THE DVINA | Eugenie Fraser | £7.99 |
| 14185 2 | FINDING PEGGY: A GLASGOW CHILDHOOD | | |
| | | Meg Henderson | £6.99 |
| 14164 X | EMPTY CRADLES | Margaret Humphreys | £6.99 |
| 14186 0 | THEIR KINGDOM COME | Robert Hutchison | £6.99 |
| 14544 0 | FAMILY LIFE | Elisabeth Luard | £6.99 |
| 13356 6 | NOT WITHOUT MY DAUGHTER | Betty Mahmoody | £5.99 |
| 10645 3 | EVITA: THE WOMAN WITH THE WHIP | | |
| | | Mary Main | £5.99 |
| 13953 X | SOME OTHER RAINBOW | John McCarthy & Jill Morrell | £6.99 |
| 14127 5 | BRAVO TWO ZERO | Andy McNab | £5.99 |
| 14137 2 | A KENTISH LAD | Frank Muir | £7.99 |
| 14288 3 | BRIDGE ACROSS MY SORROWS | Christina Noble | £5.99 |
| 14330 8 | THE TEMPLAR REVELATION | Lynn Picknett & Clive Prince | £6.99 |
| 99784 6 | FIRST LIGHT | Richard Preston | £6.99 |
| 11487 1 | LIFE AFTER DEATH | Neville Randall | £4.99 |
| 14052 X | LORDS OF THE RIM | Sterling Seagrave | £6.99 |
| 13378 7 | MIND TO MIND | Betty Shine | £4.99 |
| 13950 5 | JESUS THE MAN | Barbara Thiering | £6.99 |
| 14238 7 | JESUS OF THE APOCALYPSE | Barbara Thiering | £6.99 |
| 14114 3 | THE POPE'S ARMADA | Gordon Urquhart | £6.99 |
| 13288 8 | IN GOD'S NAME | David Yallop | £6.99 |